MIZEN

RESCUED FOLKLORE, HISTORIES AND SONGS FROM IRELAND'S SOUTH-WEST

Mike Baldwin

First published in Great Britain in 2019
Second edition, 2022

www.mike-baldwin.net

Front cover Joseph Meyer, *Grosser Hand-Atlas Uber Alle Theile Der Erde* (Hildburghausen: Bibliographischen Instituts, 1860), p. 24.
Back cover, *Principal Eminences of the British Islands*, engraved by John Emslie, in *Geological Diagrams* (London: James Reynolds, 1852).

The texts which form this book are transcribed from the School's Collection with the kind permission of the National Folklore Commission, University College Dublin. https://www.duchas.ie/en

This volume is dedicated to the children of the Mizen Peninsula's schools who so diligently rescued and preserved these stories.

EDITOR'S NOTE

This book is a direct transcription of volumes in the collection of the National Folklore Commission, University College Dublin. Every effort has been made to preserve the text as originally written. Spellings, both in English and Irish, have been maintained, as has grammatical form other than where the lack of (or excess) punctuation makes reading difficult or alters meaning. Where possible, Irish phrases have been translated and the editor accepts responsibility for errors incurred in doing so. In order to protect privacy, addresses have been removed from references – in many instances, descendants continue to live in the area. Stories that may cause upset to descendants or denigrate the memory of a deceased person have been anonymised or omitted. The editor requests that readers respect the privacy of those who live in the Mizen area today by not trespassing on private land. Please seek permission from landowners before attempting to visit any of the locations mentioned in this book. Unless otherwise stated, photographs are by the editor.

Acknowledgements

There are many people who have offered advice and support during the writing of this book. Firstly, I want to thank Claire Ní Dhubhcháin and the staff of the National Folklore Collection, University College Dublin, for permission to publish this material, and The National Library of Ireland for authorising use of images from their collection. I owe a debt of gratitude to Sheila and Jean at the e-Mizen Centre in Goleen for their encouragement and patience during my many visits there. I'd like to thank Jim O'Meara for sharing his insights and deep knowledge of local history, folklore and songs, for his enthusiasm, and especially for agreeing to write the foreword. Special thanks are due to my parents, Kathleen and George Baldwin, and my grandmother, Johanna Cleary (nee Downey) for introducing me to Goleen and its environs. Finally, I cannot finish without thanking my great uncle Mike, and aunts Nora and Lizzie Downey, for their warm and open welcome which sparked my interest in the Mizen Peninsula and wider area.

CONTENTS

Illustrations

FOREWORD

The tradition of storytelling or "scoraichting", as it is known from the Gaelic, has had a long history in Ireland. The first records date from the stories of the legendary hero, Fionn Mac Cool and his mythical warriors, the Fianna, beginning in the seventh century, the so called Fenian Cycle. The tradition continues up to the present day, for instance in the Cape Clear Island Summer Story Telling Festival and other similar celebrations. Stories are also told in the much-loved Radio Eireann program "Sunday Miscellany" which has been running for very many years.

The praiseworthy initiative by the Irish Folklore Commission in the late thirties of the last century, in requesting the pupils and teachers of the National Schools of the State (including my father, Bat O'Meara, Principal Teacher of Goleen National School) to seek out the stories and practices of earlier times from the lips of the older people of their districts, has resulted in a priceless hoard of information. We now have access to this material online and Dr Mike Baldwin has made excellent use of it. He has strong family links with this district and has gained, over the years, a deep understanding of the life of this place. He has been tireless in seeking out hitherto unknown sources of information and the outcome is that we have been presented with a fascinating account of life as it was here many years ago.

Jim O'Meara, July 2019

INTRODUCTION

In 1937, the Irish Folklore Commission issued guidance to National Schools countrywide for the collection of stories, folklore, songs, and histories; the pupils of Ireland's schools were charged with the collection, curation, and transcription of the nation's oral history. The author of this guidance, distributed by the Department of Education, put it thus, 'The task is an urgent one, for in our time most of this important national oral heritage will have passed away forever.'[i] 'Passed away' was an apt turn of phrase. Many of these stories had lived and evolved for centuries, passed by word of mouth from generation to generation. Their continuing decline risked the loss of an invaluable and irreplaceable treasure, a quintessentially Irish strand of local and national identity.

Centuries of oppression, occupation, famine, war, and emigration saw the Irish people and their folklore scattered to the corners of the earth. The world's gain (for it was certainly a gain) was Ireland's loss. Displaced, ties to their origins and communities broken, many stories became just that – stories - amorphous and disincarnate with a diminished sense of the people or places they left behind. The nation's very history became the most significant contributing factor in the demise of national narrative and prose. It is no coincidence then that the Fastnet Rock, symbolic and remote, immovable and immutable, the final sight of land for hundreds of thousands of emigrants, acquired the epithet, 'the teardrop of Ireland'.

History is a peculiarly biased thing. All too often it is the narrative of the wealthy, the famous, infamous, and the notorious. History is rarely the story of you or me. Us common people are reduced to bit parts… or are largely forgotten. If history books are to be believed, we're people of apparently little significance. The National Folklore Commission's subversion of historical convention then, just 15 years after the birth of the Irish free state, was bold. Unconcerned and disinterested with those who might wish to dictate their own histories, whether through action or oratory, it raised its common folk high, rendering their tales important, and thus, a priceless tradition was saved from annihilation. In their saving, some unexpected things happened. The students' writing preserved local dialect and aspects of regional Irish. One book in particular, that written by Bart Ó Meara, master of Goleen school, records the stories precisely as told. Albeit mostly written in English, dialect and grammatical form owes a lot to the Irish language. Irish spellings are non-standard, varying from story to story, book to book, and from school to school

---

[i] Irish Folklore and Tradition, September 1937, p.3.

– the range and breadth of which is preserved in this volume. In reading the stories, one can hear the lyrical sing-song lilt of the Mizen villages preserved in the text.

Stories were often repeated and frequently differed in their retelling, the variations perhaps reflecting the interests and concerns of the tellers. The Irish Folklore Commission emphasized that all tales mattered, no matter how short or long – everything should be written down. Each city, town, village, and townland could contribute. Subjects for composition were proposed: hidden treasure; old or funny stories; old Irish tales, riddles and proverbs; stories of giants, warriors, leprechauns and mermaids; songs, poetry and local poets; weather lore and recollections of severe weather; local heroes and happenings; old schools; marriage and festival customs; hurling, football, home-made toys, and games played; place and road names, home districts and landlords; local fairs; care of farm animals, strange animals, and bird lore; food in olden times, the potato crop, churning; local cures, herbs, and care of the feet; the lore of certain days and historical traditions; travelling folk, fairy forts, holy wells, local monuments and ruins; famine times; the local forge; locally made clothes; buying and selling; religious stories, stories of the holy family, local patron saints, prayers and graveyards; emblems and objects of value. Nothing was to be left out. And the children of the Mizen's schools, 'the collectors', took up their pens and wrote. Contributors, often family members and neighbours, ranged from 36 years (Mr W. Goggin of Enaughter, Goleen) to 97 years (Jeremiah Donovan of Gunpoint, Schull) the latter's year of birth, 1840, predating the famine. Storytelling was a collective community act.

I've been a visitor to the Mizen since I was a young child, my grandparents being from Goleen and Durrus respectively. I remember stories being told, such as one about a priest caught during penal times at a mass rock in the townland of Castlemehigan. In his rush to escape, a chalice was thrown into a lough adjacent to the mass rock, which now serves as a local reservoir. It is said that should the chalice be recovered, the reservoir will run dry – impressive if true, the area being awash with rainfall. For the most part, I have only vague recollections and wish I had listened more attentively. However, it is clear that the landscape of the area preserves its own narrative, with its farms, lanes, derelict émigré houses, churches, field boundaries, ancient monuments, and its windswept and wild sea-carved coastline, redolent of long departed people and their stories. But the landscape tells an older story still, one of the very shaping of the rock. Long before the erection of the area's megalithic standing stones and tombs, its medieval castles, and churches, glaciation scribed its indelible signature large across the Mizen. Deep striations on hills and mountain sides, the drumlins and erratics that litter the landscape, and the dendritic like ria-coast speak of glacial retreat of millennia past.

Irish place names, often descriptive, tell us something of localities and sometimes take their names from people of the past. Although spellings have varied over time, and whilst most have been reduced to their phonetic form, it is possible to take them back to their original Irish, and to extract meaning. Crookhaven becomes An Cruachán – the round-topped hill; Lissigriffin become Lios Uí Ghrífín – Griffin's fort; Goleen becomes An Góilín – the little inlet; Lowertown becomes Lúghortán – the herb garden or place where herbs grow; Schull become Scoil Mhuire – School of Mary; and Ballydehob becomes Beal an da chab – town on the mouth of two rivers. Townland names are richer still; Cloghanacullen (Chlochán an Choillín) means the causeway through or by the little wood; Knockagallane (Cnoc an Ghalláin) translates as hill of the standing stone; and Gortnamona (Gort na Móna) means field of the bog.

Considered now to be remote by some, the villages of the Mizen were originally well connected. Crookhaven welcomed ships from across the globe. This peninsula, a collection of maritime communities, was perhaps more accessible by ocean than by land. Movement by sea, until the building of metaled roads and the coming of the now lost railway, was quicker than travelling over land, particularly over long distances. Early tourism, however, wasn't uncommon. In 1783, Philip Luckombe, having undertaken a somewhat windswept variant of the grand tour, published his book, *A Tour Through Ireland.* His journey from Bantry, via Dunmanus Bay, to Kilcoe and Schull, and eventually to Crookhaven, is described. Little has changed. His description, which follows, is still recognisable today, and thanks to the children of the local schools, the folklore is as well preserved as the landscape of the Mizen peninsula.

> From Bantry we proceeded south with the river Four-mile-water close on our left, to where it empties itself into the head of Dunmanus bay, which forms another peninsula, called Minterbarry [sic], a most barbarous country, washed on the east by Dunmanus bay, and by Bantry bay on the west. At the north end of Dunmanus bay, near Four-mile-water river, is Coollong, a good seat, but the country round it is rocky, boggy, and mountainous.
>
> From there we crossed Four-mile-water to Dunbeacon castle, which stands at the bottom of the bay, about a mile south of Coollong, and three to Kilcoe, the head of Roaring-water, where also stands Ballydehob village. This whole peninsula is called Ivaugh. We passed

down the side of the peninsula to Rosbrin castle, a stately ruin, erected boldly on a rock, which hangs over the ocean. The proprietor of this castle, in Queen Elizabeth's time, turned pirate, which occasioned its demolition, and the west side is battered to the ground. Two miles more southwest are the ruins of Ardintenant castle, seated near the east point of Skull [sic] harbour. Skull, one mile west from thence, is but a small insignificant village, having few buildings besides the church and parsonage house. To the north of it stands a high conical hill, called Mount Gabriel; on the top of it is a remarkably deep lough, which is but a few yards over; it has been sounded from the north-east with a hundred fathom line; although the lead stopped, yet the hole was deeper. The water oozes out of the mountain to the north-east; and this cone is above three hundred yards higher than the level of the sea; from it is a noble prospect of vast extent, over a rude uncultivated country, from the Mizen-head to Ross, with an infinite number of islands, bays, creeks, and harbours.

On returning from this mountain, justly reckoned the steepest of its length in Ireland, towards the coast, and passing by Skull, we proceed west to Leamcon, a pretty seat near a good harbour, between Long Island and the peninsula. Near it are two castles in ruins, one of which is called Black castle, built on an island; to which is a very narrow passage easily defended; and more west, is the castle of Bally Desmond, now called Bally Divilin [sic], boldly erected on a rock projecting over the sea. More westerly stands Crookhaven, an inconsiderable fishing town, near an excellent harbour, and one of the best outlets in Europe for vessels to sail to any place whatever. The lands about are exceedingly rocky and barren. Near it are the ruins of Castle Meghan. The extreme point of this tract is Bally-Vogy-head, between which and the opposite cape, called Mizen-head, is a great bay, and another between that and Three-Castle head, so called from three square towers built on it. From thence we travelled up the western side of this peninsula to Dunmanus castle, from whence the bay on the western side has its name, which castle was formerly fortified with walls and flankers, now in ruins.

Philip Luckombe, *A Tour Through Ireland*
(London: Lowndes, 1783), pp.211-222

What of the Mizen villages now? Today the villages of Crookhaven, Goleen, Toormore, Lowertown, Schull, and Ballydehob are undeniably smaller than in former years, their populations having never recovered from famine and emigration. Most of the schools that contributed to the collection of the stories in this book are gone. Those in Crookhaven, Toormore and Lowertown have been converted to homes, their original use marked only by the inaugural stone plaques above their entrances. Lissagriffin school moved a short distance in 1958 but closed its doors for the final time in 2018 when the headteacher retired, the remaining pupils moving to nearby Goleen. Smaller does not, however, mean diminished. The villages continue to thrive. Whilst much of the local income is still made from farming, tourism now plays a very large part in the sustenance of the community. And the community continues to be at the heart of it all. There's a strong sense of self-sufficiency and entrepreneurial spirit; a friendly welcome and hospitality for all.

Here moss-grown trees expand the smallest leaf,
Here half and acre's corn, is half a sheaf,
Here hills with naked heads the tempest meet,
Rocks at their sides, and torrents at their feet,
Or lazy lakes, unconscious of a flood,
Whose dull brown naiads ever sleep in mud.
Yet here content can dwell.

Thomas Parnell (1679-1718)

CROOKHAVEN

Co. Chorcaighe
Bar: Cairbre Thiar
Par: Kilmoe
Scoil: An Cruachán
Oide: Saidhbhín ní Bhoidhbléin
11.1937 – 23.12.1938

Figure 1. Rock Island, Crookhaven, 26 July 1837. Brocas sketchbook (PD 1962 TX). Image used with the kind permission of the National Library of Ireland.

CROOKHAVEN
Local Folklore and Stories

The Glavin Mermaid

The following story is told in my district, Arduslough, Crookhaven, Co Cork about a family named Glavin who resided in the neighbourhood.

One of the Glavin men was fishing one day. He saw a girl combing her hair on the rock near the strand. She was a mermaid. He took her home with him and he married her. But she told him three special things he should never do: not to kill a seal; not to eat off a sheriff's table; not to kill a black sheep.

Everything went on well for years till one Sunday when the wife was at mass, the man went with a party of men to the seaa nd he killed a seal, skinned it, and brought home the skin. When the woman returned, she said to the man, "you have broken your promise and killed a seal, and I can stay here no longer." She then went towards the beach and shook a bridle. A saddled horse from the sea came to her. She said that seven men of the name Glavin would never be see together again. She then mounted the horse and disappeared out to sea and was never heard of again. But the prophecy seems to have been fulfilled as seven men of that name have never been since together. [1]

Collected by Mary Sullivan, Crookhaven
From Mr Denis O'Sullivan (aged 50), Crookhaven

The Serpent of Arduslough

There is a story told in this district about a serpent which lived in the lake in Arduslough a short distance north of Crookhaven. Long ago it was seen in different shapes. St Patrick banished him into the lake when he came to Ireland on a May evening. On every seventh May evening he is supposed to be seen near the lake. Attempts were not made to capture him as the people were afraid to go near him.[2]

Collected by Margaret Sullivan, Crookhaven
From Mr Denis Sullivan (aged 50), Crookhaven

The Demon of Arduslough

Cuan Cruacán, that is harbour of the round hill, takes its name from the round-topped hill of Lenane which overlooks its upper reaches. On the highest portion of this hill there is the grave of a Tuatha de Dannan chief and a short distance from the grave there are now the scarcely discernible remains of a large dwelling place of great antiquity. Less than a quarter of a mile from the grave there is a druidical altar with the little lake of Arduslough nearby. There is a legend narrated by the older inhabitants of this district. At the bottom of this lake lies an imprisoned demon of the pagan times. He is permitted to come to the surface every seven years on May morning and addresses St Patrick who is supposed to have banished him in the following words, "It is a long Monday, Patrick". The demon does not speak in the English but in the vernacular. The long Monday refers to the day of general judgement. Having expressed these words his chain is again tightened and perforce he sinks to the bottom of the lake for another period of seven years. His imprisonment will not expire till the last day.[3]

Contributed by Mr John Downing (aged 72), Crookhaven

A Moral Story

One day a number of hens lived together in a farmyard. Some were plump and others were lean. The fat hens were fond of making fun of the lean hens. "You are more like scarecrows than hens," the fat hens used to say to the lean hens. One day the farmer's wife came into the yard to choose some hens for her dinner. "I will not have those thin birds," she said. Then she caught up some of the fat hens and brought them into the kitchen. She killed them. The fat hens wished they had not been so foolish as to laugh at the lean hens that were left alive and happy.[4]

Collected by John Pyburn, Crookhaven, Skibbereen

Holy Wells

Adjacent to my district, Arduslough, which is about two and half miles from Crookhaven, is a hill called Letter hill which contains a holy well. The hill is about a few fields from my home. It is said that in former years people from far and near used go to the well and pray. They used leave beads, bottles, medals, money etc. there. On every St John's eve, flocks of people used to spend the whole night in prayer and rounds. About a hundred yards above the well is a round green spot and stones all round it and on one of the flat stones there is a cross. The people used go from stone to stone praying. It was customary to spend the night there praying, dancing, and singing. On leaving it was usual to leave some coin or other article there. This place is called the gollans. It is also believed that people were cured by praying there.[5]

Fairy Forts

There are no fairy forts in my locality but there is one in Lissigriffin. This is a townland situated about three miles to the north-west of Crookhaven. There are also some in Lissacaha and Lissihinahorac. The Lissacaha fort is situated near Dunmanus castle and the Lissihinahorac one is near Goleen. They are called *liss* meaning a fort. They are not in view of one another. They are round in shape and flat on top. There are no fences around them. They have entrance holes to them. People used go into them long ago but not now. Many still believe that there are fairies in them. A man named Griffin built the one in Lissigriffin. Lissacaha was supposed to be called after a battle which was fought there in olden times. Lissihinahorac is supposed to get its name as it was a scene of a battle in former years. They were built as defence. People never like to plough near these forts as they think it is not right to interfere in any way with them.[6]

Collected by Mary Sullivan, Crookhaven
From Mr John Sullivan (aged 60), Crookhaven

Figure 2. Dunmanus castle (top). Arduslough (High Lake) Crookhaven (bottom).

Smuggling Story

Smuggling was carried out to a great extent in my district in the past times. One of the most famous smugglers was Daniel Coughlan, brother of the admiral mentioned in the previous story. He used to go to foreign countries and bring with him wine, whiskey, tobacco, silks, and other things. Once he went to Amsterdam in Holland and got a cargo of tobacco and brandy and sailed back for Crookhaven. On the way a revenue cutter chased them. He ran under the Old Head of Kinsale and put out his lights. He then went ashore in a small boat and put a light on the rock. The English men stopped watching it as they thought it was the ship who was ashore. In the meantime, he sailed for Crookhaven without any lights and unloaded his cargo. Another time Coughlan was coming to Crookhaven with a cargo of contraband brandy. On the route an English man-of-war captured him and took the vessel into Queenstown harbour and stopped watching her. Coughlan became very friendly with the English crew, and one night he took some of his brandy on board her. He gave it to the crew to drink. When he had them all drunk, he left the ship and went unto his own boat and set sail for Crookhaven unknown to the English boat. Thus, he escaped prison.[7]

Collected by Mary Sullivan, Crookhaven
From Mr John Sullivan (aged 60), Crookhaven

The Woman's Leap

About two miles from Crookhaven there is a high cliff standing out known as the Woman's Leap. It is said that an English soldier chased a woman through the hills to kill her but she jumped over the cliff out on the strand. Though the jump was a high one, she was uninjured. That is how it got its name Woman's Leap. The story goes that the soldier was killed.[8]

Collected by Mary Pyburn, Crookhaven
From Mr J Driscoll (aged 60), Crookhaven

Crookhaven: Where the wine flows like water

The following story is told by the old inhabitants of the village of Crookhaven of the days when the O'Mahony's held sway there. The site of their castle can be pointed out today. It stood on the strand a little distance from the spot where the village shops are now situated. In those days a chieftain in the north lost his son in battle. He grieved night and day for this son. The deep grief at length caused him to be deranged. He imagined his son still lived and left his home to seek him. He went from castle to castle seeking his son. His query always being, "Is my son Diarmuid here?" Where he received the reply that his son was not there, he used to leave sadly saying, "Where Diarmuid is not, I will not stay." At length he arrived at O'Mahony's castle in Crookhaven. He enquired there for his son. O'Mahony noticed his condition. He bade him enter telling him his son was in the castle. Then O'Mahony sent for the local herb doctor. The chieftain was under his care for some time. At length he recovered his senses. O'Mahony treated him very hospitably. In departing he offered him the *deoc an dorais*. This was a rich wine. O'Mahony's cellars were well stocked with wine, as at that time Crookhaven did considerably trade with Spain. When the chieftain reached his own territory, he praised the hospitality of the O'Mahonys to his friends and said that the wine was flowing there like water. Three neighbouring chieftains set out for O'Mahony's castle to see if all that was told was true. When the chieftains arrived in Crookhaven they were treated royally. When departing, O'Mahony and his friends accompanied them to about a mile outside the village. The exact spot where they parted is where an old boiler now stands, at the junction of the Crookhaven and the Browhead road. O'Mahony, as a parting gift, brought an immense cask of the best wine. There they rested and began to drink the wine. All went well till one of the chieftains was not satisfied. He bent his head into the cask to drink. One of O'Mahony's friends caught him by the legs and plunged him into the wine, in which he drowned. The O'Mahony's then boasted that the chieftains had to admit when they returned home that wine in Crookhaven was a plentiful as water.[9]

Contributed by Mr Florence McCarthy (aged 50), Crookhaven

The Pedlar and the Black Man

The following is an old story told locally. Once there lived an old man in Dough about two miles to the west of the village of Crookhaven. He was a pedlar. He used go to Cork and buy small articles such as pins, needles, thread, handkerchiefs, etc. and then come back and sell them in the neighbourhood. On one of these occasions as he was returning the night was foggy. He saw a light in the distance, and he went towards it. It was the light of a house. He went in. There was no one inside but a black man. He was astonished to see him. The black man asked him did he ever see a black man before. He said no. He then asked him did he ever see a darkey. He said no. The black man told him he was a sailor and that he was shipwrecked at the Old Head of Kinsale. He saw this light in the distance and came towards it. While they were talking, they heard people talking outside. They heard one saying to the other "strike him". The other replied, "Strike him yourself". The black man said to the pedlar, "Don't mind them. I'll fix them." They found out it was a bullock they were killing and that the house was theirs. The black man found the hide and horns of a cow. He put it around him, and he put his head out the door and the two outside ran away. The two inside searched the house and they found a lot of gold. They found out that the two outsides were two thiefs [sic]. The black man and the pedlar shared the gold. The pedlar came home and lived very comfortably in his home ever afterwards. After his death there was a lot of money found after him.[10]

Collected by Margaret Sullivan, Crookhaven
From Mr John Sullivan (aged 60), Crookhaven

The Priest's Footprint

Near the Mizen Head, which is about seven miles west of the village of Crookhaven, there is a rock and on it is the print of a priest's foot. It is believed that during the time of the Penal Laws in Ireland, a priest was saying mass in a place called Sheep's Head in Berehaven when a flock of soldiers chased him. He jumped from that place to a place near the Mizen and the rock where he put his foot, the print of it came out on the rock. Today there is water on the print, and it is believed to cure warts.[11]

Collected by Mary Sullivan, Crookhaven

The Catholic and the Protestant

This is one of the religious stories I heard which was told long ago in this locality. Long ago there lived two men one of them was a Catholic and the other was a Protestant. They were great friends. They had only one disagreement. Each man thought his own religion was the right one. They made a bargain that the first one of them that would die should come back and tell the other which was the right religion. After some time, the Protestant man died. Shortly after his death he appeared to the Catholic and said, "Stay as you are", then he vanished again.[12]

Collected by Jeremiah Mahony, Crookhaven
From Mrs Bowler, Crookhaven

The Old Woman and her Stones

There were several religious stories related in this locality in former years. This is one of them. Long ago there lived an old woman and she used to go to mass every day. She kept a box and every day when she used to attend mass, she used to put a stone in the box. While she attended mass, she used to think thoughts about her neighbours. After a considerable time, she came to the box and opened it. She found only one stone in the box, as it was the only one mass she attended properly.[13]

Collected by John Pyburn, Crookhaven

The Giants and the Fastnet Rock

The following is a local legend regarding a giant. Long ago two giants were fighting. One of the giants lived in Cape Clear. The other dwelt in this parish. The later picked up a big piece of rock from Mount Gabriel near Schull and threw it at the giant in Cape Clear. It did not reach the island. It fell into the sea to the west of the Island and remained on the top of the water. It is now known as the Fastnet Rock.

There is also a legend regarding this rock. The old people believed that it left its position on every May morning and went sailing around the ocean but returned back again to its former position.[14]

Collected by Jeremiah Mahony, Crookhaven

Penance for Forgotten Masses

Long ago religious stories were told in the district. This is one of them. Once there was a man who went to confession. After his confession he fell asleep in the confessional box. When he awoke, he was not able to get out of the church because the doors were shut as it was night. Then he saw a priest on the altar seated for mass. The candles were lighting on the altar. After a time, the priest asked was there any one in the church who would answer mass. The man went up and answered mass. Then the priest told him to come again at the same hour for so many nights. When he went the last night, the priest told him not to come anymore. He explained to him that these were masses he got offerings for during life and forgot to say them. His penance was now done as he celebrated these masses.[15]

Contributed by Willie Mahony, Crookhaven

The Mermaid

There are no stories about the leipreachán in this district except ones which are got from books. But there is one story told locally about the mermaid. It is recorded in the first page of this book. The mermaid was able to talk. She had the head and body of a woman and the tail of a fish. When the promises were broken, she then disappeared into the sea. A family by the name of Glavin was connected with the mermaid. They resided in a townland to the west of the parish.[16]

Collected by Margaret Sullivan, Crookhaven
From Mr Denis Sullivan (aged 50)

The Bishop and the Haunted Room

Once there was a Bishop went on a pilgrimage to Rome to see the Pope. There were no trains at that time and so he had to walk. He was tired and he went into a hotel and remained there for some time. One evening as he was going out walking, he noticed that one the windows in the back of the hotel was not like the others. It was darkened. He asked the landlord of the hotel why was the window shuttered. He said that the room was haunted. This Bishop said he would like to see the room and remained till midnight. A priest appeared to him and told him that he was dead. But during his life on one occasion he was hearing the confession of deaf and dumb girl in the room. She wrote her confession on a paper. The priest was summoned to go on a sick call. When he returned, he was very tired, and he went to bed and he forgot to burn the confession. The next day he died. He came back in order to get somebody to burn the paper. He told the Bishop to take the confession out of the book in which the priest had deposited it before his death and burn it. He told him not to read it. The Bishop did as he was directed. The priest then disappeared satisfied.[17]

Collected by Margaret Sullivan, Crookhaven
From Mr W. Goggin (aged 36), Goleen

Figure 3. Crookhaven Harbour. Drawn by Foley C. P. Vereker (1896)

CROOKHAVEN
People, places and Property

Local Heroes

The men of Crookhaven were noted oarsmen and sailors. The following account was told by local men. About sixty years ago John Driscoll, Thomas Beasley and Stephen Downey set sail from Wales in a sailing vessel with a cargo of coal for South America. They had a terrible passage and the gas of the coal set the cargo on fire. They went to the Falkland Islands and unloaded their cargo. Then they went on their journey. They wanted a cargo of manure and had to wait six months for it. Once again, they set sail for Hamburg, a place in Germany, with the manure. It took them two years before they came back to Crookhaven. They also were great oarsmen. Many years ago, there was a regatta in Berehaven and a boat went from Crookhaven to pull in it. The best oarsmen were Charlie Meade and John Driscoll. They won the race and the Berehaven men were so jealous of the prowess of the Crookhaven crew, that they would not let them in, and a crew song was composed by [the] Berehaven schoolteacher about the race. The old mariners of Crookhaven went on many long voyages in sailing vessels around Cape Horn. One man was noted for his sailing whose name is John Glanville. He wrote many stories about his voyages. They also lifted heavy stones. One man from Crookhaven name[d] John Driscoll took a stone weighing six hundredweight on his back from Crookhaven to the graveyard in Kilmoe, a distance of about three miles. The best walker was John Meade, a native of Crookhaven. He walked to Cork and beat a six oared boat which started with him. The best reaper in the parish was Cornelius Mahony of Letter. It was said he could reap as much two men in one day. The best storyteller was Jeremiah Mahony of Lenane.[18]

Collected by Mary Pyburn, Crookhaven
From Mr J Driscoll (aged 60), Crookhaven

Castle Mehigan

Castle Mehigan is a townland situated to the north-east of Crookhaven. It got its name from a castle that was built there in former years by a man named Mehigan who was a French man and was an officer of Lord O'Mahony who then ruled from Mizen Head to Drimoleague. The castle was built as a defence. When any invasion came to fight them, they would hide under the ground as there were tunnels under the ground running from the castle to the hill.[19]

Crookhaven - My Home District

My native district is Crookhaven. It is situated in West Carbery, in the Parish of Kilmoe. Carbery is situated in West Cork. Crookhaven is now a small village, but it was a very prosperous place about a hundred years ago. When there were no steamboats the sailor's ships came into the harbour when the wind was easterly. Long ago, O'Driscoll ruled all Carbery, so the name most common in the village is O'Driscoll. There are also foreign names in the village. Most of the village men were sailors. The places around have Irish names. The land around is hilly. The houses in Crookhaven now are slated. Long ago the houses were more numerous than they are now. There were five or six hundred people in Crookhaven. There are 32 families there now. There is a protestant church in Crookhaven now. There is a stone in the church, and it was taken from a Catholic church that was in Kilmoe. There was a Catholic church in Crookhaven long ago and there was a priest living there. There are two old people in Crookhaven. One of them knows Irish and tells stories in Irish and English. Her name is Mrs J. Goggin, Blackpool, Crookhaven, Skibbereen. Long ago the people of Crookhaven emigrated to Australia and America and many other countries. Some people say Crookhaven got its name from the round topped hills that are at the other side of the harbour. There is a stream at the other side of the harbour called the Mill Stream. There was a corn mill working there about a hundred years ago. There are songs about Crookhaven. One song is called Crookhaven. At the other side of the harbour there are the remains of a wood. It was cut down about 1920. There is a stone quarry at the other side of the harbour. There are about 60 men employed in the quarry. The stone is very good, and it is sent to all parts of Europe. Steamboats come to the quarry for the stone.[20]

Collected by Jeremiah Mahony, Crookhaven

Figure 4. Kilmoe church and graveyard (top). Bullane to the south of Kilmoe Graveyard (bottom)

Figure 5. Eastern gable, Kilmoe Church.

Figure 6. Hiberno-Celtic window, eastern gable.

Figure 7. Southern door, Kilmoe Church.

Figure 8. Castlemehigan Lough and rock (top). Castlemehigan mass rock (bottom).

Arduslough – My Home District

My home district is Arduslough. It is situated about two miles from the village of Crookhaven in the southwest of Cork, parish of Kilmoe. This is in the barony of Carbery. At present there are only two families living there. The population only being fifteen. The houses are slated. It got its name from a lake which is in the district as the word Arduslough means high lake. There are no people over seventy years living there. One person can speak Irish and can tell stories in English but not in Irish. His name is Daniel McCarthy, Arduslough, Crookhaven. Both population and houses were more numerous in former years in the district than at the present day. In ancient times people emigrated to America from there. The land is hilly and good. There are no trees there now but there are the remains of a wood a little distance below the place. Long ago it was covered with trees but in the time of the trouble in Ireland they were cut down by the natives and were used for several purposes.

There is a lake, which is fairly large in size, and from it a stream which runs down through the land and wood and into the sea near the main road. It is known as the mill stream and got its name from a mill which was there in former years. It was a corn mill and the foundation of it can be seen at the present day. There is a story about this lake. Long ago a serpent lived somewhere near the head. He used do a lot of damage. He used kill the people and even the cattle. So, in the end the natives were greatly afraid of him. When St Patrick came to Ireland, he banished the serpent into the lake. It is said it was on a May evening he did it. So, for that reason the tradition here is that a serpent used appear in different shapes every seventh May evening. There are also two mass rocks in the district and long ago during the penal laws in Ireland mass was said on these rocks by catholic priests. They are long flat stones leaning against a bank and then there is another stone about four feet high under the outside of it to support it. There is also a king's grave in the place, and it is believed that a battle was fought there in former times by the Danes and this king was killed and was buried there. It is supposed that a treasure is hidden in the kings grave also. The place where he is buried is called fear a buideacais.[21]

Killean

Killean is a townland situated about one mile from Crookhaven. It got its name from a little graveyard which was there in ancient times as the word Killean (Cillín) means a little graveyard. It is believed that it was an ancient burial ground for the locality. [22]

Local Roads

There are many by-roads in the Crookhaven district. The two most commonly known are the old road and the new road. The new road leads from Crookhaven to Goleen and to all the other townlands and districts outside of Goleen. This road was made in the year 1876. No one can remember when the old road was made. There are many by-roads leading from the main road. There is another main road leading from the top of the strand to Lissigriffin school and to Kilmoe graveyard, and there are branches off it leading west to Mizen Head, and other townlands east of Goleen and north to any of the country townlands. Before the bridge was made on the Lissigriffin road the people of the district had great difficulty in crossing to the graveyard. The old people of Crookhaven can remember the time when the bridge was made. [23]

Collected by Mary Pyburn, Crookhaven

Tobar Mianac – The Wishing Well

There is a well in Crookhaven which was known unto the old people of the village as Tobar Mianac or the Wishing Well. It was believed in former times that whoever drank the water of the well three times and formed a wish, his wish was granted. The most propitious time to drink the water was midnight. It was also believed that whoever drank the water would die in the village, that if he travelled from it, he was sure to return. This well is not used now, and its existence is forgotten.

Collected by Margaret Sullivan, Crookhaven
From Mr M. McCarthy (aged 50), Crookhaven

The Old Graveyards

There are five graveyards in this parish, Kilmoe, Kilhanging, a graveyard in the churchyard of Goleen Catholic church, one in the Goleen Protestant churchyard, and one in the protestant churchyard in Crookhaven. Kilmoe graveyard is in the townland of Lissigriffin, and Kilhanging is in the townland of Dunmanus. The graveyards are sloped. There are no trees growing in them. There are old crosses in them. There are crosses made of wood and iron. There are ruined churches in the graveyards of Kilmoe and Kilhanging. People are buried in them. In the graveyard in Crookhaven there are very old tombs. Catholics and Protestants were buried there. Sailors who were lost at sea were also buried there. There are two underground tunnels in the graveyard. The old people think it was a smuggler that used them in the days when smuggling was prevalent in the village. Others think they were used in the time of the Danes to hide the sacred vessels. There is a graveyard in Killeen. It is not used at the present day. Long ago unbaptised children were buried there. [24]

Collected by Jeremiah Mahony, Crookhaven
From Mr John Mahony (aged 49), Crookhaven

Old Houses

Mostly all the houses in my district in olden times were thatched with straw. Some of the houses had beds in the kitchens. The beds they had were not all the same. Some of them were made of timber and they were covered all over with timber, but one side was opened for the people to get in. They were known as testers. The fire was at the gable end of the house. The front of the chimney was made of clay and stones. There were houses there long ago that had no chimney. In some of the houses there were small windows with no glass in them and other houses had no windows. Floors were made of clay and flags. At present, half doors are not common. For their fires they used turf, wood, and sometimes they used coal. They had no lamps long ago, but they melted fat and they put a rush through it for a wick. This was the light they had. Candles were made locally in past times.[25]

Collected by Mary Sullivan, Crookhaven
From Mr John Sullivan (aged 60), Crookhaven

Local Ruins

There are no ruined castles in the village at present. Long ago there was a ruined castle on the strand in the village but there is no trace of it today except one stone. This castle was built by the chieftain O'Driscoll. There are five ruined castles in the parish. There are the ruins of three castles at Three Castle Head in the townland of Dunlough about 8 miles from Crookhaven. There are also the remains of one in the townland of Arduslough, a short distance from Crookhaven. There is another ruined castle in Dunmanus. These castles were built about 1172. They were built by the O'Mahonys. They are situated in the parish of Kilmoe, in the barony of Carbery, and in the County of Cork. Long ago they were attacked by the English. They became ruins about 1600. They had dungeons. There is a ruined church in the graveyard of Kilmoe. Long ago monks resided there. There is a stone out of this church over the door of the Protestant church in Crookhaven. The stone has the mitre of a bishop on it. There are old towers in the locality. There is an old tower in the village of Crookhaven. It is known as O'Sullivan's tower. It was built by a man named Coughlan a considerable time ago. He was an admiral in the navy and he had a gun on this tower, and he saluted every British warship that came into the harbour. There are two towers at the other side of the harbour. They were built for watching smugglers. There was a poem composed about Coughlan's turret in past times. The following is one verse of this poem.[26]

In this harbour you could see the Spaniard, Frenchman, and Portuguese
Who ploughed the seas courageously to bring riches to our harbour?
And Coughlan's turret it stands as high it illuminates the cloudy sky
You'd see bunting flying there in days gone by
And big guns cannonading

Collected by Jeremiah Mahony, Crookhaven
From Mrs Bowler, Crookhaven

Figure 9. St Brendan's Church, Crookhaven.

CROOKHAVEN

Farming, Trade and Crafts

The Potato Crop

Potatoes are grown on my farm. Every year about an acre and a quarter is sown. The ground is at first manured with farmyard manure before it is turned. They are chiefly sown in ridges. The ridges are made by a plough six scrapes in width. The plough is used instead of the spade. Wooden ploughs were used in former years. There are none of them to be seen throughout the parish at the present day. Spades are usually bought in shops. The seeds are at first cut with a knife, each piece bearing an eye. Then holes are made in the ridges with a spade and one seed is thrown into each hole. Lastly the holes are closed. Some neighbours help each other to sow the potatoes. In summer, when the potato crop is of a reasonable height, a wash of blue stone and washing soda is applied. The blue stone and washing soda are put into a barrel of water. When its melted, it's put into a spraying machine. Out of the machine is a hose with holes in the end through which the spray comes out. The farmer then goes from trench-to-trench spraying as he goes. In the autumn time the potatoes are dug with a spade. Then they are picked by women and children and drawn to a pit where they are covered and left for the winter. The following are a list of potatoes sown in my district and the townlands around; champions, yankee's, British queens, Irish queens, Epicures, and various others. [27]

Collected by Mary Sullivan, Crookhaven

The Care of Our Farm Animals

I have at home three cows and three calves and a pony. The cows have names, Daisy, Summer, and Pretty. When driving the cows in or out of a field I say, "how how." When the cows are in the cowshed they are tied with a rope. The rope is tied to the cows' horns. When the hens are called, "Tuk Tuk," is said. When eggs are hatched, 13 eggs are hatched as a lucky number. In former years in this locality holy water was sprinkled on the eggs and the sign of the cross made over them before the hen is put to hatch on them. This practice has now died out.[28]

Collected by Jeremiah Mahony, Crookhaven,

Churning

We have a churn at home. It is six years old. It is about two feet tall and two feet broad. Its sides are square. It consists of four sides, bottom, top, cover, windless or beater, and handle. There is no mark on it. Butter is made once a week. Strangers who come in at the time of churning usually never help. Churning lasts about half an hour. It is done by hand. The handle is kept turning around. Butter is made when the churn gets heavier to twist. Water is sometimes poured in. The butter is taken out of the churn with a butter spade and is put into a bowl of water to get the butter milk out of it. There are no local sayings connected with it. Butter milk is kept for various uses in the homes.[29]

Collected by Margaret Sullivan, Crookhaven
From Mr John Sullivan (aged 60), Crookhaven

Old Crafts

Long ago the natives of Crookhaven and the districts around grew their corn in a different manner to the people nowadays. At that time nearly all farmers dug their ground with a spade but some of them had ploughs made of timber. The handles and beams were made from a certain strong wood while the sock was made of iron. At first, they dug or ploughed the trench. Then they scattered the grain and lastly covered it with earth. When they had it fit to be ground into flour, they never took it to a mill. They ground it with a quern. This was two round stones which rested on each other. In the centre of the top one was a round hole where the grain was put in. It also had a handle by which it was twisted. It was the rubbing of the two stones against each other that ground the flour. This is done at the present day. They also planted their potatoes in a different way. They used to turn up the ground with an iron implement. The sod was then burnt into ashes which they used as manure. They did this so well that after six weeks they would have new potatoes. This was nearly a hundred years ago.[30]

Collected by Mary Sullivan, Crookhaven
From Mr Denis O'Sullivan (aged 50), Crookhaven

Candle Making

Candle making was one of the most common Irish industries in Crookhaven. Many kinds of candles were made, such as tallow candles and candles made from the oil of fish. The older candles were rush lights. The rushes were peeled and placed in a vessel containing the oil of fish which had to be boiled. The tallow candles were made out of tallow. The tallow was melted and put into the moulds and cotton thread was put through it. They made candles also in the same way out of the oil of fish.

Other candles were also made for religious purposes. They were known as scraitheoga. They were made of tallow and cotton thread was put through them. They were very small, and the people wore them inside their clothes when they were blessed, for protection against accidents. The people in Crookhaven made those candles and when people were going to be anointed, they lit them by their bedside.

Farmers also used them when the cows were calving. The hairs on the udders of cows were burned with the lighted candle. They were unlike the other candles. They were short in size and were only used for these purposes. They were blessed on Candlemas day.[31]

Collected by Mary Pyburn, Crookhaven, Skibbereen
From Mr J Driscoll (aged 60), Crookhaven

Rope Making

The ropes which were used long ago were not like the ropes at present. They were made of hay or straw or grass. When they were making these ropes two were required. One would hold a stick in his hand about a foot long and he was twisting this stick round while the other person would be making the rope. When they were thatching their houses, these were the ropes they used, and they were known as sugane ropes. These ropes are used at present, but they are not so common as they were long ago.[32]

Basket Making

Basket making was another craft which was carried on in Crookhaven and the surrounding district in past times. These baskets were made of twigs. The twigs grew wild, but some people grew them in their own gardens. In the autumn these twigs were cut down and left under the sun for a time. When they were making the baskets, they stood a number of twigs on the ground in the shape of the mouth of the basket and they worked more twigs in between these. They kept on at this until it was the required size. When they had this finished, they closed the bottom. Baskets are still made at the present day but are not so numerous as in olden times.[33]

Ciseans and bouranes

Ciseans were square baskets used for drawing potatoes. They were made of twigs in the same manner as the ciseans they used for drawing manure. Long ago people made their own sieves for cleaning their corn. They were made of a round timber frame with a sheep skin bottom. This was pierced with holes through which the grain went. These were made about 50 or 60 years ago and the sieves were known as bouranes.[34]

Súistín

About thirty of forty years ago there were no chairs in use in our district, Arduslough, Crookhaven. Seats, which were known as súistíns, were used instead. They were made round and hollow in the middle. They were made of traced straw and were put together in such a way that they formed comfortable seats. They were packed with hay in the middle. On some of them there were backs of straw also. Some people used make armchairs out of them. When they had the straw traced, they used to call them thrawneens.[35]

Thatching

In olden times, the country houses were all thatched. There was a special man for doing this and he lived in Enaughter. His name was Cotter. He used to go around from house to house thatching. It was done with straw. The straw was placed evenly on the roof of the house. It was tied down with ropes known as sugane ropes.[36]

Net Making

In Crookhaven long ago the people made their own nets. They got the material from Cork and an old woman named Kitty Downey used to make them. My Grandfather John Driscoll also used to make all his own nets. But the two of them are dead now and net making is also finished. Then they barked their nets with what was called bark. That bark was selling in some of the shops in Crookhaven. They first put a big fire in some old, ruined house and then they put on a big iron pot and boiled the water, and then the bark was dissolved. Then the nets were dipped in and barked. Then they were taken out and put on a ditch to drain and to dry.[37]

The Local Fair

The local fairs in this locality are held in Goleen. Buyers sometimes buy cattle in the country, at the cross and at the farmhouses. There are no local traditions of fairs held on hills near graveyards. The fairs are held in the street in Goleen. When cattle are sold, luck money is given. When a bargain is made, they strike hands. The animals are marked by clipping the hair at the side. When the animals are sold, the halter or rope is not given away. The best fairs are in May and September, and at Christmas. There are no special fairs for sheep or horses or bonhams.[ii] All cattle are sold at the one fair in Goleen. In former years the fairs were not held in Goleen. The people had to go to Schull or Bantry to sell their cattle.[38]

Spinning

Long ago spinning was the most common industry in Crookhaven and the districts around. The same spinning wheel was used for the spinning of flax and wool. The wool was oiled and combed and made into rolls. Then it was attached to the end of the spindle. And the wheel which was on a long piece of wood known as the shoulder was turned by the hand. At the same time the thread was held in the other hand. Then between the fingers the thread was pulled out and at the same time the wheel was kept turning.[39]

Collected by Mary Sullivan, Crookhaven

[ii] Bonham, a phonetic anglicisation of banbh, meaning piglet.

Wool

About forty years ago the people of Crookhaven and the surrounding country made all their own clothes from the wool.[40] First the wool was sheared, washed and dried. When it was dried it was carded. The carders were something like two combs which worked on the wool until they made it smooth. When it was spun, it was then sent to the local weaver to be woven into cloth. They dyed the wool to any colour required. They got this dye from a certain plant which used to grow on rocks in fields. They boiled this plant and dipped in the wool. Then when they had the colour required got, they made their clothes. This was not done in the houses in later years but sent to Bantry to be dyed at the wool mills. This old Irish custom is dying out and very few houses in my district have spinning wheels.[41]

Flax

Flax was a plant which grew plentifully in the Crookhaven district. There is a bog in the village and the old people say flax was steeped in it. It was known as the "flax bog". When the flax was ripe, it was picked and steeped in the bog and left there for a certain number of days. Then it was taken out and left dry. In every house in that time there was a tongs with which they made the flax fine. Then they pounded it with a mallet. Every house at this time had a spinning wheel. With this they spun the flax into thread. When the flax was made into linen, the people of the houses made all classes of clothes, sheets, tablecloths, shirts and various other things. The flax was one of the principal crops in Crookhaven in the old days. The flax is not grown in Crookhaven now as everything made out of linen can be bought in the shops at a low price.[42]

Collected by Mary Pyburn, Crookhaven
From Mrs J Goggin (aged 85), Crookhaven

Lobster Pots

The making of lobster pots is a very old Irish industry. We could not go back to the days when lobster pots were first made. They are still made in our own village, Crookhaven. First the twigs are planted or perhaps they grow wild in wet places. Then they are cut down and made into bundles and are drawn home. Then a stand made of timber with holes in it is put on a barrel and the twigs are put in the holes and are worked in and out until the lobster pot is completed.[43]

Collected by Mary Pyburn, Crookhaven
From Mr J Driscoll (aged 60), Crookhaven

Clothes made locally

At present there are only two tailors in this parish. One resides at a place near the Mizen Head called Corran and the other in a place known as Balteen. These tailors work in their own homes. They sometimes stock cloth. Cloth is not woven locally now. Woollen cloth is used mostly now. When the tailor is at work, the gear he uses are needles, scissors, thread, and a sewing machine. Shirts are made in the homes. Woollen material, linen, or cotton is mostly used in the making of shirts. Both socks and stockings are knitted in nearly every home at present. The thread is not spun in most of the homes but in one house. There is at least one spinning wheel in the district. This is belonging to Mrs Helen, Dunmanus. She still spins and knits socks and stockings with the thread. Different styles of clothes are work at different periods. Black is worn at the death of a relative and various colours are worn at marriages, such as pink, white, blue, and other colours.[44]

Collected by Margaret Sullivan, Crookhaven
From Mr Denis Sullivan (aged 50), Crookhaven

Buying and Selling

Shops were not common in this locality in olden times. The people had to go to the nearest town to sell their butter and eggs. Sometimes they even walked as far as Cork city. Buying and selling was carried on after mass. This is still done. Many different articles were sold. Money was not always given. Labour was given in exchange for goods. Many words were used in buying and selling as tick, boot, cant, change, and many other words. Long ago, hucksters, pedlars and dealers in rags and feathers came to the village. Pedlars still visit the district selling small articles such as boot laces, studs, buttons, broaches etc. It was thought unlucky to buy or sell goods on certain days. The usual day that was thought unlucky to buy or sell goods was Friday. Long ago there were many different coins such as four penny pieces and ten penny pieces. These were made of silver. There were also many other coins such as crowns, sovereigns, half sovereigns, and guineas. There are no stories of coins who returned to their owners.[45]

The Local Forge

There are five forges in this parish. The smiths' names are Daniel Sullivan, Goleen; Denis Harrington, Lissigriffin; John McCarthy, Ballydevlin; John Hegearty, Dunmanus; and Hegearty, Lowertown. The forge in Goleen is situated near the roadside. The forge in Lissigriffin is situated a little distance from the main road. The forges in Dunmanus, Ballydevlin, and Lowertown are situated near the road. The forges are situated near cross roads. There are slate roofs on the forges. The doors of the forges are not made of any special shape. There is one fire in each of the forges. The bellows are not made locally. The smith's tools consist of a hammer, an anvil, tongs, a chisel, and a poker. The smiths shoe horses and asses. The smiths make ploughs, harrows, and other farm implements. Some parts of the forge work are done in the open air such as putting bands on cartwheels. There are no beliefs about forge water or the sparks that fly from the red-hot iron. People did not give any gifts to the smiths in this locality. They had not any power to banish rats. The smiths were always looked upon as strong men. There are no traditions connected with the local forges. [46]

Collected by Jeremiah Mahony, Crookhaven
From Mr John Mahony (aged 49), Crookhaven

Crookhaven
Leisure

Homemade Toys

Long ago the children of Crookhaven and the surrounding districts made all their own toys. The girls made dolls out of different material such as paper, rubber, wood, and cloth. They also made necklaces from different wildflowers. The boys made many toys such as guns, tops, slings, snares, and bird baskets. They made the guns from the branches of the elder tree. Tops were made from old threadspools. Slings were made from a long narrow twig with a cord from one end of the twig to the other. This was used for throwing stones. Snares were made for catching rabbits or hares. They were made out of snare wire with a loop at one end. They put these snares outside the rabbit burrow so when the rabbet stepped on the wire it would choke him. Bird baskets were also made out of twigs to catch birds. All these toys are made to the present day in Crookhaven by the young boys.[47]

Collected by Mary Pyburn, Crookhaven
From Mr J Driscoll (aged 60), Crookhaven

Hurling and Football Matches

There was a football matched played in this parish about 50 or 60 years ago. The teams that played were Goleen and Schull. On each side there were twenty-one men. The best players in each parish were picked out to play the match between two parishes. They played three games; Schull won one game and Goleen won two games. The score was Goleen three goals and Schull two goals. They were dressed in fancy clothes. The ball was the same kind of ball which is used at present. It was made of leather. Goal posts were four posts on each end of the field. One was to mark the goal and the other the point.

Hurling was also played in this district. It was a very common game long ago. Wooden hurleys were used. It was a straight stick and it was flat in the end. The ball was made of woollen thread and it was covered with leather. The man who was best in the field was Fitzgerald of Leenane. They also had other games such as handball and bowling. Most of these games were played in Barley Cove which is about two miles west of Crookhaven.[48]

Collected by Margaret Sullivan, Crookhaven
From Mr John Sullivan (aged 60), Crookhaven

Games I play

Boys and girls do not play the same games. The following is a list of games which we girls play in our school yard; fox and chickens, house and shop, London bridge, cat and mouse, hide and go seek, hunting, blind man's buff [sic], tig, tug of war, Mary Brown, the lost glove, and green gravel. This is the way fox and chickens is played. One child pretends she is a fox and another a hen and the rest chickens. The fox runs after the chickens and tries to catch them. House and shop is played in this way. One of the children has a shop and the rest have a house and they go to the shop buying things. This is the way London bridge is played. Two girls go away, and they take two things and they come back then, and they raise up their hands. Then the rest of them go under their hands and they take whatever they prefer best. Then they go to the back of the girl which has the best thing. This is the way hide and go seek is played. All the children go hide and one of them go seeking for them. Hunting is played like this. All the children stand together and one of them say a name and the last one out chases the rest until she catches them. For blind man's buff one girl covers her eyes and chases the rest of the girls until she catches one of them. Colours is played like this. One girl gives the colours another calls the colours. Then they all run to know which one of them would get to the den first. Nearly all these games were played by the children of my locality long ago.[49]

Collected by Margaret Sullivan, Crookhaven
From Mr Denis Sullivan (aged 50), Crookhaven

Figure 10. Barleycove beach from the sand dunes (top).
Barleycove from Chimney Cove (bottom).

CROOKHAVEN
Local Customs

Local Marriage Customs

Marriage mostly takes place during Shrove in my district and also in the surrounding districts. May is the month during which it is considered unlucky to marry. Monday, Wednesday and Friday are days which are also thought unlucky to marry. Matches are not so frequently made locally now. Money is sometimes given as dowry. Stock and goods are also given with the dowry. Long ago strawboys did visit the houses, but this custom has now completely died out. Marriage also took place in the houses in olden times.[50]

St Bridgit's Day

Customs were also observed on St Brigid's Day. It was customary for the people of the locality in the past times to put a cross on their right arm on cloth. It was usually made with a burnt furze stick. Some also made crosses of timber and hung them in their houses in honour of St Brigid.[51]

Hallow Eve

Hallow Eve falls on the thirty-first day of October. The people of this locality on that night sped a very enjoyable night. The have cake which they get in the shops. Inside these cakes there are rings, pieces of cloth, and pieces of sticks, and other things. When the cake is cut, the family is very anxious to see which of them will get the things. When they have supper eaten, they get a tub of water and put apples into it and each person tries to catch the apples with his mouth. When they get tired of this, they sit around the fire telling stories.[52]

Collected by Mary Sullivan, Crookhaven

St John's Eve

The usual Irish custom on St John's Eve in this locality is to light bonfires. These fires are chiefly lit near potato gardens as the Irish think that it prevents blight from coming on their potatoes. It is a beautiful sight to witness the hillsides ablaze on St John's Eve, but on the following day the black hillsides look dreary.[53]

Festival Customs

In my locality Crookhaven, some of the old customs are still observed on certain festivals. On St Stephen's day, boys go around to the houses in the village. They collect money. They sing a song called the Wren Song. These are the words sung here.

The Wren

The wren, the wren, the king of all birds
St Stephen's day he was caught in the furze
Although he is little his family is great
Rise up landlady and fill us a treat
But if you fill us of the small
it won't agree with our boys at all
But if you fill us of the best,
I hope in heaven your soul will rest
I met my wren on the top of a rock
I up with my cuple and broke his back
And I brought him here to your brandy shop
My money box shakes making noise and a rattle
Rise up landlady and handle your pocket
I brought my wren for to visit you here
For a taste of your liquor and a drink of your beer
Wishing you a merry Christmas
and a Happy New Year
With your pockets full of money
and your cellars full of beer
Up with the kettle and down with the pan
Up with the kettle and down with the pan
Give us our answer and let us be gone.

At present it is the boys of the village take part in the wren. The money is divided between them. Sweets and cakes are bought with the money. Some time ago it was the men of the village that took part in the wren. They spend the money collected in getting up a dance and in other ways.

The Christmas customs are still observed in this locality and great preparations are made for it. The people clean their houses, and they decorate the house with holly and ivy. On Christmas Eve they light a large candle in every window in their home. The Christmas candle is lit on Christmas Eve. It is allowed light till it burns out. On New Year's Day in my locality people consider it an important day. If a person is seen doing anything that day, it is remarked to him that he will do it for the year. They also consider it very lucky to get money on that day. The 6th of January, the feast of the Epiphany, is known locally as little Christmas day or the Women's Christmas. There is feasting and merrymaking on that day. It is thought that if a person remained up till midnight on that night, he would see water turned into wine. It is believed it occurs in memory of the time Our Lord changed water into wine at the wedding feast of Cana at the request of his Blessed Mother. Probably that is why it is known here as the Women's Christmas.

St Patrick's day is a great festival in Ireland. St Patrick's day occurs on March 17th. On that day the Irish attend mass and they wear shamrock on their coats. They also wear green badges and other national emblems.

During Shrove, the people mostly get married in this district. On Shrove Tuesday night in olden times, it was a custom to compose poems about the young people of the district who were unmarried. They went from house to house singing these songs. These verses were called Skellig's list. Much fun and amusement was derived from this custom but it quite died out in the district. On Shrove Tuesday pancakes are made in most of the homes. On Ash Wednesday most of the people of the parish go to Mass in the morning and the priest puts holy ashes on their foreheads. On Good Friday the people of this locality believed it is not right to drive in nails or strike iron or turn up sods on that day. Most of the people do not work on that day. They keep it as a holiday. West of the village there is a large cockle strand and the people of the village go there every Good Friday to pick cockles. Chalk Sunday is the Sunday following Shrove. On that day it was the custom in this district to mark the unmarried people of the locality with chalk. This custom has completely died out for a long time.

Easter Sunday is observed as a great festival in this locality. People eat meat and eggs on that day. It is believed that if a person got up early that morning, they would see the sun dancing with joy in honour of the resurrection of Our Lord.

On the first day of May the people of this locality gather flowers and furze and they hang them around the house. Some of the old people believe that if they gave away milk that day, it would decrease the supply of milk for the year. They also believed that the person who went first to a well that morning would have good luck for the year.[54]

Collected by Jeremiah Mahony, Crookhaven,

Figure 11. The Wren boys, Cork City. from S. C. Hall, Ireland: its scenery, character etc., Vol. I (London: Hall, Virtue & Co., 1843).

Hedge Schools

About a hundred years ago there were no National Schools in Ireland. The schools were called hedge schools. The teachers got no pay from the Government, and they got but little pay from the parents of the children whom they taught. Some of these schools were in our district. There was one of them in Lissigriffin. The teacher's name was Harnet. He taught in the open air where the cemetery of Kilmoe now is. In our village we had an old National School. This was a very badly built building. The teacher who then taught there was O'Mahony. Irish was not taught in this school.[55]

Collected by Jeremiah Mahony, Crookhaven
From Mr John Mahony (aged 49), Crookhaven

Food in olden times

In olden times some people in this district used eat but two meals a day, but those who could afford it had three meals a day. The two meals were breakfast and supper. Breakfast was eaten in the morning and supper was eaten in the evening. People used to work before they ate their breakfast. The meals consisted of potatoes and fish and sour milk. Potatoes were not eaten at every meal. Milk was drunk. The table was placed near the wall. When the table was not in use it was hanging near the wall. The bread they used was the wheat they ground themselves. The bread was fresh. Pork was the meat that was generally eaten. Fish was one of the chief foods in olden times in the village of Crookhaven. Vegetables also were eaten. Cabbage was the usual vegetable used. They did not eat late at night. Eggs were eaten on Easter Sunday. Fowl was eaten on Christmas day. About a hundred years ago tea was first used in the district.[56]

Bread

Bread was made in the district in years gone by from wheat, oats, barley, rye, and potatoes which were sown locally. Flour was ground locally. Querns were and are still used in this district. Many kinds of bread were used in former times: ríobún, gráinseacán, cárdi, stampy, and oaten-meal bread. Ríobún was made by first drying the wheat, ground by the quern, in a pot over the fire and eaten with milk. This is eaten at present in the country district. Gráinseacán was wheat boiled soft with milk and eaten with sugar. Cárdi is Indian yellow meal boiled with water until it gets thick. It is then eaten with milk. This is also called gruel. Stampy is raw potatoes grated with a grater. Then the water is squeezed out of it. A cake is then made out of it and baked. Potato bread was made by peeling boiled potatoes. Then braking them up and mixing them with flower and baking it into a cake. Both milk and water were used in kneeding the bread. Bread was baked every day. Bread was mostly baked in a bastable pot long ago. There are no accounts of bread being baked before the fire.[57]

Collected by Denis Sullivan, Crookhaven

Emblems and Objects of Value

There are many emblems worn on certain feasts in the locality. On St Bridget's feast the old people used to make a cross of rushes in honour of St Bridget. It used to be hung up in the houses and in the out houses. On St Patrick's day shamrocks are worn. Long ago the old people used to put a piece of furze stick into the fire and put a piece of cloth on their shoulder. With the furze stick they used to make the sign of the cross three times. This custom has now died out. On May eve certain branches and flowers are gathered. They are not brought into the house till May morning early before the sun rises. Then they are hung up in the houses and the out houses. On Palm Sunday people pick palm branches and the priest blesses them before the masses on that day. They wear a little piece of the palm in their coats and in their hats. They hang more of it in their houses. It is used also for religious purposes. It is given to the priest to sprinkle holy water with on the dying. On Christmas Eve people in this locality decorate their houses with holly and ivy. [58]

Collected by Jeremiah Mahony, Crookhaven
From Mr John Mahony (aged 49), Crookhaven

The Care of the Feet

Long ago the people of this district never wore boots or shoes till they were grown up. It is believed that there were people who never wore boots or shoes. In the old days shoes or boots were not worn except on special occasions as attending mass on Sundays or perhaps going to the nearest town or market on fair days. Usually when going to mass they did not wear their boots but carried them. When they arrived at the cross roads which is now a short distance from where our church stands, they washed their feet in a stream and then put on their boots to enter the church.

An old man, a native of the parish, tells this funny story about the time when he was a boy. One day as he was going to mass he met a woman, an acquaintance of his, a short distance from the church. She was limping and seemed in pain. He asked her what was wrong with her. She replied that "She was walking in her leather." She was unaccustomed to wearing boots and found difficulty in walking.

Children at present go barefoot in summer. The water that is used for washing the feet is usually thrown out. Boots are made and repaired locally. There are four shoemakers in the parish. Some of these shoemakers' forefathers have been shoemakers for generations. In olden days shoemakers were more numerous than at the present day. Clogs with wooden soles were and are made in some parts of the parish. Leather was not made locally in former years. No foot coverings were made.[59]

Collected by Margaret Sullivan, Crookhaven
From Mr John Sullivan (aged 60), Crookhaven

Crookhaven
Local Cures

Local Cures

In former years the natives of Crookhaven and the surrounding districts never visited a doctor to get cured. They used certain herbs and greens which they thought would cure them. If they had headaches, they used boil a plant called peppermint and drink it. As a cure for a toothache they used boil a plant called camomile and used the steam of it to relieve the pain. For strains and hurts they used wild sage. For bad stomachs they used boil garlic and drink it. For swollen or sore joints, they used march malice. For sore eyes they used put hot tea leaves on them. In this parish there was a herb doctor. It is said he lived in a place called Corran near the Mizen Head.

If they suffered from warts on the hands, they believed if they dipped the hands with the warts on it in a hollow in a rock containing water that the warts disappeared. But they should do this inadvertently. The charm would not work if they did it consciously. They also believed a snail would cure a wart if it was crushed between two stones. As soon as the snail would decay, they believed the wart would wither away.[60]

Collected by Mary Pyburn, Crookhaven
From Mrs J Goggin (aged 85), Crookhaven

Herbs

Many herbs grow on my farm but the ones which are most harmful are thistles, nettles, and dock leaf. If these herbs are seen growing plentifully it is said that the land is good. Other herbs grow also but they are seen only when the land is bad, such as the dandelion, bushes, ferns, and others. Some of these herbs were used for cures such as sage and the dandelion. The dandelions were boiled at first and then the juice was squeezed out of them and it was then drunk. Sage was also used as medicine. It was put into water and the juice was extracted from it. It was then strained and drunk.[61]

Collected by Margaret Sullivan, Crookhaven

Crookhaven
The Natural World and Weather Lore

Bird Lore

Around my locality there are many birds such as the thrush, the blackbird, the sparrow, the crow, the lark, the snipe, the cuckoo, the wren, the robin, and the whinchat. The thrush builds its nest in hedges, the blackbird and magpie in trees, and the sparrows under the eaves of houses. The crows build their nests in the treetops. The snipe builds its nest in marshy places. There are some superstitions connected with the magpie. Some people think if they see one magpie it is for sorrow and if they see two magpies it is for joy. The cuckoo comes to Ireland about April or May. The cuckoo builds no nest. If people hear the cuckoo in their left ear, it's thought that sorrow will come and if they hear it in their right ear, it is for good luck. Some of the birds go to foreign countries in the winter, such as the swallow, the cuckoo, and other birds, and they return about April or May. There are also many seabirds around this locality such as the gulls, gannets, divers, and many other sea birds.[62]

Collected by Jeremiah Mahony, Crookhaven
From Mr John Mahony (aged 49), Crookhaven

Weather Lore

About a hundred years ago, the people of my locality, Crookhaven, could tell the weather by observing the sun, moon and stars, rainbows, and by the appearance of the sky. If the sky was red in the morning it was a sign of bad weather. If the sky was red in the evening it was a sign of good weather. When a circle appeared round the moon it was also a sign of bad weather. They also told the weather by observing the islands in the distance. When the island of Cape Clear could be seen clearly, it was a sign of bad weather. They also could tell the coming storms and rain by the smoke. When the smoke went up straight it was a sign of good weather, but when the smoke was flat down on the chimney it was a sign of bad weather. When insects flew low it was a sign of bad weather. They also could tell the expected weather by the rainbow. When they saw a quarter of a rainbow it was also a sign of bad weather. The wind that brings the most rain to my home district is the southwesterly. When the gulls were seen on the land it was a sign of coming storms or rain. An old saying was, "Sea gulls on land is a storm at hand."[63]

Collected by Jeremiah Mahony, Crookhaven
From Mr John Mahony (aged 49), Crookhaven, Co. Cork

Forecasting the Weather

Long ago the natives of Crookhaven and the surrounding districts could tell by certain signs if good or bad weather was to come. They had certain ways of knowing by the behaviour of certain birds, animals, the sun, the sky, clouds, rainbows etc. If swallows were seen soaring high good weather was expected, if seen flying low bad weather was to come. If a circle was seen round the moon or sun bad weather was expected, and also if a lot of black clouds were seen in the sky or if the wind was south or west. When east it was a sign of hard dry weather, and when north fine weather was expected. The southwest wind brings most rain to this district. If seagulls or other sea birds were over the land, rain and storms were expected. Fog on hills and dust flying on the road were also signs of rain. Insects flying low and smoke ascending up from chimneys was a sign of good weather. If seals were seen in the harbour or if the sea was heard roaring against the rocks rain was expected. When numbers of fish are seen on the surface of the water, good weather was to come. Rain was also nigh if a blue light was seen in the fire, if cows were seen running, or if the wind was heard whistling. If a piece of hay or straw was seen hanging to a hen's feathers or when a dog was heard howling or crying, it foretold a death.[64]

Collected by Mary Sullivan, Crookhaven

Severe Weather

Many accounts of great storms, heavy rain, and snowstorms are told by the natives of my district Arduslough, Crookhaven, Co. Cork, and in the surrounding districts. The greatest storm that ever blew was in the year 1834. It was in the wintertime. It is said that it came without any warning and lasted for 24 hours. It blew from the southwest and caused a great damage both on land and on sea. Houses were blown down, cattle were killed, and lives were lost. Ships on the sea were blown ashore and many of them were wrecked. Many thunderstorms also occurred in former years but were not so very dangerous. About 70 years ago a great snowstorm blew and it caused a lot of damage. About 40 years ago there was also a great storm and a sailing boat was lost outside the harbour's mouth.[65]

Collected by Mary Sullivan, Crookhaven
From Mr John Sullivan (aged 60), Crookhaven

Crookhaven
Sea and Shipwrecks

The Crookhaven Admiral

To the east of the village of Crookhaven there is a turret overlooking the Atlantic Ocean. It is supposed to have been built as a watchtower by a man named Coughlan who was a native of the village. One day he left Crookhaven and set off for London in a sailing vessel. As he was walking along the river Thames, there was a pleasure yacht on the river and in her were an admiral and his daughter and crew. The boat through some accident or other turned over, all the occupants being thrown into the water. Coughlan seeing what had happened jumped into the water and saved the life of the girl. Her father was so grateful that he offered him anything in return. Coughlan asked him to give him a position. So, the admiral gave him a post in one of his ships. After a time, he left the ship and entered the navy, and he rose from rank to rank till he became an admiral. There are many stories told about this famous man. One of them was how he saved a countryman of his, and a native of his own village, from the hands of a cannibal chief in the South Sea Islands. The sailor was a great musician. The chief of the island discovered this. The chief derived great entertainment from the music of the Irish sailor and decided never to part with him. In the meantime, Coughlan's man-of-war landed outside the island. The admiral came ashore. He was amazed when he heard the familiar tunes of his native village being played so far from home. He questioned the chief on the identity of the musician. He recognised the sailor, who was very anxious to leave his exile. Coughlan approached the chief to set the captive free. But the chief would not hear of it. Persuasion or reward had no effect till Coughlan threatened to turn his mighty guns on the island unless the sailor was released immediately. Finally, the chief had to relinquish his valued musician. So, the sailor and admiral returned eventually to Crookhaven, the voyage being brightened by the music of the Crookhaven sailor.[66]

Collected by Mary Sullivan, Crookhaven
From Mr John Sullivan (aged 60), Crookhaven

Crookhaven in the Days of the Sailing Ships

In the days of the sailing ships, Crookhaven harbour was famous as a port of call for the ships of the world. The men of Crookhaven in former years were noted mariners and sailed the seven seas. The following is a typical example of the narratives remembered by the older inhabitants of the village.

Some ships I remember…

I will give a few names of sailing ships that the seamen of my native place sailed in in the days of sail. In my young days there were a number of small vessels belonging to Crookhaven, pilot cutters, lighthouse tenders, smacks and schooners, and those I remember were the Auspicious, Caroline, Halcyon, Heroine, Kate Dawson, Kingston, Lady Dentry, Mary Rowe, Mazeppa, Meteor, Nina, Osprey, Prima Donna, Robert Boyle (named after the celebrated scientist of the 17th century, Robert Boyle, who was the seventh son and fourteenth child of his father, the Earl of Cork), Union, William, Waterlily, and Yacht, the last two topsail schooners whose ports of registry were Liverpool and Bideford respectively. A few of the others hailed also from cross-channel ports. Accordingly, as the boys of Crookhaven reached the school-leaving age, they were drafted on board one or other of the small vessels, where they received a good training, with the result that when the urge came to go on deep water, they were competent to ship as ordinary seamen. The first that I can call to mind were three that returned home in 1876, after a two-year voyage in the Dundee barque, Glentilt. In 1877 there was an exodus of young sailors from the port. The following were the vessels they sailed in: City of Mobile, of Liverpool to Quebec; Archibald Fuller of Liverpool, to the West Coast of South America; King Celoric of St. John n.b. to Madras, King Cerdic to Calcutta and Peru, and barque Diana to Rio. In 1878-79 one made a voyage to Hong Kong and Manilla in the ship Commissary of Aberdeen; another in the barque Parknook of Whitehaven to South Africa and New York; and a third completed his time as apprentice in the barque, Copsefield of London.[67]

Contributed by John Glanville (aged 75), Goleen

The Toll of the Deep

In 1879 there were two men belonging to Crookhaven lost at sea; one was washed off the jib-boom of the ship, Cathcart of Greenock, and another was in the ship Wild Rose, of Liverpool, when homeward bound from Moulmein. She failed to reach port and was posted as missing.

I will give a list of the vessels that Crookhaven men sailed in in the early eighties: (Barques) Carrier, Dove, Cape Finisterre, John Milton, John C. Munro, Selkirkshire, Canada, Ruby, Araby, Maid. (Ships) G.W. Wolff, Panmure, Blair Athole, Canute and Cannonore of Liverpool. This ship ran ashore in the Hooghli when bound from Shanghai to Calcutta in 1885 and became a total wreck.[68]

Contributed by John Glanville (aged 75), Goleen

The Wrecking of the Wolverene

The local happenings that are remembered most commonly in this district are connected with shipwrecks. This is an account of one of them. On the 17th of March 1867 a great sailing vessel was wrecked in Crookhaven harbour. The Wolverene was her name and she belonged to Greenock in Scotland. She sailed from the West Indies with a cargo of rum for England. On her way, storms forced her to come into Crookhaven harbour, where she remained for a few days. A terrible storm blew from the southeast which caused her to drift her anchor. She struck the land to the east of the Lighthouse and became a total wreck. Her crew were saved by the natives of Crookhaven but her cargo was lost. It flowed up the harbour. She drifted back up the harbour and sank just opposite the village, where she remained for a number of years till divers came and cleared her away as she was an obstruction to other ships.[69]

Collected by Mary Sullivan, Crookhaven
From Mr Denis O'Sullivan (aged 50), Crookhaven

SHIELDS DAILY GAZETTE

[21 March 1867, p.3]

Maritime Notes

The Wolverine driven onshore

The barque Wolverine, Kyle, from Demerara, arrived at Crookhaven on the 16th, drove on shore under the lighthouse about 4 p.m., and had become a total wreck. Some casks of rum will be saved.

CORK EXAMINER

[6 April 1867, p.1]

The Auction of the Wolverine

TO BE SOLD by AUCTION (on account of whom it may concern,) on MONDAY, APRIL 8th at One o'clock, p.m., at CROOKHAVEN, the Colonial Built Barque, WOLVERENE, (of Greenock), as she now lies at CROOKHAVEN, with Anchors, Chains, Hawswers, Masts, &C.; also, allotted at the time of sale, a quantity of Rope, Sails, and broken Spars on shore.

The WOLVERINE is yellow metalled and copper fassened.
For further particulars apply to:-

CAPTAIN D. CHISHOLM, Clinton Arms, Crookhaven;

or to

FREDERICK P. E. POTTER.
Auctioneer, Skibbereen.

Figure 12. Types of ship. R.H Dana, *The Seaman's Friend* (Boston: Thomas Groom, 1851), plate 4.

EXPLANATIONS.

SHIP.—A ship is square-rigged throughout; that is, she has tops, and carries square sails on all three of her masts.

BARK.—A bark is square-rigged at her fore and main masts, and differs from a ship in having no top, and carrying only fore-and-aft sails at her mizen mast.

BRIG.—A full-rigged brig is square-rigged at both her masts.

HERMAPHRODITE BRIG.—A hermaphrodite brig is square-rigged at her foremast; but has no top, and only fore-and-aft sails at her mainmast.

TOPSAIL SCHOONER.—A topsail schooner has no tops at her foremast, and is fore-and-aft rigged at her mainmast. She differs from a hermaphrodite brig in that she is not properly square-rigged at her foremast, having no top, and carrying a fore-and-aft foresail, instead of a square foresail and a spencer.

FORE-AND-AFT SCHOONER.—A fore-and-aft schooner is fore-and-aft rigged throughout, differing from a topsail schooner in that the latter carries small square sails aloft at the fore.

SLOOP.—A sloop has one mast, fore-and-aft rigged.

HERMAPHRODITE BRIGS sometimes carry small square sails aloft at the main; in which case they are called BRIGANTINES, and differ from a FULL-RIGGED BRIG in that they have no top at the mainmast, and carry a fore-and-aft mainsail instead of a square mainsail and trysail. Some TOPSAIL SCHOONERS carry small square sails aloft at the main as well as the fore; being in other respects fore-and-aft rigged. They are then called MAIN TOPSAIL SCHOONERS.

R.H Dana, *The Seaman's Friend* (Boston: Thomas Groom, 1851), plate 4.

The Wrecking of the Memphis

A steamboat named the Memphis sailed from Montreal with a general cargo bound for Liverpool in the year 1896. In a thick fog she struck a rock in a place called Dun Lough a few miles distant from Crookhaven. Eleven of the crew were lost. She remained there until she became a total wreck. Another steamboat was wrecked there after the Memphis, named the Oswestern. She was also bound for Liverpool with a general cargo. The captain and six of the crew were lost.[70]

Collected by Mary Pyburn, Crookhaven

About 41 years ago a steamboat called the Memphis was wrecked at the Mizen in a dense fog. There was a general cargo on board the Memphis. The Memphis left Montreal bound for Liverpool. Nine of the crew of the Memphis were lost. Another steamboat called the Oswestern was wrecked in the same place. It had on board a general cargo bound for Liverpool. Some of the crew were lost. About eight years after the Oswestern, another big steamboat called the Irada was wrecked in the same place. The Irada left Galveston bound for Liverpool. It had on board a cargo of cotton and oak staves. The captain and six of the crew were lost. There is a very dangerous headland at the Mizen on which the boats struck. A lighthouse stands there now to protect passing vessels.[71]

Collected by Jeremiah Mahony, Crookhaven

CORK EXAMINER

[20 November 1896, p.5]

The Wreck on the Cork Coast

ELEVEN MEN MISSING
ONE BODY FOUND
SURVIVORS ARRIVE AT CROOKHAVEN
INTERVIEW WITH CAPTAIN AND CREW
GRAPHIC ACCOUNT OF THE DISASTER
A TERRIBLE NIGHT OF HARDSHIP
(FROM OUR REPORTER)

Crookhaven, Thursday.

A thirty-miles drive through a hilly and sparsely-populated country brought me to Crookhaven, seven miles from Dunlough Bay. The afternoon was well advanced on my arrival, and there was no time left for visiting the actual scene of the wreck of the steamer Memphis, belonging to Messrs Elder and Dempeter, of Liverpool, of 2553 tons register, and 350 head of cattle on board. I had therefore to content myself with driving some miles along the coast in the direction of the Mizen, during which a curious sight was encountered.

A THICK FOG HUNG OVER THE WATER oceanwards, and a heavy surging sea came dashing over the rockbound coast, bringing with it wreckage of all kinds, including carcasses of cattle from the wreck and an immense number of casks of apples, boxes of bacon, sacks with a general cargo of flour, and casks of cheese and lard.

The people near the coast were busily engaged carting away quantities of bacon and cheese, but the timber remained practically untouched.

At Barley Cove, about a mile from Crookhaven, huge lots of timber and portions of the woodwork of the ill-fated vessel were also washed ashore. It was ascertained that the MASTS OF THE MEMPHIS HAD DISAPPEARED from sight, and nothing remained to denote the scene of the calamity except the piles of planks and boxes of merchandise, etc. The survivors had all been conveyed over to Crookhaven, where they were supplied with fresh clothes, and accommodated in different houses in the little village. At McCarthy's Hotel, the proprietor of which had been most assiduous in looking after the wants of the unlucky mariners, I found Capt. Williams, master of the Memphis, and most of the survivors. They were most courteous and afforded your representative all possible information. Captain Williams, who belongs to North Wales, and is comparatively a young man, gave a very clear and concise narrative of a terrible occurrence, of course avoiding, as he was bound in justice to himself to do, all reference to questions of the circumstances which led up to the actual foundering of his steamer. That, he said, was a matter for the Board of Trade afterwards. He stated, however, in reply to my questions, that the Memphis left Montreal on Friday, 6th inst., with a general cargo for Avonmouth, Bristol. She had 47 SOULS ON BOARD, including cattlemen. Approaching the Irish coast on Tuesday morning a thick fog set in, with the wind strong from the south. All went well till about 9.30 p.m. on Tuesday evening. When nearing Mizen Head the fog became very dense. The steamer was now moving at half-speed, and a vigilant watch was kept by the look-out men. Nothing was known till there was a shout from those foreheads in the vessel that LAND WAS AHEAD close under the bow of the steamer.
In a moment, before anything could be attempted to be done, the vessel had struck on a rock – the Carrig Na Coode Rock, as it subsequently proved to be, with a crunching noise.

The vessel made water with alarming rapidity, and orders were at once given to lower the boats. At the time of striking on the rock it was the second mate's watch below, and many of his men rushed wildly on the deck with very little clothing on. In less time than it takes to relate, and while one of the boats was being lowered the Memphis gave one great spring round as if she had settled firmly down between two rocks.

Twenty men scrambled headlong into the boat, and in their wild excitement, together with the heavy seas running, THE CRAFT CAPSIZED, precipitating her crew into the water. They grasped floating timbers, and in some way held onto rocks. Efforts were made to rescue them by a small boat which was next lowered, she proved ineffective, the boat being already manned by six men. The lifeboat, with 21 men on board, was got down in a moment, but they were not able to approach it after leaving it.

Second mate Dickenson, second engineer Wilson, and fourth engineer Bryce climbed the rigging of the foremast, while the captain, who remained on deck till all had taken to the boats, made for the mainmast, but before reaching it he was washed overboard by the heavy sea amongst a lot of cattle; he managed in some miraculous manner to get clear of the struggling cattle, and seizing a floating plank, HELD ON FOR GRIM DEATH.

In a short time, he was enabled to paddle in towards land, which was but a short distance away, but was unable to land for a considerable period owing to the breaking surf. The captain could not speak of the fate of the other men, but the instant he landed took all steps to have necessary assistance sent to them. He considers his escape a most miraculous one.

Second Mate Dickenson told an equally remarkable story.

He, with Williams (second engineer) and Bryce (fourth engineer), rushed up the forerigging when they saw the lifeboat unable to near the ship. Scarcely had they reached the mast head than the ship went down, and it was by dint of strength that the three held on to the rigging, the seas breaking wildly over them.

For CLOSE ON NINE HOURS did the three cling to the mast till a boat manned by five men from the village of Aughminna named Michael Leary, Daniel Leary, Con Leary, Peter Sheehan, and Andrew Donovan put out about eight o'clock, and by means of lines got the three poor fellows on board their boat, bringing them safely ashore. Mr Dickenson speaks very highly of Leary and his companions. Leary, he said, brought them very kindly to his own hut and gave them food and dry clothes, after which they were put to bed.

Speaking of the rescue, Leary himself very modestly said that they did nothing more than what should be done by them in such circumstance. Leary, who fishes in the vicinity of the rocks, says there are about ten fathoms of water outside the rock in which the vessel went down.

Chief Mate Parry's escape was also an astounding one. After being dashed out of the boat that capsized, he with some others managed to get on the rocks. The waves were WASHING OVER THEIR HEADS, and in a very short time five of the seven who first clung to the rocks were swept away and were drowned. The two remaining on the rock, Thomas Payne, A B, and Mr Parry, were got ashore by a man named Downey by means of a rope.

The lifeboat, with twenty-one souls on board, was dashed about for several hours trying to reach a safe landing place, which they did about 5 a.m.

The news of the wreck spread rapidly, and the inhabitants near the scene came running to the top of the cliffs overhanging the rocks in Dunlough Bay.

The survivors were taken to the neighbouring homes and were very kindly treated. During Wednesday most of them went down to Crookhaven, and were followed by the remainder today.

BODY PICKED UP

The body of Edward Jones, carpenter, belonging to Weighbridge, Cardiff, was picked up about 4:30 on Wednesday off Brow Head by a fisherman named Sullivan.

Coroner Neville will hold an inquest on the body which was taken to Rock Island Coastguard Station, where it was identified by Capt. Williams. Attached to the body when picked up was one life belt.

District-Inspector Dale, Schull, and Sergeant Foran, with two men, were early on the scene of the wreck. Captain Billet, officer of the Coastguards, Crookhaven, on hearing of the calamity, set out to the scene of the wreck, about eight miles away, with a number of men with life-saving apparatus, but the survivors had in the meanwhile been landed.

One of the crew LOST OVER £400 in valuables and money on board the ill-fated steamer.

That portion of the coast where the wreck took place is considered by mariners of the most treacherous character. Already two shipwrecks have taken place in the identical spot.

Up to the time of wiring no further bodies have been recovered. The names of the drowned are:- Evans Jones, carpenter. J Montrose, A B. Albert Ferrah, steward. William Davis, seaman, of Bristol. William Davis, fireman. Frank Wiltshire, trimmer. Frank Reid, trimmer. William Owen, fireman, and two cattlemen whose names cannot be ascertained.

A Dublin man named Fitzgibbon, who was THE ONLY IRISHMAN ON BOARD is amongst the survivors.

Our Skibbereen correspondent writes – It is probable that all the survivors have been collected together by this, and in that case, they are to start for Skibbereen immediately, where they will be taken charge of by Mr Swanton, and sent to their respective destinations.

I understand that the major portion of the crew are Welshmen or Englishmen, and so were those who perished. They are all expected to reach Skibbereen this evening, Mr Swanton's instructions to the captain being to send them on immediately, when they will be dispatched to Cork by the last train. A representative of the Underwriters' Association reached here this afternoon *enroute* for the scene of the disaster and will make all the salvage arrangements. Coastguards and police are doing their utmost in this direction so far, but so enormous are the quantities of valuables being washed bout in the sea that it would take an army of them to afford proper protection for their salvage.

There is a pretty heavy swell, and the great fear that some of the poor fellows engaged in this perilous work with small craft may forfeit their own lives. It is understood that the lost steamship has been covered with very heavy if not full insurance, and it is stated that the cargo has been separately insured. Dunlough Bay, where the steamer Memphis was lost on Tuesday night, was today full of wreckage, and hundreds of tons of bacon, butter, flour, cheese, beef, &c., are being washed about.

Dunlough Bay and the Wrecking of the Bohemian

Dunlough Bay, situated a few miles westward of Crookhaven Harbour, was in the past one of the most dangerous landfalls on our southwestern seaboard. In the days when there was no warning signals on Mizen Head to apprise mariners of danger ahead, many a good ship finished her last voyage in Dunlough Bay, and many a brave and hard toiler of the sea found his grave at the bottom of its deep waters. In stormy weather the efforts of the crew to escape the doomed ship which is dashed against the inaccessible cliffs which form the landward side of the bay are absolutely futile; for them there is no chance in the raging sea and cross currents that run with irresistible force along its iron-bound coast.

In the beginning of the 18th century an English troop ship with her crew, and 400 troops, among whom were the soldiers' wives and children, was dashed to pieces against those cruel cliffs and not one escaped to tell the tale. So it was with many other good and valuable ships that had the misfortune to become embayed between the Mizen Head and Three Castles Head, and of which there has never been any trace, save the wreckage and damaged merchandise that used frequently after a storm be seen floating in the coves and inlets of the neighbourhood.

In January 1881, the Leyland liner, "Bohemian" of Liverpool was lost in Dunlough Bay. This fine steamer with a general cargo from Boston U.S.A. was sunk through a mistaken order given by her captain to the officer on watch when the former left the vessel's bridge at midnight. They had arrived in sight of Dursey Head steering a course due East, which would take them round Mizen Head and on towards the Fastnet Rock, and as there was a strong south-west breeze, the vessel was under sail as well as steam, this being the custom with steamers in those days whenever a fair wind offered. The captain on leaving the bridge gave the order to keep the ship "two points off", meaning two points of the compass off the land, but his first officer took it to mean off the wind, which was of course blowing towards the land. If the order had been carried out as the captain meant it, the ship's course would have been E.S.E., a course that would have taken her safely up channel, but the chief officer altered the course to E.N.E., with the result that the steamship "Bohemian", under a full press of canvas and a full head of steam, struck the cliffs in Dunlough Bay, one mile north of Mizen Head. She quickly went to pieces on the rocks, but not before one lifeboat with seventeen men succeeded in getting away. They got around Three Castle Head, a distance of two miles north of them, and gained the comparative safety of Dunmanus Bay, where they were able to land. Another boat was capsized, and all the occupants drowned, except the boatswain who had a marvellous escape. He grasped a floating bale of cotton, a part of his ship's cargo, and hanging on to it, he was taken by the tide, south to the point of the Mizen. Here the tide turned, brought him back past the shipwreck, and deposited him in a little cove under Three Castle Head. He had drifted four miles while on the bale of cotton, and when found at daylight by the late Mr Peter Sheehan of Dunlough, the poor fellow was in an exhausted condition. Mr Sheehan took him to his home, where he received the tender care, which had ever been given to the shipwrecked mariners by the people of our coast.

The captain and 32 men of the "Bohemian" were drowned. The most poignant incident in connection with the tragedy, was that two men who got on some outlying rocks, where they clung on until three o'clock the following evening, were washed off by the rising tide and increasing storm in the presence of hundreds assembled on the cliffs. The lifesaving apparatus was brought from Crookhaven, but they were beyond rocket range, and the sea was too rough for a boat to go to their assistance.

Twenty-six years ago, a powerful fog signal was installed on Mizen Head, and recently the place has been fitted with the latest type of wireless-direction-finding apparatus, having a working radius of 500 miles. At the present day the dangers of Dunlough Bay to ships and mariners exists no longer, and vessels can now approach that dangerous coast with confidence and safety no matter what weather prevails.[72]

John Downing (aged 72), Crookhaven

THE BELFAST MORNING NEWS

[10 January 1881, p.4]

The Bohemian Disaster – Narrative of survivors

Crookhaven, Tuesday Night

Today there is nothing to mark the scene of the wreck beyond the wreckage which has been washed ashore in large quantities. The masts have entirely disappeared, and the rocks stand out bold and grim as before, as if nothing had occurred. It is now ascertained that 35 persons belonging to the Bohemian perished, and another victim was today added to the death roll. A man named Sheehan, while engaged in snatching up waifs from the ill-fated ship was drawn in by the sea, and was drowned in the presence of a number of people, who were unable to render assistance. Among those who went down with the ship were:- W. M. Grundy, master; James Rennie, first officer; Walter Saunders, third officer; Edward Thomas, forth officer; Allen Dunsmore, chief engineer; Mr Hastings, second engineer; Mr Voce, third engineer. The fourth engineer, whose name did not transpire, was also among the lost, with Quartermaster J. Mulligan, and J. Whitman and Brows, invalided sailors, who were sent from Boston by the British Consul, were also drowned. The survivors are- Stephen McIsaacs, second mate; John Riordan, boatswain; William Clancy, steward; Peter Kelly, storekeeper; R. John Lyness, boatswain's mate; Henry Mathew, fireman; James Nolan, fireman; Denis Callaghan, fireman; Thos. Hynes, fireman; George Gray, fireman; Robert Stringer, A.B.; Daniel O'Neill, fireman; Matthew Hickett, second stewart; Cornelius Sullivan; and a stowaway, whose name was not ascertained.

The crew consisted of 49 all told, but there were in addition four men engaged in refrigerators on board, one cattle driver, the two invalids, and one stowaway – in all 57 souls. The news of the disaster reached the coastguard station at Rock Island, opposite Crookhaven, at half-past one in the morning. The information was brought by a resident at Mizen Head, who, having heard the steamer's whistle going, suspected something was wrong.

When the coastguards reached the place it was so dark and thick that nothing could be seen. They remained till daylight, when the topmasts were observed over water near Caher Island, on the southern point of the Mizen Head. This island is only separated from the mainland by a deep and narrow ravine, into which the sea rushed with fearful force. Just outside the island are two rugged pieces of rock, rearing themselves about fifteen feet above water, and extending from them is the reef upon which the Bohemian struck.

Upon the larger of these two rocks two men were seen clinging on for hours, apparently beyond human aid. They were first seen about ten o'clock, when they were waving a pocket handkerchief or some other cloth, in order to attract attention. The people became excited and seemed not to know what to do. They could not launch their boats, for the only landing-place they had could not be used in consequence of the surf.

The scene was a terrible one. There were two poor creatures abandoned and left to the slow process of a horrible death, which was gradually closing around them as the waves lashed against them with fury.

The two fated men were supposed to be no others than the master and his first officer, who were recognised by the clothes they wore. At half-past two o'clock word was sent to the coastguard station for the rocket apparatus.

By the time this arrived it was late in the evening, and probably the two poor fellows were drowned. At all events it would have been of no service, even had it been there before, on account of the difficulties of the place and the distance of the men from the shore. Two hookers put out from Crookhaven to render assistance, but they also failed in their humane mission. This morning there was nothing seen of the men. The circumstances which led up to the disaster are clearly related by the survivors and leave no doubt as to the cause of the melancholy affair. Robert Stringer, able-bodied seaman, a native of Dublin, states – The Bohemian left Boston ten days before the occurrence. Nothing remarkable occurred on the passage. We had easterly winds, but of a moderate description. I was on the look-out that night. We passed the Calf light about eight o'clock. It was then calm, and I distinctly saw the three rocks which mark the Calf Light.

There could be no mistake as to that. After we passed the Calf, the weather got very thick, and the next thing I heard was a telegraph signal to the engineer to stand by. Almost ten minutes after that I reported breakers ahead, and sang out, "Hard-a-port; full speed astern." The mate on the bridge heard the call, and the order was executed. About five minutes afterwards the steamer struck. The whistle had been going previous to that on account of the fog. When the steamer struck, I came down to the bridge, and the crew were rushing about.

The captain, who was perfectly calm, told them to be quiet and to prepare the boats. We all made for the two starboard boats and got them swung. Five or six got into the first boat, but it was stove in. The second boat was also damaged owing to the rolling of the vessel on the rocks. We succeeded in launching the port lifeboat. There were four of us in the boat, including Mr McIsaacs.

We got a line and hauled the boat aft. The captain said nobody was to get into the boat before the two sick men, but when they were looked for, they could not be found.

The boy was put in and others followed, making eighteen. The engineers were waiting to go in, but at this moment the line broke, and we drifted astern. We were pulling back to the ship when she heeled over and sank, stern foremost. We subsequently heard men calling for assistance, and we found five men in a damaged boat, two of whom died before we reached land.

The steward, Clancy, makes an important statement to the effect that when the captain found the fog setting in he gave the third officer instructions to keep her two points off. He then proceeded to consult the chart, and on going on deck and looking at the ship' course, he exclaimed, "Good God, what are you doing? Hard a-port." She struck very soon afterwards.

The second officer, who was below at the time the accident occurred, attributes the accident to a mistake on the part of the third officer in carrying out the captain's instructions. He thinks it possible that, as the wind was blowing on the starboard bow at the time, the third officer misinterpreted the captain's orders, and kept two points off the wind, instead of two points off the shore.

John Riordan, the boatswain, who was washed ashore on a bale of cotton, after being several hours in the water, says:- About ten o'clock I was standing near the break of the forecastle, when the look-out man called out "Breakers ahead." The captain was on deck with the chief officer, and gave orders, "Stop engines; full speed astern." The steamer, however, crashed on the rocks, and I assisted in launching the boats.

The steamer began to roll heavily from side to side, and stove in the first boat. After the third boat was launched and filled, we got out the pinnace, into which the remainder of the men and captain were to get.

We were backing astern when the mainmast fell and struck the pinnace. The third officer jumped out, as well as the two other men. I clutched at a bale of cotton and got on it. The third officer seized a hatch. The vessel was sinking when the mainmast came over the side. I remained on the bale of cotton all night, until I was washed ashore in a very weak and exhausted state on the following day. The boatswain is confined to bed, suffering from bruises and the effects of long immersion and exposure. John Lyness, boatswain's mate, a native of Newry, states that he was in the first boat with four or five others, having jumped into her from the steamer. She was stove in and so damaged that she also sank. We were subsequently picked up by the second mate's boat, but two of the men died before we reached land.

James Brown and a Greek named Constantine had been injured by the dunnage, and they suffered heavily from exhaustion. We landed finally in Dunmanus Bay, with the assistance of a shore crew, who towed us in. We were so exhausted we were not able to pull ashore.

The chief officer of coastguards, who directed the operation of the rocket apparatus, has since informed me that he only saw one man on the rock; that the rocket apparatus was dispatched with all haste; and that the line was twice shot over the place where the man was clinging, and that on the third occasion the line got entangled in the rock and remained so attached until morning. Mr McIsaacs, the second officer, states that it is not a fact that the Calf was mistaken for the Fastnet Rock light. The captain had told him before he went below that he intended signalling to Brow Head.

The watch who were on deck at the time of the disaster were all drowned, with one or two exceptions, and those who were below generally escaped, some of them without their wearing apparel. Several of the survivors have, in consequence of their scant wearing apparel, been unable to leave the farmhouses where they were harboured after their rescue.

The cargo of the Bohemian is being washed ashore.- Cotton, bacon, and other matters are being picked up and taken in charge by the receiver of wrecks. The Liverpool tug steamer cruiser returned to Crookhaven this evening after leaving home some distance to the west in search of a missing vessel. She reports that 450 miles to the west she fell in with a water-logged vessel that appeared to have been run into.

Several men of the Bohemian are Irish men and two of the survivors, named William Clancy and John Riordan, are from the City of Cork. Stringer belongs to Dublin, and Lyness to Newry. William Saunders, the ill-fated third officer, belonged to Cork. The Bohemian was two thousand tons burthen and had on board and immense quantity of fresh meat and other provisions, in addition to 28 bullocks. None of the bodies of those who perished have been washed ashore.

CROOKHAVEN
Songs

The Day Star

In the year 1879 a sailing vessel came into Crookhaven harbour. She came in as some of her crew were ill. She was bound for Queenstown and had a cargo of oil cake on board. She was wrecked on the north side of the harbour. When she came in a wind blew from the southeast. The local people took some of the cargo and she was towed to Cork to get repairs. There was a song composed about the vessel and it is known as the Day Star. The following is the song, composed by John O'Mahony, pilot, Crookhaven.

On the 9th day of January in the harbour there came,
A ship loaded with oil caked the Day Star by name.
Mike Cadogan being pilot he had plenty to do,
For he had no room for to round his ship to.

That very same night there came high wind and tide,
Which caused all the vessels in harbour to drive.
The mate being on board, he thought it was right,
For the safety of ships to burn a white flare up light.

The ladies assembled when they saw this white light,
And they told Captain Sawyers his ship was on fire.
"Oh dear" said the captain, "how can that be?"
He consulted his agent on that instantly.
"Now sir," said the agent, "you must take it quite cool.
For I'm sorry to say she's in old Granny Pool."

"Agree with those boatmen for a lump sum.
And I'm certain they'll bring her in deep water quite soon."
The lump sum was mentioned and immediately agreed,
And everything went on to save the Day Star.
"Tut tut," said James Downey, "this never will do,
I'll launch down my whaleboat and save the ship's crew."

On the whaleboat arriving alongside the ship,
"Be gone," said the captain, "I don't want your help.
If you come much further, I'll blow off your head,"
He pulled out a revolver and then they all fled.

"Begad," said James Downey, "you don't want to save your ship,
And I'll let the Board of Trade know all about this.
I launched my whaleboat your ship for to save,
And I pledge you my word I will have to be paid.

Long life to James Noonan and may he live long.
For he gave employment to many around.
To sky farmers and loobeys he gave £3 a man,
From Crookhaven to Cork to pump the Day Star,

Chorus

For the honour of Crookhaven is lately run down,
Since sky farmers and loobeys got the run of the town.[73]

Contributed by Mr James Ellis (aged 74), Crookhaven

The Day Star had already experienced its share of disaster. In July 1867, shortly after leaving Bathurst, the crew contracted a fever from which only five survived. The crew of The Golden Dream rescued the remaining mariners and the brig.

THE DUBLIN EVENING MAIL

[27 August 1867, p.4]

The Day Star – Horrors of a fever ship

The brig Day Star arrived off Gravesend yesterday, in charge of the chief mate and portion of the crew of the ship Golden Dream, now on her voyage to Japan, having picked her up at sea, with a portion of her own crew dead, under shocking circumstances. The report made by the chief mate of the Golden Dream is as follows:- At 5.30 a.m. of the 15th of July, St Nicholas, one of the Cape de Verde Islands, bearing NE., distant 45 miles, saw a sail two points on our starboard bow. As we approached, saw that she had a signal of distress flying in her main rigging, and her sails all set aback. On getting within hail, asked what was the matter. A very feeble voice answered, "The ship is half full of water, and the crew are dying with fever." Our captain ordered a boat to be lowered, and put off to the vessel, but captain giving strict orders to be careful in boarding. On getting alongside found her to be the brig Day Star from Bathurst, Rio Grande, bound to London in ballast.

On boarding her found the crew in the last stage of exhaustion; they were lying on the deck, some evidently dying. The chief mate could just manage to crawl about, and he referred me to the logbook for information. In it I found the day after the ship's sailing from Bathurst a fever broke out, which, in a few days, completely prostrated the entire crew, two only being able to navigate the ship, and these were subsequently stricken down, and the ship laid helpless.

On the 10th July an able seaman, named H. Nichols, was the first to perish from the effects of the fever. He was found dead in his berth. His corpse was at once committed to the deep. The next victim was the master, Captain Lever; then a cabin boy, and so it went on till only five remained alive, and these were considered in a dying condition when I went on board. The survivors implored to be taken into my boat, as they knew they should all die. I told them not to think I intended to abandon them, but I must report the condition of the vessel to my captain, and that I would soon return.
I then had the steward lowered into the boat and took him with me to the Golden Dream.
Captain Wise, on hearing the condition of the ship, determined to remove the survivors to his ship, which was directly done, where they received every comfort and attention. Five of our crew volunteered with me to return to the brig, and took to the pumps, and succeeded in pumping the water out. They then well washed and fumigated the cabins and made sail for London. The crew of the Day Star went on in the Golden Dream to Japan."

SUNDERLAND DAILY ECHO AND SHIPPING GAZETTE

[13 January 1879, p.3]

Gale in the Atlantic Terrific Voyage and Wreck of a Sunderland Barque

The barque Day Star has gone ashore and remains in a bad position at Crookhaven. She is a vessel of 321 tons register, was built by Mr Wm Pickersgill, Sunderland, in 1863, and is owned by Messrs. Anderson, Horan, and Co. The following narrative of her voyage, which has terminated so badly, is from the report furnished to the owners by the master, Capt. T. Sawyer: - The vessel left New Orleans on 27 Nov. 1878, bound for Liverpool, with a cargo of oilcake, valued at £3,500, and insured at Liverpool. Fair weather was experienced until December 8th, when at noon the wind from the NE freshened fast, and by midnight blew very hard, the vessel shipping considerable quantities of water.

At 10 p.m. on the following day, the vessel had only lower main topsail set, but the wind blew terrifically, and a very nasty sea occasioned by the Gulf Stream made matters worse. There was no change in the weather until 9 a.m. on the 10th, when the wind suddenly hauled to the SW, the sea making a complete breach over the vessel. From 3 p.m. to 6 p.m. on that day the squalls of rain and wind were most awful, and it took two men at the wheel to keep the vessel anything near her course. Later on in the evening, the weather was now so bad, and after a rest of two hours the mate came on deck at 8 p.m.

An hour later the captain and mate were standing near each other, when the sea came over the stern of the vessel in an unexpected manner. The captain endeavoured to get hold of the weather rigging, but missed, and was knocked down and washed away to the main rigging, where he became entangled among the gear.

Being much exhausted, it took him some minutes to pull himself together again, and when he had done so, he observed the man from the port side of the wheel was gone.

All that the other man knew about the matter was that his companion had been near him before the sea came over, and he had not seen him since. The captain again looked round, and also missed the mate.

The deck was thoroughly searched, and all hands called on deck, when the melancholy surmise that the two men had been washed overboard resolved itself into a certainty. It was also evident that they had been carried clean over the bulwarks, as they could not have gone through.

The barque was then going at the rate of ten knots an hour, and of course nothing could be done to save the unfortunate men. The sea which had thus carried the men overboard had struck the vessel with a most awful crash, and did considerable damage, the stern being shaken, taffrail started, the topgallant bulwark gone entirely, topgallant bulwark on the port side gone, and the deck stripped of all things lying about it. A seaman named Jas. Baird was also knocked down, and his shoulder dislocated, injuring him so much that he was disabled for the rest of the voyage. Clearing away after the damage was very hard work and occupied all night and until four o'clock the next morning, the number of hands being so much reduced – two overboard, one sick, the little apprentice almost dead with fright, and two hands at the wheel.

There were thus only four hands, including the captain, left, and they looked awfully scared.

On the 30th December, while lying to in a gale of wind, a sea broke on board at 3 a.m., took three stanchions off by the covering board, the main rail and bulwarks on the starboard quarter, main rail both sides between fore and main rigging being also carried away.

The starboard side of the skylight was also stove in, and the cabin almost filled with water. On January 9th the vessel had been two days off the Fastnet Rock, unable to make headway against a whole gale from the SE, the crew being completely used up and unable to work.

At 10 p.m. on that day a complete hurricane raged, and several vessels, as already reported in the *Echo*, dragged their anchors and were damaged at Crookhaven Harbour.

The Day Star, which was lying off the harbour, notwithstanding that all available means of prevention were used, drifted onto the beach, and remained with seven feet of water in the hold. No further information from her has been received.

NORTHERN WHIG

[18 January 1879, p.5]

Gales and shipwrecks

VESSELS arriving at Liverpool report very heavy weather in the Atlantic during the past few weeks. Today several of the crew of the Day Star, from New Orleans, were landed at Liverpool from Cork. The Day Star experienced terrific gales during the greater part of the voyage from New Orleans. The mate and a coloured seaman were washed overboard, and on the 7th the vessel went ashore off Crookhaven, when the crew left her. The brig Parry, also from New Orleans, was abandoned 2,000 miles of Cape Clear, and the crew were picked up by a steamer. In February 1879, an official enquiry was ordered into the wrecking of The Day Star.

SHIPPING AND MERCANTILE GAZETTE

[3 February 1879, p.6]

Official inquiries ordered

The Board of Trade have requested their solicitor to take the necessary steps for holding an Official Inquiry into the circumstances connected with the stranding of the barque Day Star, of Sunderland, in Crookhaven Harbour, on the 10th inst.

Shipping and Mercantile Gazette

[13 February 1879, p.4]

Queenstown

Feb. 13, 9.37 a.m. – DAY STAR – Arrived – The Day Star, from New Orleans and Crookhaven (oil cake), leaky; towed round here to effect repairs.

Pall Mall Gazette

[20 February 1879, p.5]

Inquiry into the stranding of the Day Star

An inquiry into the stranding of the ship Day Star was concluded at Liverpool yesterday. On her return voyage from New Orleans the vessel met with very heavy weather in the Channel, and the Chief Officer and one of the men were washed overboard and drowned.

A pilot was afterwards engaged, who took the ship in Crookhaven Harbour, when she dragged her anchors and stranded during the captain's absence on shore. The court held that the captain was to blame for going ashore, but otherwise he had navigated his ship in an able manner. His certificate was returned.

The Hoche Expedition

In 1796, one of the ships of the Hoche Expedition, which Wolfe Tone procured from the French Government, was wrecked near Dunlough Bay.. There were 1100 men on board but only five survived. They succeeded in reaching Barley Cove, two miles east of Dunlough Bay in safety. This event is recorded in the following poem entitled the Mizen Head.

One evening all for pleasure's sake
I rambled o'er the hills,
Listening to the small birds singing,
And the murmuring of the rills.
The setting sun had filled the sky
all in a rosy red,
When I strayed for recreation
out to the Mizen Head.

The view that there had met my eyes
was a rare one to be seen,
Her lofty cloud-capped mountain
was bedecked in nature's green.
Her lovely hills and valleys,
Her red and rosy dells,
While round about on either side
the blue Atlantic swells.

If you look back in history,
back to the penal days,
'Tis there you will find the Mizen bold,
to fill a glorious page.
'Twas there you would find our Irish boys
bedecked in war's array,
And how the French were quartered there
back in Bantry Bay.

But mo mhuirnín', disaster came,
their hearts got cold as lead,
Where the gallant French transport was wrecked.
Here off the Mizen Head
'Twas there they lost their precious lives,
As you may plainly see,
beneath the secret water of *tobar na cláraige.*[74]

This poem was composed by the late Mr Cornelius Leary, Goleen

Caledonian Mercury

[7 January 1797, p.3]

French frigate cast away at Barley Cove

DECEMBER 31

This morning certain intelligence was received from Admiral ELPHINSTONE at Crookhaven, that one of the French frigates had been cast away at a place called Barley Cove in that neighbourhood, and every person on board (save five) perished, to the number of 570. Two of the enemy's ships of the line and lugger had returned to Bantry in a crippled condition, and I would gladly hope Lord BRIDPORT's fleet will soon appear and give a good account of them. Our danger, however, I do not by any means consider over, and you may conceive the condition we are all in upon so alarming an occasion. The banks continue to shut, and all business at a stand.

The Wrecking of the Memphis

Long ago many songs were composed in this locality. There was a song composed about a steamboat, the "Memphis", which was wrecked in Dunlough Bay in a dense fog. This bay is situated a couple of miles to the west of Crookhaven. The name of the song is "The wreck of Dunlough Bay".

The Memphis she left Montreal,
the weather it was fine,
Said the captain to his officers,
"We'll have a jolly time".
But when they neared the Irish coast,
they ran into a thick fog,
And the captain lost his reckoning
by an error in the log.

The man upon the forecastle
thought he saw a light,
He thought it was the Fastnet Rock
on a stormy winter's night,
And it was by that fatal error
that she was lost in Dunlough Bay.

When the ship struck on the rock
the captain he did say,
"Now lower your starboard lifeboats
and try your lives to save.
I hope, I pray, I trust in God
none of us will meet with a watery
grave.

The fore lifeboat was lowered down,
and she was fully manned.
Before she reached the water,
the forehead tackle jammed.
The aft one went by the run
and the boat she swung around,
And the crew got in the water
and nine of them were drowned.

The aft lifeboat was lowered down,
and all the crew got safely in,
the captain for the last,
But one huge wave came rolling on,
and swept the boat away,
And left him to his precious life
that night in Dunlough Bay.

He tried to reach the rigging,
but it was all in vain,
For another sea came rolling on
and swept him away.
The first landing he got
was on a bullock's back,
Until he struggled to the rocks
where he all night was fast.

He was rescued by fishermen
at the dawning of the day,
And that ends my story
of the wreck of Dunlough Bay.[75]

Composed by John Mahony, pilot, Crookhaven, grandfather of the collector
Collected by Jeremiah Mahony, Crookhaven

The Parish of Sweet Kilmoe

Farewell, my dearest Mary,
to America I must away,
Tho' many the pleasant evening
together we did stray,
It breaks my heart to have to part
and to bid a fond adieu,
To the friends so kind I left behind
in the Parish of Kilmoe.

It was at the fair of sweet Goleen
I spent a happy day,
With dancing and singing
the time we passed away,
A flowing glass around did pass
our spirits to renew,
I can't forget those happy days
I spent in Sweet Kilmoe.

'Twas well I knew Crookhaven
that place so grand,
Where on holidays we used to meet
old friendships to renew,
colleen with her smile serene,
And heart so good and true
Her sweet face will haunt
My native home, Kilmoe

'Twas from Queenstown Harbour
our gallant ship did sail,
We had cheerful boys and
cheerful girls
from dear old Granuaile,
When I was forced to leave my
home,
a new one to pursue,
I thought that day my heart would
break
for my native home Kilmoe.

Now to conclude and finish
I hope to see the day,
With parents dear and comrades,
once more to sport and play,
My own colleen we'll meet again,
old vows we will renew,
And roam the green hillsides
of the parish of Sweet Kilmoe.

This poem is a very familiar one throughout the parish and is sung up to the present day, but the author seems to be unknown.[76]

Collected by Jeremiah Mahony, Crookhaven
From Mr J. Ellis (aged 34), Crookhaven

Figure 13. Irish emigrants leaving home, Illustrated London News, 10 May 1851, p.387) (top). Irish imigrants leaving Queenstown Harbour, Illustrated London News, vol. 65, 1874, p.219) (bottom).

The Berehaven Regatta

The following poem was composed about 80 years ago about a regatta held in Berehaven. A boat from Crookhaven pulled in the regatta and won the race. It is supposed to have been composed by a Berehaven school master.

In the fair month of June when the trees were in bloom,
Mr Beecher consented to Berehaven to go.
He was challenged for racing for rowing or sailing
By the heads of Berehaven those Sullivans you know

Mr Hungerford coxswain he steered the gig for them
And soon the Berehaveners astern did go
As they were mistaken by the lads from Crookhaven
For they were the boys that could feather their oars

When the Harriet crew landed they though little of them
And compared to the men of their shore
But they were mistaken in the boys of Crookhaven
For they were the boys that could feather their oars.[77]

Collected by John Pyburn, Crookhaven
From Mr Jeremiah Driscoll (aged 75), Crookhaven

The Loss of the Lady Charlotte

This song was composed about a sailing ship that was lost on the Barrel Rocks outside Schull harbour long ago.

Come all you jolly mariners and listen unto me
And I'll tell you of the hardships and dangers of the sea
I belong to the Lady Charlotte from Lima we set sail
Homeward bound for Liverpool with a sweet and pleasant gale.

Our cargo it consisted of dollars, a good store
Hides, seeds, bark, wool, and tallow, gold dust, and silver ore
Our captain's name was George McGill, a man of skill profound
A jolly crew in perfect health, and a good ship tight and sound

For ninety days we sailed the seas, the weather being fine
Until we made the Fastnet on March the twenty-nine
The wind it blew from the south-south-west regardless of our might
And tossed us on the Barrel Rocks on a dreary winter's night.

Early the next morning a small boat I espied
Pulling off towards me not little was my joy
Propelled by six brave fellows who boldly did succeed
To rescue me from danger, and noble was the deed

Their names for to make mention, to them great thanks is due
There was Tom and Andy Beasley, there was Lynch and Brady too.
There was Starleen the coast guard, they had no fear of strife
And boldly they succeeded to save my precious life
They took me down to sweet Schull town where I did safely lie
And sweet Schull town I'll never forget until the day I die.[78]

Collected by Jeremiah Mahony, Crookhaven
From Mr J. Ellis (aged 34), Crookhaven

Belfast Commercial Chronicle

[29 October 1838, p.2]

Shipwreck and melancholy loss of life

A most melancholy and total wreck occurred at about three a.m. on Tuesday morning, on the Barrel Rocks, at the West entrance of Long Island Channel, of the Lady Charlotte, of Liverpool, from Callao, South America, laden with hides, wool, specie, and bark. Captain Bartingall, and eight of the crew perished; only one man, John Maddington, sailor, was saved in a most providential manner, from the circumstance of his handkerchief hitching on the points of a rock, on which he and two men, poor fellows, were dashed. The latter were washed back into the sea, whilst he was most miraculously preserved, and afterwards rescued from his still perilous situation, with the great difficulty, on the part of Mr Henry Baldwin, chief officer of coast guard, and his intrepid crew, and at the imminent risk of their own lives.

Very little, if any, of the cargo of the vessel is likely to be saved. Some wool has been floating about, but little else. *Cork Standard*

Southern Reporter and Cork Commercial Courier

[20 November 1838, p.1]

The wreck of the Lady Charlotte

About 50,000L sterling has been saved from the wreck of the Lady Charlotte, consisting of bars of silver, dollars, &c. It will be remembered that particulars of the wreck of this vessel have already been published. The passengers, and, with the exception of one of the crew, were all lost, and a very valuable cargo sunk.

CROOKHAVEN
History and Archaeology

Historical Tradition

There is a coast on the north side of Crookhaven called Coísín Franncai. During the war of 1715 between France and England there was a French warship and an English warship fighting off Kinsale. The English warship was winning. The French warship ran before the English one and took shelter in Crookhaven harbour. There were many men dead on board. The captain landed on that coast and ordered the men to be buried in a field near it. After that it was called Coísín Franncai. When Wolf Tone was sailing from France with a troop ship of guns and soldiers in 1796 one of the ships was wrecked in a place called Dunlough Bay about eight miles from Crookhaven.[79]

Collected by Jeremiah Mahony, Crookhaven
From Mr John Downing, Crookhaven

Famine Times

During the famine, many people died of hunger in Crookhaven. Before the famine there were four hundred people in Crookhaven but many of them died of hunger and also they emigrated to foreign countries during the famine times. Today many ruins can be seen of old houses where the people lived before the famine. The famine was caused by the potatoes decaying in the ground. The very poor people of the locality used to go to a place called Leenane, a district about a mile and a half from Crookhaven where they got food made from yellow meal and it was known as stirrabout. The relief work from the Government did not reach Crookhaven. The people died in large numbers by the roadside and even walking the streets. During the famine, America sent a cargo of meal and meat to Crookhaven but the landlord that ruled the place took the meal and put it in a store in a place called Rock Island. He would not give any away but to the people that were able to pay for it. After some time, it rotted in the stores and after the famine they sunk it at the bottom of the harbour.[80]

Collected by Mary Pyburn, Crookhaven
From Mrs K Driscoll (aged 82), Crookhaven

A Local Legend

There is a stone in Arduslough, a townland to the north of Crookhaven, on which are very old characters or ancient writing. It is very difficult to discern these markings now as the centuries of weather have obliterated them. The following story explains their origin. In ancient times there lived in Toureen a man named Pilib. He informed on a party of Irish soldiers who were hiding in the heather there. The enemy came on them and burned the heather round them in which the soldiers perished. The stone was erected in this spot and the event was recorded on the stone. Years passed and the language changed. The people went to the parish priest asking him to interpret it. He translated it as follows - that every sin will be forgiven but the sin of the informer Pilib an Fraoic.[iii] [81]

Contributed by Mr Sylvester Downing (aged 50), Crookhaven

The Blacks

On the north side of the Cocklestrand (two mile west of the village of Crookhaven) there are a number of stones standing about a foot over the surface. They are known as the Blacks and got their name from black men that are buried there. It is believed that a ship came into the harbour whose crew were from Africa. Disease broke out among them and a number died. They were thrown overboard, and their bodies floated up to the strand. Locals buried them and put the stones over their graves about eighty years ago.[82]

Mass Rocks

In the Penal days any Priest was not allowed to celebrate Mass in Public. So, they had to hide in the houses of the people and had Mass when and where they could. They had large flat rocks erected in many places which served them as Altars. These were generally in high places where they could see any invasion coming. Two of these Mass rocks are still to be seen in the townland of Arduslough.[83]

Collected by Mary Sullivan, Crookhaven
From Mr John Sullivan (aged 60), Crookhaven

---

iii Pilip an Fraoic – Fraoic may be a variant of fraoch, meaning heather, the name becoming Phillip [of the] heather.

Mrs James Downing and the Fenian Flag

There was an old inhabitant of the village of Crookhaven, Mrs James Downing, who used to recall the time of the Fenian rising. She died about 11 years ago having reached the age of 87 years. She was fond of telling the following event of the Fenian's days. When she resided in Oldcourt near Skibbereen, the Fenians had many supporters there. She was also in sympathy with them. As she was skilled in needlework and embroidery the Fenians of the locality asked her to make a Fenian flag. When it was completed, it was to be sent to America. She proceeded, working secretly at night. However, the police got to suspect she was aiding the Fenians. One night they made a raid. She was working on the flag when they arrived. There were three large volumes over the fireplace in the room where she was working. On hearing their approach, she folded the flag up and placed it in the centre book. They made a thorough search even opening the top and bottom book. Strange to say they did not examine the centre book. The police had to leave without finding anything incriminating. The flag was completed and was the first Fenian flag to fly over the American Fenians.[84]

Collected by Jeremiah Mahony, Crookhaven
From Mr Sylvester Downing (aged 60), Crookhaven

Standing Stones

There are many standing stones to be seen throughout this parish. They are to be seen in the townlands of Arduslough, Carrigicat, Dough, and Lissigriffin. These stones are mostly in fields. There is a king buried near the standing stone in Arduslough. There are many stones in the district with markings and strokes and hollows on them. There are two of these stones in Arduslough and one in Castle Mehigan and one in Dough. The one in Castle Mehigan is a large stone and on this stone there are hollows and crosses worn in to it. On the stones in Arduslough there are writings and lines on them. It is believed that the people long ago used eat nuts and they used break the nuts in the holes in the flag in Castle Mehigan. In the townland of Arduslough there is a druid's altar. There is one headstone in my townland which was erected in memory of a dead king who was buried there many years ago.[85]

Collected by Mary Sullivan, Crookhaven
From Mr Denis O'Sullivan (aged 50), Crookhaven

Figure 14. The 'Blacks' at low tide, Cockle Strand, Crookhaven.

LISSAGRIFFIN

Co. Chorcaighe
Bar: Cairbre Thiar
Par: Kilmoe
Scoil: Lios Uí Ghrifín
Oide: Seomsamh Ó Dhuibir
June 1937

Figure 15. Three Castles, above Dunlough Bay.

Lissagriffin
Songs

The Bold Three Castle Head

This poem was written by Daniel O'Leary of Oughtmennia who emigrated to America. Its the only poem of his remembered now.

Come all you lads of pleasure, give ear to what I'll say.
I will sing a few verses to pass the time away.
Concerning that historic spot, you've seen or else have read,
The lofty peaks and craggy creeks, of the Bold Three Castle Head.

To sing into it praises, I'm really at a loss,
To paint its beauteous picture, my pen it will surpass,
Where nature spreads its beauty and charms, they are all dead,
And they fade when they are compared, with the bold Three Castle Head.

And still crowning all this beauty, there in the foreground stands,
The relic of old ancient times, of pirates armed bands,
Hemmed in between those mountains, like lovers' shady bowers stands,
The form of ancient beauty, three strong and lofty towers.

There is a supposition, an old and fabulous tale,
That those castles were built by pirates, who sailed the ocean main.
They were built by high sea robbers, for plunder they did call,
God help the ship or ship's crew who fell into their thrall.

There's more who do object to this, they say it is a lie,
Some say they were built by O'Sullivan Beare, from the castle of Dunboy,
In blood-stained fields and valleys, where man for man fell dead,
There's no account in history of The Bold Three Castle Head.

If O'Sullivan Beare had built this place, I'll tell you how it was,
It was built as a protection, against strong and deadly wars,
And from the fields returning with joy, their hearts aglow.
For this was the place to shield them from the ruthless Saxon foe,

And now when all is over, and bygone days have fled,
Many the pleasure seeker, their hallowed walls have tread,
Some on those beauteous mountains, a pleasant walk may take,
Whilst other with a rod or line, go fishing in the lake.

'Tis sad to say those ancient ruins are fast going to decay,
Those massive moss-grown crumbling walls are falling day by day,
Just like the little shamrock, one wall unites the three,
So may we be united, for all eternity.[86]

The Hipped Old Horny Cow

The man who wrote this poem is living in Mileen. He is alive still and he is about sixty years of age. His name is John Donovan. He wrote a great many other poems also. The best known one is The Hipped Old Horny Cow.

My name it is Tom Barry,
I'm a jobber out of sight.
I thought I'd make a fortune
and I bought a cow last night.
I earned honest money
by the sweat of my honest brow,
And I gave it to Dan Maurice
for a hipped old horny cow.

Very early the next morning,
I took her to the fair,
It was my whole intention to make
money on her there.
The first jobber that I met,
he asked me could she plough,
Or where had I the chance to get
that hipped old horny cow.

When I was returning from the fair
my tears did fill,
The very first thing I did see
was a stick with Mary Phil,
Oh, take away that ugly beast,
Oh, take her away from me,
Down the road went Jobber Tom,
To Dan Maurice's old ash tree.

When he was passing Paddy
Reilly's premises,
she gave an awful roar,
"Um baiste fein" says Paddy,
"the ship she is gone ashore."
And when he met Dan Maurice,
to him he made a vow,
Oh, give me my fourteen notes,
and here is your hipped old horny
cow.[87]

Dan Hurley's Daughter Han

My name it is O'Donovan, they call me handsome Den,
I courted a farmer's daughter, I thought I had her won,
But when old brangie heard of it, some angry words said he,
You will not get the farm, you must cross the raging sea.

It was early the next morning, I struck the road for Schull,
And when I reached the station, my head was getting dull.
I went down to the tramway, the tram bells sweetly rang,
I thought I'd throw myself before the wheels, when I missed my darling, Han.

I went on board an eastbound train, from Schull to Skibbereen.
I said to the conductor, I wish it was Milleen.
For the girl I adore, she there resorts, with her fair and curling hand,
She's the red, red rose of Erin's Isle, Dan Hurley's daughter, Han.

I was thus content and away I went, to Queenstown quay and Cork.
And I went on board the White Star line for the City of New York.
I was on the tender gang-board, when the bells of Shandon rang,
But for the Captain I'd jump down, when I thought of my darling, Han.

For eight long days in the Celtic, I ploughed the ocean wave.
I prayed to be in Ireland, in some cold lonely grave.
You can imagine how I felt, when the bells for supper rang,
For that is the time I used to meet Dan Hurley's daughter, Han.

When I landed in great New York I thought my heart would break.
And when at night I went to bed, dreaming, I would wake.
I'd shake the sheets and blankets, to find her was my plan.
I'd look beneath the mattress springs, to find my darling, Han.

Now I am landed home again, I feel a happy man.
When I was crossing Barley Cove, I could see the home of Han.
And I would hear Snap barking, like I did in days of yore,
And I could hear her sewing machine, Three miles outside the Brow.

I tried to stay away some time, but I could not stay with fright.
For every day it seems a year, and my head is getting white.
I was a lady dazzler, and my girls they were a gang,
But I could see none that I could compare,
With Dan Hurley's daughter, Han.[88]

Old Charlie

Charlie was bought in Bandon,
And he cost about seventy pounds.
He was a credit to McCarthy,
Who lived in Goleen town,
He has paid his master well,
He's the best horse to be seen,
For he can pull thirty-hundred weight,
From Schull to green Goleen.

Now he is in the home for incurables,
In the valley of Dhurode,
He had plenty of grass and water,
And he's lively as a toad,
He has plenty of mungee,
And a dry ground to lie down,
He may bless the day he went away,
Three miles from Goleen town.

Now he can stretch his weary bones,
He can sit and he can lie,
He can go up the green hillside,
And fool the old gad fly.
He has a fine broad stable,
And high it is his roof,
He can walk within the shady grove,
To put fine shell on his hoof.

He was boarding all last summer,
In Florrie Donovan's old sléibhín,
His eyes were fairly dazzled,
Looking at fields so green,
And then he would see brave Florrie coming,
With a whip in all his hand,
Saying, "Get up you lazy Bandon horse,
And we'll fetch a butt of sand."

His sides were bare all from the chains,
For he would never let him walk,
And he would always shake his head,
Like he was going to talk,
Now he's living happy,
He has plenty of grass to eat,
His place of board is in Dhurode,
On the southwest of the free state.[89]

The Land of Cannawee

As I roved out one evening,
to get poor Charlie shod,
My heart it was in motion,
from gazing at the strand.
I gazed upon the lovely lake,
most pleasant for to see,
The swans they glide along the tide,
at the shores of Cannawee.

And beside it stands a black smith's shop,
so everybody says,
Where all the horses of the place,
are shod without delays.
Dennie Harrington and his anvil,
rings most sweet to me,
And there he shoes those lamed old plugs,
at the shores of Cannawee.

Besides it stands a huckster shop,
to you I will refrain,
They say he is a noble man,
he is Mahony by name,
He sells all sorts of tobacco,
and the best of blarney tea,
Which makes old women jump with glee,
at the shores of Cannawee.

I sold my Charlie to a man,
whom they say a wife will take,
He has already boarding in
a hut nearby the lake,
He can fetch her with a race horse,
he can fly from all you see,
They all can look at Charlie's tail,
from the land of Cannawee.[90]

Dhurode's Fair Hills and Valleys

Dhurode's fair hills and valleys,
are the fairest that I know;
Like sparkling gems of silver,
and shining lumps of gold.
The stone crushers and water wheels,
and fine machinery
Are all in charge of old Pad Long,
from the English company.

They were erected by McCormick
from the heart of Goleen town.
He drained this lovely valley,
forced the water up and down.
And he built that great hydraulic
to make the big wheels go,
"Am baiste fein,"[iv] said old Pad Long,
"I see tons of copper ore."

"My boys, throw away your cibbles,
let them in the drivin's lay,
And we'll put water whistling,
down through Dunmanus Bay."
And to sit above this valley,
on a dark and dreamy night,
You'd think it was a city,
lit by electric light.

And if you searched this wide world
o'er,
no happier lads you'll see,
Than Con Coughlan and Dan Reilly,
and the three sons with Curly.
And as they walk a shady grove,
the pretty girls to see,
They are happier than the Prince of
Wales, who rides in his buggy.

And now once more I'm landed here,
but I'm sorry to have to say,
The valley it is darkened,
and the miners gone away.
The shores are dim, the hills look grim,
and I heard poor Richard say,
There are tons of gold and silver,
at the bottom of the bay.[91]

All the above poems, "The Hipped Old Horny Cow", "Dan Hurley's daughter Han", "Old Charlie", "Land of Cannawee", and "Dhurode's Fair Hills and Valleys" were composed by John Donovan, Mileen, Goleen

---

[iv] Am baiste fein – the holy one -an expression of surprise.

Paddy Hegarty's Old Leather Breeches

At the side of the knell on the road to Clonmel,
Paddy Hegarty kept a "nate" shebeen,
He sold pigs' meat and bread, he kept five lodging beds,
And was liked in the country he lived in.
And Judy his wife as they struggled through life,
On weekdays Pat mended the ditches,
On Sunday he dressed, in a suit of the best,
But his pride was his old leather breeches.

Last winter's snow put "vitals" so low,
That Paddy was ate out completely.
The snow coming down, he could not go to town,
Thoughts of hunger did bother him greatly.
One night as he lay, adreaming away,
Of ghost, fairies, "sperrits" and witches,
He heard an uproar outside his front door,
He rose and he pulled on his breeches.

Says Brian MacUrp, with a voice like a Turk,
"Pray, Paddy, go get us some atin",
Says Big Andy Moore, "We'll burst open the door,
Sure this is no night to be waiting."
They swore by the hob, if they didn't get prog,
That they'd eat him right out of his breeches.
The words were scarce spoke, when the door it was broke,
And they crowded round Paddy like leeches.

Paddy in dread slipt up to the bed,
Where Judy his old darling wife was.
And there 'twas agreed, for to get them a feed,
So he slipped out and brought his big knife in.
He cut down the straps of his breeches, the best,
He ripped out the buttons and stitches.
He cut them in stripes, in the way they do tripes,
And he boiled then his old leather breeches.

The boys sure they smiled, for they thought he had boiled,
Some mutton or beef of the richest.
But little they knew, that 'twas leather ragú,
That was made out of Paddy's old breeches.
And they smiled at the stuff, but says Larry "Tis tough",
Darby jumps to his feet and he screeches,
Says Larry, "make speed, and send for the priest,
Oh, holy St Patrick, I'm finished.

"Be the hokey", says Pat, "Sure I thought it was fat",
Says Larry, "You're no judge of mutton",
When Brian MacUrp on the point of his fork, held up a big ivory button.
They all flew at Pat, but he cut out of that, he ran when he saw them all rising.
Revenge for the joke, they had, for they broke,
the chairs and the tables and dishes.
And since that very night, they'll put out your light,
If they find you wear old leather breeches.[92]

This old song was recited by James Cotter of Coosheen, and is very popular in this area. The writer is unknown.

GOLEEN

Co. Chorcaighe
Bar: Cairbre Thiar
Par: Kilmoe
Scoil: An Góilin
Oide: P. Ó Meádhra
1.11.1937

GOLEEN
Local Folklore and Stories

Old Stories

A man went to clear briars around the headland before cutting his wheat. A hare jumped out as he was cutting, and he threw the hook at the hare thinking that he'd kill him. He went home to get the machine to cut the corn and when he came back the hare had all the corn cut.

When a ship used to be wrecked they used hear the sailors talking and the noise of the rigging before the storm. A ship was 'drowned' in Dunmanus Bay and the cooper was to be heard always for years after working in the cove.[93]

Long ago, when old women were selling eggs for hatching, they used want to know how the tide was when they were putting down the eggs. If the tide was coming in they'd have all cocks, and if the tide was going, all hens. If a cow was calving with a coming tide she'd have a bull calf, and if the tide was going out, she'd have a heifer.[94]

They say that people with piseógs could take milk and butter from the neighbours.[v] They believed that eggs found in crops were unlucky and that the crop would be no good, and that the one who'd put the eggs in the crop would have the good of the crop himself.[95]

There was a weaver east near Schull. Cole was his name, and they say that he used to be going with the fairies. There was a haunted house nearby, and Cole was sent for. He went upstairs and he spent the night in the loft. In the middle of the night, he heard noises, and a crowd came in dancing around the kitchen. He told the family to leave the house for the crowd were up to nothing good. He had a journeyman working with him and they stayed working late one night. They had no tobacco so went to Schull for tobacco and a couple of pints. The hens used to be inside that time, and when they were going to the door the cock crew. A most awful crow he gave. They stopped and he crew again, and he crew a third time and he flew down on the floor and dropped dead. When they examined him 'twas choked he was for they saw the sign of the fingers on him. They'd get the same if they went out that night. 'Twas well for them that the cock was there to warn them.[96]

---

[v] Piseóg – a charm or curse

Púca

There was a fellow east in Ráthúra – his name was Gosling and he used to be always going away north storytelling to Drishane and places. Several nights he used to meet a horse and this night he felt a kind of tired and he said he'd ride the horse away north. He went up on his back, and when he did the horse galloped away and took him through every road and field in the country. Gosling was afraid for his life. He took out a knife and he said he'd drive it through him if he didn't take him home. The horse turned and galloped towards Gosling's house and near Ráthúra there was a big soft patch of mud and he threw him head long into it and went away cracking his sides laughing.[97]

Piseóga

Tis said that if you were travelling at night along you should never speak to anyone, nor answer a call, or you shouldn't speak to anyone at night if you were going for a nurse. The herons were at Hungerford's wood and they make a terrible racket in the nighttime. Paddy Hall from Clochán was going east one night on a saddle horse and he heard all the noise and thought what the herons were saying was, "Paddy Hall from Clochán go home." He turned his horse and cleared away home as fast as he could.[98]

From Tim Lucy (aged 70), Goleen

The Dreamer

I heard tell of a man once that was always dreaming that if he went to London Bridge he'd find a crock of gold. He left home and off he went to London Bridge, and he was walking up and down there. A man came up to him and asked what he was doing. "Well" says the man, "I'm always dreaming that there's a certain man in a certain place with a white thorn bush growing on the ditch outside his door, and if I searched under it, I'd find a crock of gold." "Begor", says the man, "for I have a white thorn bush growing outside my door. He came home and he found his crock of gold under the bush.[99]

Old Tom Love's advice

I heard old Tom Love saying that long ago they used to sow seed in meithals.[vi] There was once a travelling man staying in the house this night and they were to have the meithal the following day. In the morning when the traveling man got up, he went out on the ditch and looked around him. He told them not to sow any seed that day for that it wouldn't grow. They went home and came again the next day. The next day he told them not to sow for the seed wouldn't grow. Some of the men said that if he was not going to set the seed that they would, and they went off to another man and sowed his seed for him. The third morning the meithal came, and the travelling man went out and had a look around. "Let ye set all the seed today", – they did. Tom Love hadn't a failure in his crop that year, and a third of the seed didn't grow to the man who planted on the second day. He had to sow in a hard north wind.[100]

Walking Pigs to Schull Fair

Long ago the men and the women used to walk their pigs east to Schull fair. They'd start the night before and they'd make a fire in the pike[vii] and cook a bit for themselves. East at Caom there is a balick and it is said to be haunted. This man and his wife were passing east one fair morning. When they were passing the balick at Caom, they heard the voice calling the woman by name saying to come in and give her child a suck. The woman said that she wouldn't, but her husband told her that 'twas as well for her to go in and feed the child. She did, and when she came out, she was nearly crying. She said that the child nearly ate the nipples off of her.[101]

Collected from Tim Lucy, Goleen

[vi] A meithal is a group of workers. Some tasks were onerous, so people would come together to share the workload.
[vii] A country road

The Unwanted Lodgers

There was a woman one time and I heard that she had a lot of children. One night, a few women came to her and asked if she'd give them lodging for the night. She was a kind-hearted woman, and although she had a lot of children, she promised to keep them. They were inside sitting around the fire when a neighbouring woman ran to the door and said that all Cnoc Osta was on fire. Up the ladies jumped and ran out. The neighbouring woman closed the door after them and bolted it, and she told the woman of the home to stretch the tongs on the floor, and to turn the three-legged stool upside down, and to throw out the water that the children had been washing their feet in. She told her when she'd go to bed to remain lying on her right side and to put all the children lying on their right side too. She did but she had a baby, and the baby was at her breast and lying on its left side. They came back some time in the night and wanted to come in. She pretended not to hear them. They asked the tongs to let them in. The tongs said he couldn't for he was on the floor on his back. They asked the stool to let them in and the stool said he couldn't for he was on the flat of his back. They asked the feet water and it said that it couldn't as 'twas under their feet. They couldn't get in and they had to go away. In the morning the baby was dead.[102]

The Second Wife and the Fairies

I heard of a man who got married to the second wife – the first one was dead for a couple of years before he married. He wasn't long married to the second one when the second one sent him an account to come for her and that she'd be passing on horse at a certain place at a certain time. She told him to bring a bottle of holy water and a black handled knife. She said that she'd be riding behind a man on a certain horse and to pull her off and to make a ring with the holy water on the road, and to be standing in the middle of the ring, and to pull her into the ring. They (fairies) couldn't get inside the ring. She promised him that if he'd do that that she'd be no more bother to him. He went to the appointed place and did as she told him. He brought her home and she cleared off to America.[103]

King and the Skinned Horse

There was a fellow by the name of King, and he was living in Caolfada. His wife was going to have a child and he sent a messenger on horseback to bring the nurse and says he, "bring the nurse or the old horse's skin". They went away and he was bringing the nurse with him and there about Lowertown the horse gave up, and he told the nurse to be going away ahead of him. She did. He turned to and skinned the horse and brought home the skin. As he did, the horse followed him. Coming on day they saw the bae horse in the yard. "If the police sees him, they'll take him", says the man of the house. "Take him away", says he to the fellow who went away for the nurse, "up to Mount Gabriel and take the skin with you." Put the horse into a little garden there and put the skin on him. The skin did not fit properly and there was a patch about the size of your hand without any skin. He took a sod of grass out of the ground and put it in the bare place. There was a little cherry tree growing in the sod. A year or so after he went to see how his horse was getting on, and wasn't there a fine cherry tree growing on his back and grand red fruit on it up to the sky. He went picking the fruit. There was a hole in the sky and in he went and went walking around for himself above. When he came back to the hole there was no tree there, but a little woman sitting near the hole, and she had a pale of sand longside her. I'll let you down, says she, with a ladder of sand. She made the rope of sand and left it down, and when he was halfway down, the rope broke, and down he fell on his head. His head came between two stones and broke his neck. He went home for a bar to take out his head, and when he took it out there was twelve cherries longside it.[104]

The Mare

I knew a man and he had a nice little mare, and he was very fond entirely of her. She used be within in the kitchen every night – everyone used keep the horses in the kitchen that time. One morning when he got up, he noticed the mare all sweat and foam, as if she was out being ridden all night. He wiped her and brought her to. He did not tell anyone about it. There was a woman – a neigbour – and she called to the house. "You have a great mare," says she, for she heard them all racing in Eylach strand last night. "I was looking at her myself," says she, "and anyone of them couldn't come near her. Your brother was riding her and a good hand he was at it." The brother who was supposed to be riding her was dead for years before that.[105]

Collected from Tim Lucy, Goleen

The Child on the Red Ground

They say that it is not right to leave a child alone out in the red ground. There was a man there and his wife and they had one child. The husband was one-day preparing the garden, and the wife came out after the dinner and brought the child with her. She put the child sitting on a bag in the corner of the field and she went closing holes. Some time out in the evening a cow gave a roar in the yard and the woman ran to see what was the matter. When she went in, one of the cows had another cow horned and all her side was torn. She ran out to the field and told her husband to come in as quickly as he could. He left the spade in the ridge after him, and ran in. They penned up the cows and when they came out the child was stretched on the bag and there wasn't a stir in him. They didn't know what happened, but there was a weaver living at that time who had the name of going with fairies. The wife told the husband to go off and tell the weaver about the child. Off he went to the weaver and when he went in the weaver was working away at his loom. The man told him how he had a sick child. Well says the weaver, I don't know what I can do for you but if you will stay the night in my home, I might be able to do something for you in the morning. There's a bed up there in the loft says he, and go up there and sleep in it for the night says he, and I'll be working away here for it is at night I do most of my work. The man went up in the loft and indeed he did not sleep very much for he was troubled about his child. Out in the night, about one or two o'clock, he heard all the noise coming into the yard, like geese would be flying into the yard and screeching. He heard the weaver getting up and going out the door and closing the door after him. He spent a troubled night, but begor, coming on morning he heard the geese as he thought flying into the yard again. 'Twas short till the weaver came in and told him to get up. 'Twas I had the troubled night over you he said, and why did you leave your child out in the red ground alone, and only for my friends you'd be without your child today. I had to go all the way to the Mizen to get these and he pulled a bundle of herbs out of his pocket. When you'll go home now says he, make nine parts of these herbs and have three plants in each bundle, and boil one bundle each night for nine nights and give the drink to the child nine mornings fasting. But be very careful, says he, when boiling the herbs, and do not let the pot boil over, because if you do the cure will be no good. The man went home and he told his wife the story. He put down a bundle of herbs the first night and they gave the drink to the child in the morning. The wife boiled them the second night and they gave the drink to the child in the morning and they were that way for seven or eight nights. They were worn out by this time as they used to have to be working every day and up a night minding the pot and the child, and they thought that maybe it would be better to send for the wife's mother to watch the pot for the last night. His mother-in-law came and she was watching the pot the last night, and you may be sure she was dubhach[viii] about it. She was sitting by the fire and watching the pot and lifting the cover every now and then to see if it was boiling. The pot was not boiling, and, in the finish, tiredness came on her. What woke her out of it was the water overflowing out of the pot and it boiling. The cure was gone for no good and the child died.[106]

The Ghost Funeral

There was a fellow around here one time and he came from Kerry. Jimmy Barnett often told me that the two of them were coming home one night, and they had the biggest job they ever had to go through a funeral between Caodfada bridge and Coom. Jimmy Barnett walked away from his pal, and when he got up to Jimmy afterwards, he asked him why he did not wait for him coming through the people. Jimmy didn't see the funeral at all. The Kerry man told after that that 'twas the biggest funeral he ever saw.[107]

Johnny Machine and the Blind Horse

They say that Johnny Machine was surely going with the fairies. There was a travelling man came to him one day and Johnny was after losing his horse a few days before and was looking for another one to replace him. He asked the travelling man where he might get one to replace him. He said he knew where there was one for sale in the west side of Mhuintir Bháire.[ix] He described the horse and it appeared he was a nice one.
"A pity I did not know that before, and I'd go to see him"
By the by, Johnny got up and he told the travelling man to stay there a while, that he wouldn't be long. He was about an hour away, and when he came in says he, "That's a nice horse but he's blind in one eye."
The travelling man said he was, but that he forgot to tell him about it. Sure you know he was over. How else would he know the horse was blind? For twould be thirty miles to go around to it.[108]

Collected from Tim Lucy, Goleen

[viii] Gloomy
[ix] The Sheep's Head

The Boys, the Old Man, and the Flying Pigs

I heard two fellows saying that were out late 'scéalaíoct'[x] one night, and one of them came home with the other. There used to be a saucepan of milk left boiling for the lad of the house every night. When they came in, they got two cups and made two halves of the milk. They hadn't a sup out of it when a little old man came in and asked them for something to eat. They gave him one cup and they divided the other between the two of them. When the little man had enough to eat, he asked them if they'd care to go for a spin. They said they would. Out they went and what was outside before them but a garden full of pigs, and saddles on every one of them. The little man went up on a big sow, and he told the others to mount two pigs, but not to speak a word for their lives, or the spell would be broken. Off they went flying through the country. No ditch, nor river, nor lake, nor harbour was any bother to them. One of them was riding close to the little man, and the other fellow was the last. At last, when they jumped some great thing the last fellow said, "that was a great jump for a pig." The spell was broken, and it took him days to come home.[109]

Strange Goings on at the Forge

My father was working in the forge late one night, and we were only young nippers playing the hob. The curate of Kilmoe, a Father O'Leary, brought his horse to be shod at the forge. He left the horse at the forge to be shod while he was away in Schull that night. My father was working late, and we were running around the place. He made four sets of shoes and nails while the priest was away. He was working away and wasn't long until he got a blow off a little stone in the apron; he got a second and a third. There was a big stick of his lifted up and it struck the priest's horse. The horse jumped up and he broke the chain that was tying him. My father tied him again, and when the priest came home, he told my father not to ever work in the forge again after eight o'clock at night. My father did not get up until next day and he had to go to work that evening. 'Twas Fr O'Leary called to see him and cured him of whatever was the matter with him, and he warned him not to be caught working in the forge late at night.[110]

Collected from Richard Notter (aged 85), Goleen
(heard from his father 50 years ago).

---

[x] Scéalaíoct: Storyteller

A Crookhavener's Search for Tobacco

There was a man in Crookhaven long ago and he was mad out for tobacco. This night there was no tobacco in Crookhaven, and he went to Toormore looking for it. There was no tobacco there, and begor, off he went to Ardravinna, but he could get no tobacco there. He was coming back the back road by Ballensmeagh chapel that was kind of a short cut for the Toormore people. He met three men and he asked them where they were going. "We're going to Gansy for tobacco", says they. Will you come with us?" Off the four of them went to Cruagh strand there near Florry Mahonys. When they went there, there was a white little boat on the strand, and they shoved her off and went into her. They told her to fly off for Gansy. When they arrived at Gansy, they went into a little shop full of tobacco, and there was a little dog minding the tobacco in the shop. The Crookhavener caught the little dog and put him inside his coat. They filled up the boat with tobacco and sailed away for Cruagh. When they landed there, they were dividing out the tobacco between them. They were making no share for the Crookhavener. He asked them why and they said why didn't he bring his own share. He opened his coat and left out the little dog and as he did, away they cleared, and he had the boat of tobacco to himself.[111]

Collected from Richard Notter (aged 85), Goleen
(heard from his father 50 years ago)

Jackie the Lantern

Jackie the Lantern was a shoe-maker, and a stiff surly old boy he was. He never gave to charity nor a hello to anyone. He was out this night and he met a poor dejected little man. He brought him home, and he put him up for the night. This was the first person he ever did a good turn to. When he awoke in the morning, he went into the room what he put the old man in, and the room was shining and sparkling. There was a grand, well-dressed man in the room. "Now", says the gentleman, "since you were so good, I'll give you three wishes, but don't forget the grace of god."
"I've a little box there," says Jackie, "with awls and wax ends in it and everyone that comes in there puts his hand in it fiddling with me awls and wax ends. I wish that the next hand that will be put into it may stick in it."
"You have two more wishes says the gentleman – don't forget the grace of god."

"I've a chair there," says he, "and everyone that comes inside the door sits on it and often breaks it. I wish that the next fellow might stick in it."
"Don't forget the grace of god," says the Gentleman.
"I've a laurel tree growing outside there in the bawn,[xi] and everyone passing on their way to a fair or market breaks a smitch off it. I wish that the next fellow that will put his hand on it may stick to it.

The man went away. A short time after a man came to Jackie the Lantern and told him to come along with him, that his master had sent for him.
"And who is your master?" says Jackie.
"The Devil," says he.
"Hand me that fine awl in the box," says Jackie, "I want to draw my shoes together for the road." He put his hand in the box, and as he did it stuck there. There was never such a walloping anyone ever got as Jackie gave him, but he had compassion on him and left him home in the finish. It wasn't long till another fellow came.
"Come on with me to my master", says he to Jackie.
"Who is your master?" says Jackie.
"The devil!" says he.
"Take your care over there a while," says Jackie, "and sit on the chair." He sat on the chair and as he did, he stuck there. Jackie had an iron flail and he nearly beat the life out of him with it, but he let him go in the finish. Another fellow came in later, but Jackie saw him coming and shut the door on him.
"You'll have to come to my master the devil," says he.
"I'm old and feeble," says Jackie, "but I suppose I'll have to go. But like a good boy, break a good strong stick there for me to help me go along with you." He went to break the stick and as he did, he stuck to the tree. Jackie nearly finished him with the iron flail. When Jackie died, he wouldn't be left into heaven, and he was sent to hell. When the ones in hell saw him coming, they ran and bolted the door and wouldn't let him in. That's why he's going around the world since with a lantern, putting people astray.[112]

Collected from Jeremiah Coughlan (aged 70, died 1935), Goleen.
Jeremiah heard this story from his father who died circa 1905

[xi] Bawn - an enclosure around a farmhouse or castle, commonly built of stone or mud walls.

The Haunted Pig House

I heard a travelling man saying that he used to be going around Mhuintir Bháire. He was telling me one night how he used to call to Donovans of the white house. When he'd call to them, they would tell him call back at such and such a time as they'd have bonhams to mind.[xii] He used to spend a week minding the bonhams with one of the house. Anyone of the family wouldn't stay a night alone in the house for 'twas haunted. They didn't ever tell the travelling man how the house was haunted. This night the boy of the house was to stay up minding the bonhams with the travelling man. As he was going to a fair in the morning, the girl of the house told him to go to bed, and that she'd stay up with the travelling man. The travelling man told her to go home and he'd stay alone. (They were living in another house for they couldn't live in the white house). He was alone and the room door was open. There was a man came up out of the room, dressed up in trousers, a black swallowtail coat, and a carline hat. He came up and he nodded his head at the bonhams and walked out the kitchen door towards the stables. The travelling man did not like to speak to him, for they say it is not right to speak to the dead. He followed him out and when he came back, the best one of the bonhams was dead. I think he asked him what was troubling him, and he said it was a bit of money he had hidden in the stable.[113]

Collected from Tim Lucy, Goleen

[xii] Bonhams - piglets

Jer Lucy's lame leg

I heard old Jer Lucy saying that his father before him lived in Meall an Duine.[xiii] Everyone use to carry back loads on the horses that time; 'twas by back loads they used to do everything. He was a big man then, very well off, and had a fine place. There was a great mountain there for grazing horses, and all Jer's friends used put their horses grazing there and they'd be fat in a short time. There was a friend of his living in Long Island, and he told young Jer to go with him this day and send out his horses to graze on the mountain for a spell. They sent out a sailing boat to Callagh, young Jer jumped out on the rock, and as he did a terrible pain started in his leg, and he could hardly move. He was coming along for Meall an Duine and the pain was getting worse. He met a man on a horse and he told him to go up behind him and only that he'd never get home that night. 'Twas worse his leg was getting every day and his mother tried all the doctors in the place to cure him. At last, she took him to a weaver, north of Skibbereen. The weaver used to be going with the fairies.
"'Twas no friend of yours did that to you," said the weaver, "but I cannot tell you anything tonight. Come back tomorrow and I'll tell you what I know." He did and the weaver examined his leg.
"You went into an island,' says the man.
"I did", says Jer.
"And you came out in a sailboat," says he. Jer said he did. "You jumped out of the boat onto a rock," says he. Jer admitted that his did.
"Well," says the weaver, "there was a foxy woman watching you and you did not see her. 'Twas she who wounded you. I can't cure you now," says he, "because you did not come to me in time. But I'll take the pain out of it, and you'll have no more pain in it anymore, but you'll always be lame." He always had a short leg ever after.

Collected from Tim Lucy, Goleen

[xiii] Mauladinna, a townland near Schull.

GOLEEN
People, places and Property

Johnny Machine

Micky Coughlan had a boat in Spanish Cove long ago, and four of us used to fish herrings. Myself, Tom Barry, Micky, and John Driscoll (Johnny Machine). It was said that Johnny Machine used to be going with the fairies and that he could see the future. Johnny was old and he used to give us his net - he used not to go fishing, we used to give him a share of the fish. He used to salt his share of the fish and very often he gave them away afterwards. This night we had a good catch of fish. Micky made four shares and Tom Barry picked up a row and he said he would give none to Johnny. Micky was very honest, and he would not have it that way. He made the four shares. Johnny Máchin was in Micky's house that night asleep on the settle and Mrs Micky was working around the house. He jumped up and started to run around the house scolding. The poor woman got a fright. But when he calmed down, he said, "the man with the white wrapper is trying to do me out of my share of fish." Micky came home with the two shares, and when he came in, he said to him, "'twas lucky for me that you were there tonight or I'd get no share."

Another night we were out and after shooting the nets in the strand we went home. About ten o'clock we came back to Micky's and Johnny was there. 'Twas a grand night without a puff of wind there. When we were ready to go to the nets, Johnny came out and looked around. "Bring the nets ashore tonight", he said, "and pull up the boat because twill be a very bad night." We went to the nets and there was five hundred fish in them. We all said we'd leave them till morning, but Micky said we'd do what Johnny said. After a lot of work, we brought the nets ashore and when it came to hauling up the boat, we pulled her up on the green about two boats lengths farther up than she was ever before. We went home and out in the night about four 'clock I heard the wind and rain. Such a storm never came before. It went up on the green to the boat – 'twas lucky she was so far up. You may say that after that we believed what Johnny said.

Long ago, in the fall of the year, a lot of people from here used to go over to the north side fishing. This year, old Andy Donovan of Ballydevlin was fishing there. One night when he was coming home across Cnoc na Púca he met Johnny. 'Twas a very dark night and Johnny gave Andy a hazel stick. "Keep that says Johnny and you'll get home all right." But Andy threw away the stick. He was travelling all night and at the dawn of day he found himself in the same place. Sometime after he met Johnny. "Why did you throw away the stick?" asked Johnny. If you took my advice, you wouldn't be going astray all night.[114]

Collected from Patrick Collins (aged 75), Goleen

Old Bat Downey's Ditch

There was a man by the name of old Bat Downey living at the back of Goleen. He had a small farm. There was an old road running back of the house. It was covered with grass. Bat said that he'd build a ditch across it and that it would help to feed a cow. He built the ditch, but he left a step in it. Next morning when he went out the step was red with blood. This happened several mornings, and shortly after this a son was born to him and he had a clubfoot – the Lord save us. The ditch was there for a good while afterwards, and one morning Tim Bob Sullivan was passing that road and he saw the blood on the step too. Old Bat must have got some other warning because he took away the ditch, and even today they say that Tim, his son, goes out every night and takes down a stick that he had across the road during the day. It is unlucky they say to have anything to do with old roads or old paths because the Good People use them at night, and it would not be good for anyone that would make them cross or put them out of their road.[115]

Collected from Patrick Collins (aged 75), Goleen

GOLEEN
Local Customs

The Perils of Disturbing a Cíll

They say it isn't right to disturb a keel (cíll). There was a man ploughed up a keel one time and he sat spuds in it. The spuds grew all right, but they could never boil them. When they used be boiling, to look at them you'd think 'twas a mass of meat was boiling in the pot. That man died in the trench afterwards.[116]

Burial of Drowned Corpses

People say that if a corpse came ashore you should not give it up at all, but bury it in the land. They say that religious people wearing scapulars and so on would float if they fell into the sea. There was a man drowned in the north side (Dunmanus Bay). William Downey was his name. 'Twas the way that he was taking a wreck. They were looking for the body for days. They sent for Father Desmond who was parish priest in Goleen at that time. He went north and they showed him the place where the man was drowned. He picked up three small stones; the second one he threw in, the body floated up.[117]

Goleen
Songs

Come all ye jolly sailors bold

Come all ye jolly sailors bold,
who plough the raging main,
And landsmen pay attention,
while I relate the tale,
I belong to the Lady Charlotte,
from Lima I set sail,
Homeward bound for Liverpool,
with a sweet and pleasant gale.

Our cargo consisted of
dollars in great store,
Gold, wool, hides, and tallow,
and a lot of silver ore,
Our captain's name was James McGill,
a man of skill profound,
A jolly crew in perfect health,
and a good ship light and sound.

Our hearts were light and merry,
and our spirits they were great,
Until we reached the Irish coast,
no dangers we relate,
If the wind blew in a hurricane,
we were regardless in our might,
Till it drove us on the Barrel Rocks,
on a dreary winter's night.

The first stroke we did suffer,
'twas for mercy we did call,
Our noble ship in splinters went,
and in the deep went all,
A violent surf upon the rocks,
my mangled corpse did throw,
While all my brave companions,
lay in the deep below.

In that painful situation.
I lay until next day,
With a foaming tide going over my head,
which caused me great dismay,
From the shore I was espied,
and many was the tears,
That flowed away from my sad eyes,
for Irish hearts to bear.

About eight o'clock next morning
a small boat I espied,
She was making fast towards me,
against the running tide,
She was manned by brave young Irish
lads,
who timely did succeed,
To rescue me from danger,
how daring was the deed.

Their names for to make mention,
to them great thanks was due,
There was Tom and Andy Beasly,
there was Lynch and Grady too,
There was Strahen of the coastguard,
they never dreaded strife,
And boldly they succeeded,
to save my precious life.

They brought me down to sweet Schull
town,
where I was safely moored,
Where I was clad and nourished,
and my health it was restored,
Till a birth I got on board the ship,
where now I safely lie,
And the boys of Schull I'll ne'er forget,
until the day I die.[118]

A Lay of the Mizen Head

Jeremiah Joseph Callanan

It was the noon of Sabbath,
the spring-wind swept the sky,
And o'er the heaven's savannah blue,
the boding scuds did fly,
And a stir was heard amongst the waves,
o'er all their fields of might,
Like the distant hum of hurrying hosts,
when they muster for the fight.

The fisher marked the changing heaven,
and high his pinnace drew,
And to her wild and rocky home,
the screaming seabird flew;
But safely in Cork haven,
the sheltered bark may rest,
Within the zone of ocean hills,
that girds its beauteous breast.

Amongst the stately vessels,
in that calm port was one
Whose streamers waved out joyously,
to hail the Sabbath sun;
And scattered o'er her ample deck,
where careless hearts and free,
That laughed to hear the rising wind,
and mocked the frowning sea.

One youth along bent darkly,
above the heaving tide
His heart was with his native hills,
and with his beauteous bride;
And with the rush of feelings deep,
his manly bosom stove,
As he thought of her he had left afar,
in the springtime of their love.

What checks the seaman's jovial mirth,
and clouds his sunny brow?
Why does he look with troubled gaze,
from porthole, side, and prow?
A moment – 'twas a death-like pause –
that signal! – can it be?
That signal quickly orders out,
the Confiance to sea.

Then there was springing up aloft,
and hurrying down below,
And the windlass hoarsely answered,
to the hoarse and wild "heave yo;"
And vows were briefly spoken then,
that long had silent lain,
And hearts and lips together met,
that ne'er may meet again.

Now darker lowered the threatening sky,
and wilder heaved the wave,
And through the cordage fearfully,
the wind began to rave,
The sails are set, the anchor weighed,
what recks the gallant ship?
Blow on! Upon her course she springs,
like greyhound from the slip.

O heavens! it was a glorious sight,
that stately ship to see,
In the beauty of her gleaming sails,
and her pennant floating free.
As to gale, with bending tops,
she made her haughty bow,
And proudly spurned the waves that
burned, around her flashing prow!

The sun went down, and through the clouds,
looked out the evening star,
And westward from old Ocean's head,[xiv]
beheld that ship afar.
Still onward fearlessly she flew,
in her snowy pinion-sweep,
Like a bright and beauteous spirit,
o'er the mountains of the deep.

It blows a fearful tempest,
'tis the dead watch of the night –
The Mizen's giant brow is streaked,
with red and angry light, –
And by its far-illuming glance,
a struggling bark I see.
Wear, wear – the land, ill-fated one,
is close beneath your lee!

Another flash – they still hold out,
for home and love and life,
And under close-reefed topsail,
maintain the unequal strife:
Now out the rallying foresail flies,
the last, the desperate chance –
Can that be she? – Oh heavens it is! –
the luckless Confiance!

Hark! heard you not that dismal cry?
'Twas stifled in the gale –
Oh! clasp, young bride, thine orphan child,
and raise the widow's wail!
The morning rose in purple light,
o'er ocean's tranquil sleep –
But o'er their gallant quarry lay,
the spoilers of the deep.

The subject of the "Lay of the Mizen Head," was the wreck of the Confiance, sloop of war, lost April 1822, about a mile west of Mizen Head. All on board perished; among the rest many young midshipmen who had just joined the service and were going to join their respective ships.

Gems of the Cork Poets: Comprising the complete words of Callanan, Condon, Casey, Fitzgerald, and Cody (Cork: Barter & Sons, 1883), pp. 73-74.

[xiv] The old head of Kinsale. Such is the meaning of the Irish name.

DUNMANUS

Co. Chorcaighe
Bar: Cairbre Thiar
Par: Kilmoe
Scoil: Dunmanus, Toormore
Oide: Helena Lucey
11.1937 – 12.1938

Dunmanus, a bay or sea-lough in the barony of West Carbery, co. Cork, Munster. It enters between Sheep's Head on the north, and Three Castle Point on the south; is separated from Bantry Bay by a rugged upland peninsula of 2¾ miles in maximum breadth; measures 3½ miles across the entrance; has from 10 to 30 fathoms of depth of water; penetrates the interior to the east-north-eastward, to the extend of 11 miles; receives at its head the rivulet called Four-mile Water; and embosoms the islets of Carbery and Furze, and a number of insulated rocks. As seen from several points on the shore, it has the appearance of a spacious mountain-environed lake; and at its head is an extensive vale which forms a fine foreground to the water-views. In consequence of the immediate vicinity of the almost unrivalled bay of Bantry, Dunmanus Bay is in no repute for navigation or commerce; but it forms an important fishery-ground. On the eastern shore are the ruins of Dunmanus Castle, a fortress of considerable extent, erected by the Mahonys; and 4¼ miles farther up the bay are the remains of Dunbeacon Castle, another fortress of that sept.

The Parliamentary Gazetteer of Ireland (1814-1845)
vol. 2 (London: Fullarton, 1845), p.159.

DUNMANUS

Local Folklore and Stories

The Cripple's Leap

Away down in the south coast of Ireland lies that sheltery bay of Dunmanus, which presents in general the appearance of a widespread lake girded by a zone of mountains of the boldest outline. It is up to twenty miles in length, and from three to four miles wide, and in some places forty fathoms deep. At the south side, near the entrance, the mountain barriers which confine it seem to start up abruptly from the water's edge, and its northern shores are equally stern and precipitous. There are two Islands of small dimension in this large expanse of water, the first which stands farthest out to seaward lies about the centre of the bay and the second lies closer into the south shore. A little farther inland from this Island is the little inlet or cave called Irálára, the rocks enclosing this little cave are of the wildest character, singularly broken and irregular in their outline, rocks and stones, some of enormous dimensions, are flung together in strange confusion. On one of those stones far up in the little strand is seen the print of a shoe and the ferule of a stick or crutch, and so the old shannachie's story goes on:

In the time of the Penal days in Ireland, a man and his wife and their only son, who was deformed from childhood, were living in a cottage somewhere in the vicinity of this little cave. One evening, as the man was out in his boat fishing and his wife was telling her beads for his safety, their son, who was passionately devoted to music, took down his harp and began to play one of his favourite tunes. All at once the sound of horse's hoofs were heard coming towards the cottage. The good woman, thinking some party had lost their way (as there was a boreen convenient to the place) went to open the door, when the red coats - for it was they - seeing the beads in her hand, stabbed her through the heart and she fell dead at the doorstep. The son, seeing his mother dead, evaded the soldiers through some back opening in the cottage and made the best haste he could to the shore to warn his father of the approaching danger. The soldiers, seeing his intentions, quickly followed and overtook him at the summit of this precipitous cliff, and the boy seeing no way of escape jumped over and his body was never found. And even up to this day the marks in the stone are quite plain, although the sea washes over it constantly at high water, and the people of the surrounding districts will tell you that often when passing that way on or about twilight, they can hear the strains of music emerging from this little cave, always before a storm. And some fishermen go as far as to say that always when a storm is brewing, they can see from their boats the figure of a boy sitting on this very stone playing a harp.[119]

Collected by John McCarthy, Dunmanus

Strange Happenings in Dunmanus Bay

One day four men left Dunmanus pier to spend a week away lobster fishing. They were two Driscolls and two McCarthys. They shot their pots near Dhurode and when they had the work done, they put down the anchor and three of them went asleep and one man put a coat over his head in the stern of the boat. He was the watchman and did not go asleep. After a while a man stood up to his waist in the water. He was alive and wore a black jersey, but he did not speak. The man awakened his companions and when they had all seen him, he disappeared. They hauled their pots immediately and made for home. No sooner had they reached shore than a terrible gale blew, and they felt they had only barely escaped with their lives.[120]

Collected by Teddy O'Driscoll from H. Lucey (aged 90)

An Old Story

Once upon a time there lived a king with his wife - a beautiful woman - and his sister in-law. Now, his sister-in-law was very jealous of her sister because she was much nicer than herself and the king loved her dearly. When the first child was born the sister-in law took the child and put him in a basket and put it floating in a canal near the palace. The basket floated on 'till an old gardener and his wife rescued the child, and as they had no children of their own, they kept him. The queen's sister did the same to the next two children, a boy and a girl, and they were very handsome children. When the king found his children missing, he cast his wife into prison. The old gardener and his wife died without making known to the children the secret of their birth and they grew up thinking they were the gardener's children. One day, as they were out hunting, they met the king, and he was so charmed with their beauty that he invited them to the palace, and then the king returned the visit. They prepared a great feast, and a wise old woman told the princess to stuff a cucumber with pearls and place it before the king. When the king sat at the table he said, "What a very queer dish!". There was a parrot in the room, and he said, "What a much queerer story to have your children in this house without you knowing it," and the parrot went on to tell about the wicked act of his sister in law. The king went home, took his wife out of prison, brought home his children and punished his sister-in-law severely.[121]

Collected by Hannah McGrath, Gurtyowen

Mermaids

Mermaids were seen more frequently in olden times than they are now. They were generally seen on the seashore sitting on a rock combing their hair. Once a Glavin man who lived in Lissigriffin saw a mermaid on the seashore. He got into conversation with her, and she promised to make him very prosperous if he would comply with her wishes. He said he would, so she went home with him. When they reached the house, she made him promise never to kill a seal, never to invite a landlord to the house, and never to kill an ewe lamb.

She kept house for him for seven years and everything prospered under her care. Now, when the man became so rich, he became friendly with the landlord, and one day he invited him to the house. The mermaid did not accuse him of his breach of promise, and they lived happily as before. Next, he killed the lamb, and even then she said nothing. Lastly, he killed a seal, and even though he kept it a secret the mermaid found it out and was very angry that he had disobeyed her. She had been faithful to what she promised, and he had broken his three promises, and in killing the seal he had killed her brother. She stood on a rock outside the house and pronounced a curse on him for his want of loyalty, that seven Glavin brothers would never be seen together in Lissigriffin again. This has come to pass. Then she opened a purse which she carried and took out a little bridle and shook it. There appeared a beautiful black horse on which she rode away in the direction of the sea, and was never seen afterwards.[122]

Collected by Hannah McGrath, Gurtyowen

DUNMANUS
People, places and Property

Local Heros

The strongest man in the district was Thade Driscoll of Dunmanus, he is now over 80 years of age. He was remarkable for his strength at weight throwing and lifting loads. He was also a famous oarsman as were most of the Dunmanus people. They challenged Whiddy island, Crookhaven, Durrus, and Bantry, and each time they were the winners. One of the best rowers in this locality was John Kennedy of the Prairie (Lisnachan). Dunmanus was also famous for its expert swimmers. They used to swim from Dunmanus to Carbery island, a distance of about half a mile. Many Dunmanus people often walked to Cork with their butter. Simon Hoddnett's mother used walk to Cork with a basket of butter on her head. She would start at sunrise, remain in Cork that night, and be home the following evening at sunset. Simon Hoddnett himself also walked to Cork one time. It was also said that Frank Hellen's mother in Rathoura used put the dinner potatoes on the fire and used walk to Schull, a distance of six miles, for fish to cook for the dinner and would be back in time to strain the potatoes. Willie McCarthy of Dunkelly was known by the name of Willie the Hare. It was said he spent half a day hunting a hare and caught it. Tom Horrigan who lived about 50 yards from this school caught a thrush after running six miles after it. He was the seventh son, and it is said that the seventh son always gets some special gift. Frank Hellen's father was a great jumper. It is said he used to put his hands on the crate and jump into the car from the road. He used also stand on the horse's back while he galloped. There also lived a man in Crookhaven who made a speech standing on a horse's back going through Goleen.[123]

Collected by Hannah McCarthy, Dunmanus

Long ago there were very strong men here. Some of the strongest and greatest of these were Timothy Driscoll, Din McGrath, Jerry Murray, and Tom Wilcox. They were also the best oarsmen. And they were never beaten at any regatta, except one time when they pulled against Kilcrohane, a distance of about three miles, and the men of Dunmanus had a heavy boat. But they challenged them again for the following Sunday and Tim Sullivan of Tureen put down five pounds, and the men of Dunmanus won. Jerry Murray threw the half hundred weight 22 feet, and Timothy Driscoll took two hundred weight under each arm and stepped from the boat on to the pier at Dunmanus.

Dunmanus people were also great swimmers and a man called Cornelius Ganey swam to Carbery Island and that record has never been beaten. If the people of this locality who had a good amount of butter heard that it was dearer in another market, they would walk there, and one time my grandfather and Jim Dennis walked to Cork. They left home at sunrise, and they were home that night. On one occasion, as my grandfather and another man were out fishing in Dunmanus bay, it happened that the boat overturned, and the man took my grandfather on his back and they both came safely ashore. They swam from the south of Carbery Island, home.[124]

Collected by Bridie Walsh, Lissacaha

John Cole and John Hellen were noted mowers. It is said they were once challenged by two policemen from the barracks in Lissacaha (where Jeremiah Kennedy now lives). The policemen took the lead in the field opposite the barrack, followed by Cole, and Hellen was last. The policemen were forging ahead, Hellen asked Cole if he could do any more. On his saying he was doing his very best, Hellen cut around Cole and got ahead; he soon reached the policeman and did likewise. He reached the second policeman and passed him in the same manner and proceeded to the top of the field without ever stopping. The distance was over two hundred yards.[125] John Kennedy who lives in Lissacaha and is now nearing 70 years was a very strong man. In 1896 he was engaged in building his dwelling house. A pig that had been slaughtered was hanging from a pole lying horizontally on two beams of the kitchen. He walked across the house - 13ft - with the pig suspended from a rope around his shoulders. He walked in a bent position with his hands resting on his knees or thighs. He did this after a number of men present had failed to lift the carcass. He could also catch two beams and lift himself up 10 times without leaving his feet touch the ground. He was a great mower and cut down 8¾ acres of hay in 5½ days. Jerh Minihane of Cashelfein, who is dead over 20 years, went into Hegarty's forge in Lissacaha, and walked out of the forge with the anvil in one hand and threw it over the ditch. Denis Mahoney of Larne, who is dead about 25 years, wrote his name on a door in McCarthy's in Goleen with a ½ cut weight suspended from the little finger.

Walkers: Maurice Kennedy's mother used take 65lbs of butter on her head to Schull, a distance of 6 miles, and Maurice Kennedy travelled from his home in Lisscaha to Schull, a distance of 6 miles and back in 55 minutes. I have the knowledge from himself.[126]

Strong Men

Long ago the strong men here were, John McCarthy, Dunmanus, Den McGrath, Dunmanus, John McCarthy, Knockeens, and my grandfather was also a strong man. Once upon a time my grand-father took four-hundred weight of cement, two hundred weight under each arm from the end of the pier to the top of the pier. The best man for throwing weights was Jerry Murray. He threw the half hundred 22 feet. Long ago the men in Dunmanus were great oarsmen and they won several races. They won every race in which they competed except one which they pulled against Kilchroane. This race was about three miles long, and the men of Dunmanus had a heavy boat but they were ahead all the time until the helmsman of the other boat helped the weak side of his own boat.[127]

Collected by Paddy Driscoll, Dunmanus

Local Poets

Mark Lucey of Rathoura, an old man of 90 years, tells me that just before his day, Sullivan, a Kerry poet, often visited this area. He was held in great respect and the songs he made were much prized. The old people of his day spoke affectionately of him and sang the songs he composed. Those he remembers are *Famed Gubbeen Shore*, *The Phoenix of the Hall*, *The Rakes of Saint Giles*, *Kathleen Trial*, and a song about Napoleon which he has forgotten.

Kathleen Trial

It is in Saint Helena lies Boney well chained
Which left us all drained from money those years,
The tradesman's wives were deprived of the tea
Ever since that sanguinary Waterloo Day
The labourers likewise did pine and decay
Which made and encroachment in Kathleen Trial.

Landlords – Mr Baylie and Mr Fisher

The only landlord that any of the old people around here heard tell of were Mr Baylie and Mr Fisher. Mr Baylie, although a protestant, was a very good man, and all his tenants were catholics, in fact the Catholic curate of the parish was living in a cottage on his lands where Mr Hogan now resides. All his tenants were living in peace and comfort until he was forced to sell all his property to the Church Body, one of whose agents was a Minister named Mr Fisher. The first act that he did was to issue notices, that any catholic that did not pay the running half gale within a month would be evicted. All the catholics paid. And the next notice issued intimated that any catholic that did not go to Church on the following Sunday would be evicted. Some of the catholics remained steadfast, but as Fisher had the law in his own hands, he had no trouble in evicting all those who he knew had the best of the lands. Those farms he divided into smaller lots and gave to those whom he got to go to Church.

There were two catholic schools in Toormore at that time, one for boys and the other for girls. These were closed so that the children should go to the Altar Protestant school. As the time went on, the people got poorer as a result of evictions, and Mr Fisher keeping constantly going amongst the poor people with his charity and prayers, he got some of them to go to Church to save themselves from starvation. But others endured the greatest privation and kept the faith. Some of those that were evicted were given houses by their old landlord, Mr Baylie.

Mr Fisher was supposed to have contracted what was called a slow fever, he was taken from the Altar to Dublin where he died. There is a National School to be built in the Altar in the future, and this school is to be dedicated to his memory.[128]

Collected by Mary O'Sullivan, Toormore

Landlords – Mr Callahan

The landlord who held sway in this district was Mr Callahan. He resided in Knockeens where the Wright family now live. The land he owned belonged to Lord Bandon who got back his land again on Callahan's death as his son, who was to take over the Lordship, pre-deceased him. He was a non-practising Catholic and was very inconsiderate both to Catholics and Protestants. None of his tenants could reconstruct or improve their dwellings as he would raise the already unfair rents. When the house where Mike Shanahan now lives was being built, the masons were about to slate it when he prevented them thinking it would be too like his own. If his tenants owned a cow which he cared to buy, he would give his own price for it. Once he gave an old man a calf on condition that he would marry some old woman who lived near by within two years. The man took it for a joke and reared up the calf and when she was about to calf the landlord came and took back the cow because the man did not marry the woman he wished. On his death there was an awful thunder-clap and the old people used to say for a joke that it was a shot from the devil's gun shooting him to hell.

In olden times there were many in this district. The landlord who owned Lissacaha North was Mr Somerville. This land was first owned by Beecher. It was said that this man could hunt on his own property from Cork to the Mizen Head, except in a few ploughlands, the time of the famine. He went bankrupt and his lands were sold to small landlords, and Mr Somerville bought the land of Lissacaha North. Mr Somerville was a good man to his tenants even though he was a Protestant.

The landlords of Knockeens, Barnatonicane and Ballyvonane was Callahan. He was a very bad man to his tenants. He wouldn't leave them improve their houses as he did not want them to be better than his own. The place in which he lived is now occupied by the Wright family. He was a Protestant but during his life he never practiced any religion, it is said that he died a Catholic. Hull was the landlord of Leimcon and he owned twelve ploughlands around Lowertown.[129]

Collected by Bridie Walsh, Lissacaha

Travelling People

Travelling people come around this district often, especially in the summer. They generally travel in families, on donkeys and carts, and some have ponies and caravans. Sometimes you would see one man travelling by himself, and he would get lodging in a house, and he would sleep on the seat in the kitchen, but when they travel in bands they camp along the road. Some of the travelling people sell safety pins, hairpins, needles, and camphor, but if a person did not want any of these articles, they would give them money, eggs or bread. About twenty years ago they would be satisfied with meat or potatoes, and would sell them again. Other travelling people make tins and saucepans. The travelling people that come round the oftenest are, Coffeys, Spooneys, Sullivans, and Cronans. They generally bring some good story of the places or people they've visited, and what they saw, and they sometimes tell about your friends so as to entice you to give them something better than usual.[130]

Different bands of travelling people visit my home at different times. In the summertime you would generally see them, and at Christmas. Different families camp on the roadside and remain there a few days. Gipsies visit this district nearly every year, they sell lace, cloth, and soap, baskets, chairs and small tables. Some of them come from Limerick and Waterford. There are always two of three families together. They generally have a lot of ponies and donkeys which they also sell. They tell a lot of stories and are always anxious to tell people their fortunes. A man named Coakley visits this district sometimes. He sleeps in barns or sheds. Long ago there were many more travelling people here than there are now.[131]

Gurtyowen

I live in Gurtyowen. There are seven families in it, two catholic families and five protestant ones, twenty-seven inhabitants in all. The land is for the most part low and very productive. There is a ruin in my district where a man named Spillane lived. He was working for Sam Hunt's people, and he lived on the farm with his sister. He was afterwards lost in a boat wreck in Dunmanus Bay. Long ago most of the houses were thatched, but now they are slated and in good condition as most of the people have availed of the new Government Grant. There is but one very old woman in my district and she cannot speak one word of Irish.[132]

Collected by Helena Lucey

Dunmanus

The townland in which I live is called Dunmanus West. There are seventeen families in it, about seventy people at present, and about six old people. There is no good storyteller. Long ago people were much more numerous in Dunmanus because there was a fishing industry which employed a lot of the people. There were four seines there, and a steamer used to come into the harbour for the fish. After the fishing industry declined, a lot of the people emigrated. Most of the houses in Dunmanus are slated. The family names most common are McCarthy and Driscoll. There are three families of McCarthys, eight people in all, and there are three families of Driscolls there, sixteen people in all. Dunmanus has three townlands – Fán mór, Cumar, and Stiuch, but they all go under the name of Dunmanus now.[133] There are only a few old ruins in Dunmanus, one in our land where the Cullinane family lived. The field that Dunmanus Castle is built on is called the Mount, because it is very high ground. There is another placed called Pointe na blósach. This means the point of the pits, because long ago there used to be a lot of potato pits. A boat came for those potatoes occasionally. There is a strand near this point called Tragh Leachan because it is very wide. There is another place called the Sleabh because it is rough and rocky. There is another field called Tobar because there is a well in it.[134]

Collected by Patrick O'Driscoll

Place Names

Gurtyowen or Owen's field is so called because in the townland there is a bog which lies along the eastern side, stretching from the southern bounds to the northern. It was a great turf bog in olden times, but all the turf has been cut away now. The turf bog is over a mile long. Sam Hunt owns a part of it, Dick Hegarty owns another part, and Mrs Hunt owns the northern side. The bog was once in possession of a man named Owen. In Richard Helen's land there is a field called Tuargain and it is believed that in that field the potatoes were first struck by the blight in this district. Tureen is one of the townlands in Dunmanus. It is so called because in olden times a lot of sheep and cattle used be reared there. There is a rock in my townland called Toirteóg. This rock is so called because it is covered with grass and heather.[135]

Collected by Hannah McGrath, Gurtyowen

Toormore

The district in which I live in is rich in folklore. Túarmór (a black-green) was so called because in the olden times the people used bleach their clothes on a high green field here. Carrigín Dubh - is a rocky little island very near the shore on which black weeds grow. Cathaoir is the name of a field near us. It is so called because the shape of an armchair is cut into a big rock in the field. Gort na Neacaire (The Fairy Field) is the largest field in this townland; it contains two and a half acres. There is a subterranean passage where the sea beats against the fence, extending about half a mile in a westerly direction. An old tradition says that it was used by the Danes when they came to Ireland. The old Catholic school was also built in the same field, but it had to be removed over to Dunmanus, the site of the present school, for no Catholic school would be allowed in Toormore by the Minister of that time.

Lissacaha North

The district in which I live is called Lissacaha North. Long ago a gentleman named Somerville, who was the landlord of this place, planted a big wood there, and ever since it has been called the Prairie. This wood was bigger in olden times as it covered up to three acres of land. In this wood the ruins of Somerville's houses are still to be seen. In my district there are eight families and about thirty-eight people. There are only three old people in my district, the oldest woman is Mrs McCarthy. People were much more numerous long ago in my townland than they are now. There are only a few ruins in my district. There is one ruin to the west of Glanville's house, and it was there a Daly woman lived long ago. The land is divided into small farms. It is great land for growing oats and potatoes, but it is not good for growing wheat. There is also very good turf to be got in the Prairie. There is a big river in my district it rises in Gloun and flows into Dunmanus bay. Long ago most of the houses were thatched, but now you seldom see a thatched house and the people have availed of the new Government Grant and have repaired their houses. The family names most common in my district are Kennedy and Driscoll.[136]

Local Place Names

Faill a' Glóir (The cliff of the echo) is so called because there is an echo in the rocks. There is a subterranean passage through the rocks, but its opening is now closed up with briars and brambles. Corrach Liath is the name of the bog about fifty yards from this school. It was so called because many years ago there was flax growing in the same place. Lissacaha (The fort of the battle) is a townland about two and a half miles from here. It was the scene of a battle in the olden times between the Irish and the Danes. Poll Muslaí is a small deep strand very near us, it is always filled with mussels hence its name. Cúas Gorm is so called because the water looks blue at all times. It is a little inlet of the sea. Oileán Gabhair is an island opposite the Altar Church. In the olden times poor people used keep their goats on that island. Cúisín a' Ghainimh is a little strand in the Altar. It is so called because it is always covered with lovely white sand. Góilín a' Bháid is a field near the sea where boats were built long ago.[137]

Holy Wells

Ireland from the Christian times has been celebrated for holy wells and healing fountains. People believe that long ago a saint or a hermit lived there, or drank from them, or baptised people in their waters. There are not many wells in this district. The nearest one is situated among the hills at the back of this school. It is called the "well of the warts", as it is believed to cure warts. When a person used go to the well, bathe the affected part or limb in the waters, and leave some relic (token) after him, such as a rosary beads or medal, it was believed that he would be cured. Nobody likes to interfere with the well, they think it would be unlucky. There is a three-cornered stone in front of the well, and long ago when boys were coming to this school, they threw away the stone from the well, and afterwards when they returned it was in the same place in front of the well. There is also another holy well about 300 yards to the back of Killhomane school. Long ago people used pay rounds at this well, and they used to pay three visits in order to complete the rounds. Once a man took water from the well, and put it in the kettle on the fire, but it never boiled. Since then, the well has never been interfered with.[138]

Collected by Mary O'Sullivan, Toormore

Local Roads

I live about fifteen yards from the main road that leads from Schull to Goleen, and from the branch road that leads to Bantry. These roads were made about the year 1847, the grant being given by the government for relief works. Of late years the roads are kept in a very good state of repair. In the course of a few years the road from Schull to Crookhaven will be steam-rolled, as it has been steam-rolled now one and a half miles at this side of Schull. Before these roads were made the people had very bad roads to travel. Some of them were scarcely wide enough for a horse's cart, but as motors were unheard of in those days the people were satisfied. The road which we travel from Toormore to Ballyskneigh was then the main road to Cork, and it was called the Old Cork Road. This road was improved recently. £150 was granted for it.[139]

Collected by Mary Sullivan, Toormore

I live on the side of the road that leads from Goleen to Bantry. Long ago all these roads were but pathways or boreens, and no cars could travel them, the first man that had a common cart in this district was Tim Minihane, and in the time of the famine he was paid for taking dead bodies to the graveyard. This man lived in Barnatonicane near the graveyard. The main road that leads from Goleen to Bantry was made in 1847, the year of the famine, and every working man got fourpence or sixpence a day, and sometimes they would be satisfied with a pint of meal for payment. To the north of Kilthomane school there was a pathway in olden times, this road was made during the famine. The people had to work very hard as the road had to be made through hills and bogs. It was planned to take the road through Hungerford's wood, but as Mr Hungerford was the landlord, he would not allow it to be made through his own land, so it had to be cut through a hill. The old Cork road from Goleen through Skibbereen to Cork is still to be seen. A part of it from Toormore on to Ballinaskea chapel, (a convenient road for the people in Toormore to go to the chapel) was improved this year. The new road at Toormore bridge was also improved recently. The tide used to cover the road and cars could not travel there until it receded. A man was drowned there long ago.[140]

Collected by Dick Lucey

The School

The Catholic school of Toormore was built in the top of the townland of Toormore. At the time Toormore was made church property, the catholic school was done away with for no catholic school would be allowed in Toormore by Mr Fisher, the Minister of that time. There was an old house occupied by a woman named Mary Barry, convenient to the site occupied by the present school (Dunmanus), and the parish priest of that time took the house over from her and built an extension to make a school for the catholic children of Toormore & Dunmanus. In the meantime, he got another house built for Mary Barry which is at present occupied by Ida Hayes. The river running to the back of the school is the boundary between Toormore & Dunmanus. The old school was built in a field called Gort na Neacaire. There is a subterranean passage where the sea beats against the fence and extends for about half a mile in a westerly direction. An old tradition says that it was used by the Danes when they came to Ireland. The late Mr Baylie's grandfather was landlord of Toormore & the Altar. He sold his property to Mr Fisher and that is how it became church property.[141]

Collected by Mary O'Sullivan

Old Houses

About seventy years ago there were no slated houses in this district. The first house that was slated around here was that of Denis Mc Grath in Dunmanus. All the houses were thatched and were one storied for the most part. Those that were two-storied had no stairs but a ladder from the floor to the loft. In the mud cabins there were no windows but slits to leave in the air. In the thatched houses there were not more than two windows which were not made to open as the people did not realize the good of the sun and air then as they do now. The doors were made of fir plank, and rush and straw mats were made and put against the doors at night to protect the people from the draught. The walls were very thick, and they used mud mortar. The chimney was made of wild rods worked like a basket and lined with mud so as to prevent it from burning. At that time oil lamps were not in general use among the people. They used fir splinters to give them light. They also made candles from tallow. The fat of the cod when melted also makes oil. The oil was put into a vessel, a rush was peeled and placed in the oil and when the rush was alight it burned brightly through the night.[142]

DUNMANUS
Farming, Trade and Crafts

Local Forges

There are forges in Toormore, Lowertown, Ballydivlin, Goleen, and Lissagriffin. The local forge is situated in Toormore, but recently the last of the Sullivans died, and there is no smith work carried on there now, and Lowertown forge is the nearest. In olden times there was a forge in Lissacaha owned by Michael Hegarty. This man learned his trade from Jerry Murray's grandfather who lived in Knockeens. It was situated to the north of Jerry Murray's house, and the place on which it was built is now called the forge rock. There was another forge in Dunmanus owned by Michael Hegarty, but no work is carried on in this forge now. In olden times there was a forge in Ardravinna owned by William Wilcox. It too has fallen into disuse. It is said that he was once working in his forge until midnight. He had only retired when he heard the noise of horse's hoofs. He thought some man may be badly in need of a shoe for his horse, and so he went in haste to the forge, but when he went there, he could see nothing, he never worked so late in the forge afterwards. Most of the forges are thatched, and there is one big door in each of them large enough to admit a horse. There is a big fireplace in the forge, and near the fireplace you would see a bellows, and the smith uses this for blowing the fire when he is heating iron. Convenient to the forge you would see an iron platform which is used for shoeing wheels. There is a hole in the centre to put in the stock, they put the wheel down on that platform and light a fire around the band. When the iron is hot, two men take it out with a tongs and strike it down on the wheel, and then they pour water on it to make it tight and firm, and to prevent it burning the wood.[143]

Weaving

Weaving was a great trade long ago and in every house, there was a spinning wheel. A man named Andy Donovan who lived in Ballydevlin was a weaver. Every farmer in this district kept sheep. When the wool was cut off, the women washed it, then carded and spun it into thread. The weavers made it into frieze. In olden times all the houses were thatched and a good, thatched roof lasted twenty years. Straw and read were used for thatching. In every district there was a thatcher. The people made súgáns from hay and the hair of the mane and tail of the horse was also made into ropes. The local smith made nails from rod iron. It was the smith who made the spades and all the farm implements.[144]

Collected by Mark Lucey, Ballyrizard

Crafts

Long ago the people in this district made their own baskets. They used cut the rods and season them. Some people used grow their twigs and others cut the wild rods. When there were no carts, the people made back loads. Two baskets used to be put accross the horse's back for taking loads. They made whips from rope. The children made whips of rushes. Before nails were bought in shops, the people got nails made in the local forge. Long ago nearly all the houses in the district were thatched. A man called a thatcher went around thatching the houses. The wheaten straw or reeds cut in bogs were used for thatching. The straw was sewn on the roof. There was a cooper in Lissacaha for making churns. The people made candles from tallow, the fat of the sheep and cow. The wick was put through a mould and over a nail at the top. The mould was stuck in a sod of turf and the melted tallow was poured in. When it was cool the mould was heated to the fire and the candle was pulled out by the nail.[145]

Collected by Dick Lucey, Ballyrizard

Clothes made locally

There is not any tailor in our immediate vicinity but there are three tailors in Schull - the nearest village to us. Two of them stock the cloth - tweeds and serges. The materials are not home spun as they used to be in past times. There was a weaver in Ballydevlin called Andy the weaver. Long ago the tailors used go round from house to house and mend the clothes for the people. There is one of those tailors still in Lowertown, named John Callaghan, known as Johny the Tailor. He is nearly seventy years and is lame. He makes clothes for the people of Lowertown and Ardravinna. He has no home, but he stays at certain houses. Tailors are looked down upon and considered inferior. Once nine tailors presented themselves before Queen Elizabeth. She saluted them saying, "Good morrow gentlemen both" which meant that it took nine tailors to make two men. The women of this parish knit socks for the boys and men, and they also knit jerseys for them. There is but one spinning wheel in my district which is owned by Mrs Hellen of Dunmanus. She still spins her thread. This was not unusual in past times as every farmer kept sheep. There was a spinning wheel in every house, and when the wool was clean and dry the women would spin it.[146]

Collected by Hannah Mc Grath, Gurtyowen

AN IRISH INTERIOR, SHOWING A HAND LOOM WEAVER AND A SPINNER.

(From a Sketch by Charles Whymper.)

Figure 16. An Irish Interior. Richard Lovett, *Irish Pictures* (Dublin: Religious Tract Society, 1888).

DUNMANUS
Leisure

Dancing

Mike Kelleher of Glason had a dancing school about 66 years ago. The people in that district knew nothing of dancing till he set up school. This man settled down in Glaun on his marriage in 1866. He and his people came from Ballyvourney in 1855, the year of the big snow. The townland in which they dwelt was Ardeen, the next townland to Liscarragane, in the parish of Clondrohid and he was a schoolfellow of an t-achair Pearse ó laoghaire. There were confirmed at the same time and place at Carraig-an-tire. He was taught catechism in Irish and spoke no English till he was 16 years. On the removal of the family to Rathoura, Michael walked all the way from Ballyvourney driving a herd of cattle. He rested one night with friends in Kealkil. He remembered that poets used come into their house. On one occasion two poets, Creed and Binny Prigheasóra, met there. The news of their arrival soon spread and in a short time the house was filled with people listening eagerly and with great enjoyment to the battle of poetry between the two. His grandson Michael Kelleher gave me this account. He set up a school for dancing and was paid in work by the pupils. He also taught the fiddle. He was a wonderful step-dancer and taught Mike Hegarty of Dunmanus dancing and fiddle-music. He was also a great storyteller and loved to tell about Fionn and the doings of his famous dogs. This pupil of Kellehers, Mike Hegarty composed a song on Glaun.

I often think of the bygone days
The merry fair in town.
When herds were on the mountain side
And happy homes in Glaun

A sporting place, a charming race,
A land for music famed
Sure Rambler lived behind the hill
We was lord of Tureen Cain

Where Nancy great a lovely lass
A star was Nelly Brown
Oh, life was well worth living for
Those sporting days of Glaun.

The dancing school was there in bloom
A wealth of pleasure reigned.
With flocks and herds to roam the glen
And graze the mountain range

Famed Cormic would cross the mountain pass
From Schull his native town
Acourting Mary of the Glen
The sporting lass from Glaun.[147]

DUNMANUS
Local Customs

Lore of Certain Days

I have always heard it said that no one should start on a journey on a Friday as it would be very unlucky. Monday is also supposed to be an unlucky day for travelling. A person who is ill in bed for some time never gets out of bed for the first time on a Friday as it is said that he or she would have to go back to bed again. It is also said it is unlucky to remove from one house to another on a Friday. Good Friday is considered a good day for sticking potatoes. Some people would not like to plough the ground on Good Friday, and it is also considered unlucky to work in a forge or drive nails or heat irons on that day. Long ago, the people used to say that everyone should have his potatoes sown before St Patrick's Day. Some people would not spend money on a Monday because it is said they would be spending it all week, and the old saying says, 'Good Monday, good week.' Tuesday, Thursday, and Saturday are supposed to be the best days for gathering herbs, especially if it is near full moon. People never get married on Friday, and some years ago they did not get married on Wednesdays, but of late years they do. Some people would not cut their hair or manicure their nails on a Friday, and some men would not care to shave on that day either. I have often heard a rhyme about sneezing on the different days of the week: Sneeze on a Monday, sneeze for a letter, sneeze on a Tuesday, sneeze for something better, sneeze on a Wednesday, sneeze for danger, sneeze on a Thursday, you will meet a stranger, sneeze on a Friday, sneeze for sorrow, sneeze on a Saturday, you'll meet your best friend tomorrow.[148]

Old Customs

To meet a person on the stairs is a sign of disappointment. A cat with his back to the fire, or seagulls inland are portraits of bad weather. To carry inadvertently a lighted lamp in one's hand or to put on an article of clothing inside out are signs of good luck. To see a pin in the morning is a great omen of good fortune, and so the old saying is, 'Meet a pin and pick it up, and all the day you will have good luck, meet a pin and pass it by, you will need a pin before you die.' Before sowing wheat some people here mixed the grain with ashes made from the holly that was bought in to decorate the house at Christmas. An old shoe used be thrown for luck, after those going out fishing or seining.[149]

Old Customs

The people in this district still adhere to many customs that were prevalent in ages past. Outsiders may laugh at these observances, but the people say, make no law and break no law. Our forefathers did these things, and they did not do them for nothing. It is considered an omen of ill-luck to meet a red-haired woman at the beginning of a journey. Spilling salt portends a quarrel. A dog crying in the night is an omen of death. If a honeybee enters the house buzzing it is a sign of news. If a knife falls off the table or if you dropped a knife by accident, it means that you'll have a gentleman visitor, and if a spoon falls you will entertain a lady visitor. To find a horseshoe is very lucky and some people hang one on the back of a door to bring luck. It is very lucky to find a black cat and it is said, 'If a black cat to you strays, butter his feet and make him stay'. To see a moth flying around you means you will get a letter. To see a spider creeping on your dress means that you will get a new one. A tea leaf swimming on top of your tea means that you'll have a visitor.[150]

Collected by Hannah McCarthy, Gurtyowen

Care of the Feet

Long ago there were many country people who seldom or never wore shoes or boots. In remote country places some of the women never wore any shoes, and those that did had them always for special occasions, such as for attending Mass. Some women walked to Mass barefoot, and then put on their boots near the Church. Afterwards clogs came into use. Captain Somerville who lived in the Prairie was the first person who brought clogs to this district for his workmen. The clogs had timber heels and soles with cloth uppers and fastened with two straps on each side. The children growing up never got any shoes until they were almost men and women. All the shoes were handmade as there were no such thing as machines. Denis Sullivan of Dunmanus and John Driscoll of Gloun were two men who never wore shoes. There are many people who would never throw out the water with which they wash their feet at night as they consider it unlucky as the fairies would have power over them.[151]

Churning

There are three kinds of churns, the barrel, the box, and the end over end churn. In olden times the dash-churn was used, this was similar to those that are used now for taking milk to the creamery, but they were made of wood. There was a hole in the centre of the cover for the staff. The staff was a handle with a flat piece of timber fixed on one end. With that they used make the butter, but nowadays the barrel churn is in general use. The churns are made of oak with an opening to put in the cream and to take out the butter. There is a small hole near the big one to let out the buttermilk. In winter the churn is scalded before putting in the cream so as to raise the temperature, but in summer it is well rinsed with cold water so as to lower the temperature. The churn is fixed on a stand about three feet high. It is an old saying that if you go into a house while butter is being made you should give a twist to the handle for fear the butter would not come. The people do not leave out their cows on May Eve for fear some evil-minded neighbours would milk them and take away the luck from them.[152]

Bread of the Olden Times

Long ago the people depended chiefly on the potato for their sustenance. Besides boiling the potatoes they also made them into bread. They used to make stampy and potato cake which are still made and are looked upon as a delicacy whereas they were the ordinary food of our grandfathers. To make stampy the potatoes are first washed and peeled, then a grater was provided by opening a cocoa tin and making holes in it. Then it was nailed on a piece of timber and on this the potatoes were grated, and the pulp squeezed in a strong calico bag. Then it was kneaded with sour-milk or cream after a pinch of salt had been added. It was put into a pan very thinly and when it was baked on one side it was turned over to bake on the other side. It is very tasty if eaten with butter when hot.

Long ago the men used to work in the morning before eating their breakfast and the women used have a hot cake or a pot of potatoes ready for them. They used to have yellow meal gruel for their supper. In every house long ago, there was a quern for making reboon. Firstly, the wheat was well dried in a bastable over the fire and then ground with a quern into very fine flour. It can then be eaten with sweet milk and is very palatable.[153]

Collected by Hannah McGrath, Gurtyowen

Food in the Olden Times

Long ago the people ate but three meals a day. And in the very early times they had potatoes for breakfast, dinner, and supper. They used milk and fish with the potatoes and sometimes they used only milk and salt. In olden times fish was very plentiful, and those who lived by the seaside were never short. In some houses where there was a big family, the table was placed in the centre of the floor, and a pot of potatoes were thrown out on it, and the family gathered around the table for meals. In the olden times the bread the people used was wheaten bread and yellow-meal cake. They called the wheaten bread black bread. On Christmas and Easter, the people used have better food. Easter Sunday and Patrick's day were great days for egg eating. At Christmas the people used have a goose or turkey and a currant cake. About 80 years ago, tea was first used in this district, and then it was used only among the women as tea was very costly. It was said as a joke that when tea came to this district first, the people didn't know how to use it and they used boil it and eat the leaves. Long ago mugs and tin cans were used before cups became common. In later years some farmers killed a pig or a cow, and they used it all the year round with their own vegetables, such as turnips, cabbage, and parsnips.

Collected by Bridie Walsh, Lissacaha North

Old Emblems

People were very devoted to holy emblems. After Christmas, holly was burnt, and the ashes were mixed with the wheat to bring a blessing. The people used to take palm branches to Mass on Palm Sunday to get them blessed, and these they kept in the house. On St. Patrick's night, and on St. Bridget's night, the people wove crosses and hung then in each room and the outhouses to invoke a blessing. They had great faith in Holy Water and each night they blessed themselves. The candles blessed on Candlemas day were used when burning the hair of the udders of cows after calving. The people used to rise early Easter Sunday morning to see the sun dancing and the Fastnet sailing. The people used to usher the summer in on May morning by bringing in a bucket of spring water. Many people from this district used to go to Our Lady's Well in Ross to pay rounds there. They also paid rounds at a holy well at Kilthomane and at Fr O'Connell's grave, Goleen, for during his lifetime he cured many diseases.[154]

Figure 17. Prospect of Dunmanus Bay. British Library. Shelf mark: Ktop LII, no. 41.

DUNMANUS
Local Cures

Herbs

There are several herbs highly valued in the past for their medicinal properties, and long ago nearly all the people treated their ailments with herbs. Of these the wild sage, penny leaf, sorrel, dandelion, garlic, and yarrow, are the best known. The wild sage is very good for a cold or a hurt. The month of May is the best month for using it. It is taken from the roots, and the leeks washed and put into a saucepan of cold water, brought to the boil and allowed to simmer slowly for a few hours, it is then strained, and the liquid is mixed with port or sugar to make it more palatible before using. It is drunk fasting. Penny leaf is used as a cure for boils and corns. It is heated, lightly peeled and put on the sore. Sorrel is a common plant in this country. It has a sour juice and is used for a cough and is eaten raw. It is sometimes used as a salad. Dandelion is boiled and used in the same way as wild sage. It is said to cure liver complaints and rheumatism. Garlic is a plant with a bulbous root and a very strong smell, it is used for whooping cough. The old people use put it into the children's stockings to prevent them from whooping. It is good for the lungs and is used for bad colds. Yarrow is treated in the same way as dandelion and wild sage. It is good for rheumatism.

The cupóg is a harmful plant because it spreads very quickly and is regarded as one of the noxious weeds. It is said to grow best in good ground.

There are several other herbs that would be useful if we could only understand their cure. The people long ago used these herbs when there were no doctors or chemist shops to be had, but now unfortunately many of these cures have fallen into disuse.[155]

Collected by Bridie Walsh, Lissacaha

DUNMANUS

The Natural World and Weather Lore

Weather Signs

When we are going to get bad weather, the sea is very rough at the shore, and the water boils from the bottom and it is called ground surge. The gulls gather cúining (keening) on the mainland. The cat sits at the fire, the dog eats grass, and the hens are constantly picking their feathers. The cows go gadding, and the curlews shriek. The sky gets cloudy, a circle comes around the moon, the stars twinkle, and a very cold wind is blowing from the south. A day before rain you would see cobwebs on the ground, the water increases in the springs, and the fog comes on the tops of the mountains. When the wind blows from the north, we often have snow.[156]

Collected by Bridie Walsh

Storms

About the year 1902, a terrible storm caused the Bohemia to be wrecked off the Mizen Head. She was an American vessel laden with general cargo. The wreckage was picked up by the people of Dunmanus. The captain came ashore on a bullock's back. Many of the cattle were sold by the neighbouring people at Bantry. All lives were saved but two. This storm did a considerable amount of damage in the district. Many hay ricks were thrown down, houses were stripped, and trees uprooted. Masons were at work for several weeks repairing the damage. Later still, in the year 1928, we had a severe storm. It began on Christmas night and did not cease until St Stephen's night - hay and turf ricks, hay sheds, and out houses suffered, and cattle were killed by falling houses. Our local river, which rises near Mt. Gabriel and flows into Dunmanus Bay, overflowed its banks and brought turf from Gloun to Dunmanus Bay. Many sheep were lost in the snow, and some were found hidden in holes in the hills. It is said that these sheep had eaten their wool which kept them alive.[157]

Collected by A. O'Sullivan

DUNMANUS
Sea and Shipwrecks

Local Happenings

About 35 years ago there was a sad drowning in Dunmanus Bay. Two boats left Muintevara to shoot nets off the lug of Míláin at this side of Dhurode. One of the boats was called the Coffin. The crews were bad friends. As they were leaving for the fishing ground the father of one of the crew of the doomed boat - the Coffin - ordered his son out of the boat, he taking his place, as he had a premonition - a foreshadowing as it is called - of disaster. They shot the nets and set sail for home at nightfall. It appears the evening got squally. Each had lug sails. They did not anticipate danger and the sheet-line of the Coffin was bound to the boat so that when the squall came it overturned. The first boat noticed the disaster but went on and never went to the rescure. Six were lost. A mother whose two sons were lost went out of her mind. The boat drifted back and righted itself at the fishing ground where she was found with two bodies aboard. All those in the first boat left for America soon after. The supposition was that they were haunted.[158]

Wrecks

Hibernian (or Iberian): Bird Island in Dunmanus Bay about 48 yrs ago.
Bohemian: over 50 years ago in Dunlough Bay.
Memphis: Dunlough Bay near Mizen Head in Nov. 1897 - 7 or 8 lost.
Oswestry: March 1899 at Mizen Head (General cargo - copper, timber, flour, carriage wheels).
Queensmore: caught fire in Dunmanus Bay.
Irada: Clohane Island near Mizen Head over 30 years ago. Cotton and wood chief cargo.
The Memphis had a valuable cargo of cattle, timber, bacon, lard, cheese, matchwood, margarine, butter. Cheese and butter saved from this wreck were sold in Bantry. The Hibernian, Glerian & Bohemian were sister ships and were all lost within ten years. The Glerian was wrecked on Cape Clear, wither a cargo of rum.[159]

Collected by P. McGrath, Gurtyowen

DUNMANUS
Songs

Batty Hegarty's Bit of Moonshine

When the springtime tints the hedges
And when autumn fields are brown
'Tis a pleasant thing to wander
Through the fields of Aughadown,
And to gossip with the husbandman
Of matters grave and gay,
Reminiscent of folks and times
That long have passed away.

By the roadway, in the meadow
Relic of the past is shown,
Hoary pile of crumbling ruins
All dismantled, ivy-grown,
Round which circles a quaint stone-wall
Workmanship of curious hands,
With the background of a story
Passing current in the land

You have never heard the tale then.
But 'tis true beyond a doubt
How that stonewall one occasion
Tricked the bailiffs out and out
'Twas the park wall of Squire Beecher
And a man well-known was he
In the foxhunt and the steeple chase
And old time chivalry.

And he lorded in his hey-day,
O'er that smiling countryside
Sloping down in hills and pastures
To the Roaring-water tide.
'Mongst his goodly host of tenants,
Batty Hegarty was one
Whom it would be hard to beat
For pure Irish wit and fun.

But the pity was that hard times
Came to steal in at the door
And his cares and disappointments
Seemed to deepen more and more.
As the gale-day drew near quickly
In the stealthy flight of time
And he lacked the landlord's money
Then as now, the heinous crime.

He was upright and hard-working,
His intentions all were bent
To be fair and square in dealing,
But intentions are not rent.
Let that fail to be forthcoming
On the next accounting day
And adieu to merry Batty
He must bundle and away.

Now, as ever, man's resourcefulness
So sorely tried as that
He straightway must shoot the landlord,
He must rob a bank or what?
Yerra no! behold that twinkling
Brightening up the roguish eye!
And how cleverly he'll manage
You will learn by and by.

For a ride, used go the landlord
Every morning just at nine.
In that circumstance and moment
Batty's plot must fall in line.
Out of doors betimes he sallied
And he slyly took his stand
By the landlord's flanking stonewall
With the crowbar in his hand.

There he waits in expectation,
Whether will he win or fail?
Meeting with opposing forces
Batty ne'er was known to quail.
When at last it is the landlord,
Hear his horse's hoofs to sing
Up jumps Batty, grips his crowbar
Wields it with a mighty swing.

Brings it clanging on the stonewall
Rising sparks that madly flashed
Just as round the bend, the great man
On his prancing hunter dashed.
"Ho there, rascal! what the duce then
Are you doing to my wall?"
Feigning wonderment, the schemer
Quickly lets the crowbar fall.

"Top-o-the-morning, to your honour, sir,
And faith, you're looking fine!
There's no gentleman in Cork, Sir,
That could cut so grand a shine!"
And says Batty, "By your lave sire,
All about it, I will tell
How I went to Skibbereen yesterday
A thing or two to sell.

Now the rent was due to-day, sir,
And I am in duty bound,
To square matters with yer honour,
For that little bit of ground.
But last night when stepping homewards
Faith a thought came to my mind,
That if Peggy trucked my guineas
They would scatter with the wind.

So I stopped here, thinking of it,
And for fear such would befall
I found out a secret crevice
And I hid them in the wall.
Now the moon was shining brightly,
And the shadow of a tree
Fell across that bit of roadway
That lies just 'twixt you + me.

But the moon makes people quare set.
And if I were to be shot
I couldn't say the minute
Whether this or that's the spot.
But when the moon will shine tonight,
I will come again and see.
And I'll surely come anear it.
By the shadow of that tree

And I'll search, and dig, and delve sir,
And my gold again I'll find
If I have to fell the wall sir,
A few perches you wont mind."
"Tut! You ruffian!" cried the landlord
"Not for those few coins of gold,
Nor for all the farm produce,
You have ere bought or sold

"Would I let you break that stone wall,
That I look upon with pride,
So away with you immediately
And from this place keep wide!"
"Míle murther!" whimpered Batty,
"What am I to do at all?
Must I starve, and be evicted
While my money's in the wall?"

So went on the wordy warfare
Thrust and parry fairly dealt
Till the soft tones of relenting
In the landlord's voice was felt,
Then he said in kindly accents,
"As it thus befell on you
I'll remit the whole instalment
Of the rent that's hanging due

But I stringently enjoin you
On a clear command from me
That you daren't touch that wall again
Or punished you will be."
Of course, Batty thanked his honour,
And homeward straight he went
Chuckling how the ancient stone wall
Paid the missing half year's rent.

That's the story as they tell it,
So it is and let it be,
And of Batty's bit of moonshine
In the shadow of the tree.[160]

You True-bred Sons of Erin's Isle

You true-bred sons of Erin's Isle
Pay attention to my song
And if you will attention pay
I wont detain you long.
I am a true bred Irishman
From a land so green
And I love that soil called Erin's Isle,
That reared an Irishman

John Bull my boast of battles
And victories he won.
But only for our Irish boys.
What would those lads have done.
Our Irishmen are genuine
They are foremost in the van
I will tell you true that Waterloo
Was won by an Irishman.

Their deeds on sea as well as land
They make my blood to boil
Did they not fight with Nelson
At trafalgar, on the Nile
On board the good ship Victory
When their odds were two to ten.
Old Erin's sons held to their guns
Like genuine Irishmen.

If the Duke of Wellington were alive
Some tales he would relate.
How our Irishmen, they fought and won
And the enemy did defeat
Old England she should bear in mind
She will want those men again.
And not to make foes of those we know
Who are genuine Irishmen.

An Irishman is genuine
Whatever his faults my be
But to hang three men for the death of one
That's more than I'd like to see
There was Allen Larken and O Brien,
The judge did them condemn.
Although they are dead, their memory dwells
In the hearts of Irishmen

May Ireland soon be happy
And from all oppression free
May the North and South of Ireland
Be one in unity
May discontent soon disappear
And as true as my name is John
I will stay at home
In my dear island home
And die like an Irishman

Lonely Banna Strand

It was on a Good Friday morning
At the early dawn of day
A German ship was signalling
Far out upon the Bay
With thirty thousand rifles
Just ready for to land
But they could get no return signal
From Lonely Banna Strand

A motor car came dashing fast
The early morning bloom.
A sudden dash and down a cliff
It fell to meet its doom
Two Irish boys lay dying
Just like a rose so grand
But they could not give the signal
From lonely Banna Strand.

We have no return signal from the land
Sir Roger sadly said
No comrades here to welcome us.
Alas they must be dead.
But I must do my duty
This day I mean to land
So in a boat he pulled away
To lonely Banna Strand.

A German ship was sailing in
With rifles galore
Saying, Here you are a fore
You are the Empire's enemy
We will fight you now so stand
For a German boat shall never be put
On the lonely Banna Strand.

We sailed to Queenstown Harbour
Say the Germans we are done
The British ship our master
Man for man and gun for gun
With thirty thousand rifles
And none of them left land
We'll dump them all and bid farewell
To lonely Banna strand.

The R.I.C. were searching
For Sir Roger high and low
They found him in McKenzie's fort
Saying here you are a foe
My name is Sir Roger Casement
I came to free my native land
But I could never free my country
From lonely Banna strand.

Where the Beautiful Rivers Flow

I sing tonight of a fairy land
In the lap of ocean set
And of all the lands I've travelled o'er
'Tis the loveliest I've met
Where the willows weep and roses sleep
And balmy breezes blow
In the dear old land, that sweet old land
Where the beautiful rivers flow.

But oh! alas how can I sing?
'Tis an exile breathes the strain
And that dear old land of my youthful love
I must never see again
And the very joy that fills my heart
Must ever change to woe
For that dear old land, that sweet old land
Where the beautiful rivers flow

But I'll sing of the lonely old churchyard,
Where our forefather's bones are laid
Where the cloister stands in ruins grand
That tyrant foes have made
And I'll strike this harp, a mournful touch
Till the glittering tears will flow
For that dear old land, that sweet old land
Where the beautiful rivers flow.

And I'll sing of Emmet's mournful fate
And of his lonely grave
Of his early doom in his youthful bloom
And his spirit more than brave.
And oh how blest and calm his rest
Though his grave be cold and low
In that dear old land, that sweet old land
Where the beautiful rivers flow.

And I'll sing of Tone and Geraldine proud
Edward true and blest
They won the crown, the martyr's crown
And they sleep in shade and rest
In heavenly mould their names are rolled
They died in manhood's glow
In that dear old land, that sweet old land
Where the beautiful rivers flow.

I'll sing of Ireland's ancient days
When her sires were kingly men
Who led the chase and manly race
Through forest, field and glen
Whose only word was the shining sword
Whose pen the patriot's blow
For that dear old land, that sweet old land
Where the beautiful rivers flow.

'Twas on a Sultry Summer's Day

'Twas on a sultry summer's day
When tired from worken at the hay
I lay and watched a regiment
march by to foreign war
I don't know how it came about
I must have slept beyond a doubt
I thought I took the shillin's
in the town of Mullingar.

Scarce had I drawn my belt to place
When all my dark and dire disgrace
Burst on me with a bitterness
that left my mouth ajar
For who would think a dacent boy
A son of honest Mike Molloy
Would join his countries enemies
Forsaken Mullingar.

Then cried I Seargent Gra Machree
Will you swap back again with me
My own old coat and breeches
they were warmer by gas
Sure with shame my heart would break
If all the neighbours I'd forsake
And wear a highland petticoat
Disgracing Mullingar.

Then spoke the sargent sharp to me,
You may as well contented be
You went and took the shillin free,
in Martin Hogan's bar
And as to those you leave behind
You may as well make up your mind
You went and put your foot in it
To-day in Mullingar.

'Twas then I wept with rage and pain
But all my protests were in vain
We marched through Monastereven,
with the General on a cart
And when we came to Wexford town
Straight to the transport we went down
And sailed away to India
My sorrow! Mullingar

The heat was dreadful overhead
We fought till all were nearly dead
From Sutledge to the Kyber
Till we came to Kandahar
Those Afghans were a savage lot
They whacked it to us hard and hot
I lost my leg by cannon shot
And mourned for Mullingar.

Upon the bloody field I lay
In deep despair I couldn't pray
I cursed the day I listed
And my joy in life did mar
Then someone near me gave a shout
I woke right up and looked about
Thank God twas but a nightmare
I was home in Mullingar.

I gazed around me with delight
And felt my own two legs alright
I kissed the sod of Ireland
And thanked my lucky star
No soldering I swear I'll try
And unless for Erin's sake I die
John Bull may suck his shillin
I'm content in Mullingar.

The Cottage by the Sea

Childhood's days now pass before me
Forms and scenes of long ago
Like a dream they hover o'er me
Calm and bright as evening's glow
Days that knew no shade of sorrow
When my young heart brave and free
Joyful hailed each coming morrow
In the cottage by the sea

Fancy sees the rose trees twining
Around that old and rustic door
And below the white beach shining
Where I gathered shells of yore
Hears my gentle mother's warning
As she took me on her knee
And I feel again life's morning.
In the cottage by the sea.

What through years have rolled above me
Though mid fairer scenes I roam
Yet I ne'er will cease to love thee
Childhoood's dear and happy home
And when life's long day is closing
Oh, how pleasant it would be
Oh some faithful breast imposing
In the cottage by the sea.

Famed Gubbeen Shore

One morning in May as Phoebus resplendently shone
For pure recreation I carelessly wandered alone
By a clear crystal stream convenient to famed Gubbeen shore,
I espied a fair maiden, she's the fair one I love and adore

Her fine golden traces spontaneously in ringlets did flow,
Her eyes animated displayed a pure vivid glow,
Her voice more enticing than Cynthia on the Cyprian shore
Or the harp of Orpheus, she's the fair one I love and adore

Her carriage is neat, her waist is slender and small,
Her breast elevated, her stature majestic and tall
Her skin like the snow or the foam of the Aegean shore.
And her limbs like tall cedars, she's the fair one I love and adore

She's spotless, engaging, endearing, civil and kind,
Affable, graceful, in learning and wit most refined,
She's a paragon of beauty, mostly truly I never before
Beheld such a maid, as the fair one I love and adore.

Were I as rich as Croesus, that famed legend monarch of old
Or Solomon, the sapient, whose temples were decked with pure gold
Were I king of all Asia, or heir to the Peruvian ore.
All I'd confiscate for the fair one I love and adore.

That matchless Creatus whose faith the Great Brutus inspired
Or the Lavonian dame whose fame the whole world admired
Susanna the chaste, or the Egyptian princess of yore.
Were not to be compared to the fair one I love and adore

That brave gallant Paris who treacherously Achilles slew.
Hector, Pyramus, bold Ajax and Hercules too.
With numberless heroes whose names I pass silently o'er
Would be captivated by the fair one I love and adore.

Sad, sad is my fate should she my entreaties disdain
For here I'll bemoan and condone in grief sorrow and pain
In some lonely retreat, perpetually I will deplore
For that lovely fair maid, she's the fair one I love and adore.[161]

Drowning in Dunmanus Bay

You mariners and fishermen,
Come listen to my song,
And if you will attention pay
It won't delay you long
How six poor men did lose lives
It grieves me for to say
Nigh to the shores of Kilcrohane
That lies in Dunmanus Bay

On the 20th of September
All in that present year
That was the night of a terrible gale
Through the country far and near
Just as the sun had gone to rest
They went their nets to cast
They little thought upon that night
That it would be their last

Those six young men
Were in their prime
And healthy for to view
Two of them were McCarthy's
Tim Spillane and Donovan's two
And also Charles Coughlan
As the public papers tell
But I hope for all eternity
In Heaven their souls will dwell

The night was wild and stormy
As they ventured from the shore
The sea it rolled then mountains high
Against them more and more
And soon the boat upturned
It grieves me for to tell
It was then they met their awful fate
Beneath that deadly swell

Oh Lord! it was a fearful sight
When the boat and two were found
Close into Bird Island
It being near the fishing ground.
And the other four with deep regret
They fill a watery grave
May the Lord have mercy on their souls
Against the judgement day.

Now to conclude and finish
I have no more to say
May the Blessed Virgin Mary
Pray for their souls this day
And may Her Son the King on high
Their parents now console
Who are weeping for their darling men
Lost off Dunmanus shore.[162]

The Rakes of Saint Giles

Here's long life to the sons of old Erin
In Poplar, Wapping, Blackwell,
Whitechapel, the Borough of each station
That we have been place in at all
Success to the lads and young lasses of Erin
From Bloomsbury down to the Doyles.
With full pots and sparkling glasses.
Toast still the Rakes of Saint Giles.

Thus tortured by remorseless tyrants
And stripped of our paternal rights
We're forced to mix as intimates
With sectarian infidel sprites
When our shoulders get sore from full monkeys
Of mossy brick, mortar and tiles
And we bore with the patience of donkeys.
Lamenting, our fate in Saint Giles

Through rivers of blood how we waded
Our tenets and rights to maintain
Until Cromwell our country invaded,
With his black bloody, gut-ripping train
Still cherished by rank persecution
By a system both putrid and vile
Has alas then inflicted our ruin
And then we know naught of Saint Giles.

Let us be united and steady
And show in the season of need
That we came determined and ready
To stand by our clergy and creed
Its then our degenerated Milesians
The wreck of rack gibbet and toils
Shall soon gain the emancipation
And free the poor slaves of St Giles

Lamentation of Mrs O'Donovan Rossa for her Husband

Pity the fate of a heartbroken lay,
Repining in sorrow and grief
I'm deprived of all comforts
There is nothing can eace me
Alas I can find no relief.

For the love of my darling
My heart did feel sore
Away from my arms, my love he was tore
And banished for ever from his native shore
He is gone, will I ne'er see him more?

Sad was the hour when my darling was taken
And exciled away from his home.
At his cruel fate he became undespairing
As if he were placed on a throne

His motto was freedom, his courage was bold
No money could buy him, neither silver nor gold
When I think on my darling, my blood it ran cold
He is gone, will I ne'er see him more?

Never again shall I gaze on the face of my darling
Or listen to his manly sweet voice
Shall I ever again, either night, noon or morning
At his fond loving smile e'er rejoice

Oh where shall I wander or where shall I go
My heart for my husband shall ne'er cease to flow.
He is gone, will I ne'er see him more?[163]

Dunmanus
by M Hegarty

Evergreen and fair Dunmanus
O'er your hills I long to stray
And around your sheltered harbour
Where the winter was like May
Oh to roam along that quarter
Where the lofty castle stands
And to see the rippling waters
O'er the bright and silvery sands

Pleasant times were in Dunmanus
When the boys would step genteel
The charming Bantry hornpipe
And the sporting Bandon reel
There was football in the Prairie
And a dance house in Dreenane
And on Sunday ever we went sailing
O'er the bay to Kilcrohane.[164]

The sporting lad from Glaun

This song on Glaun was composed by Michael Hegarty, Dunmanus, and the 'Shaun' of the song is Michael Kelleher. This was given me by his grandson M. Kelleher of Glaun.

It's sixty years since Shaun was young
And well known in Schull town
A favourite with his dog and gun,
The sporting lad from Glaun
A land renowned for dancing
That fine old Irish game
For Dan the Yank and Clancy
And Thade from Toorincane

In frost and snow 'twas only play
When Shaun was in his prime
At shooting cock to climb his way
For lonely Poull-an-ine.
The eagle there had built her nest
High o'er the heather glen,
The badger goes to sleep and rest
As reynard leaves his den.

He often tracked the moor and vale
And sheltry wood for game;
A shot rang out he winged his prey,
And seldom fired in vain.
With Fosco down the rolling plain,
Where partridge would be found,
He broke the laws the tyrant framed
The sporting lad from Glaun.

The Fenian boys cross the stream
And down Ratooragh hell,
Where Shaun trained the hurling team
To pike and rifle drill
His violin times were a rich treat
At every ball around;
His dancing was correct and neat,
The sporting lad from Glaun.

On Sunday we, each lively boy,
Would step the hornpipe
Those jigs and reels they did enjoy
And dance with keen delight;
"Follow me down to Carlow,"
The winsome "Bonny Kate",
"The wind that shook the barley" grain
"The pigeon on the gate".

Their sports were on the velvet green,
And down the ring side -
The football match, the hurling team,
And crowds from far and wide
For manly boys came down the hills
For dancing in the dell,
And colleens fair came o'er the glens
Of lovely heather bell

The crowd would join the dance,
When Sunday's sport was o'er,
The leading pair were lovely Nance
And Jack from Poul-an-ore,
The breeze was cool and grand,
The violin music sweet
For dancing on the riverbank,
Down where the waters meet.

Those lively boys and charming girls
Of sixty years ago,
Have left the sore and dreary world
Of wars, of toil and woe.
An aged few are lingering on
Old Fenians to the ground
Who loved to join at freeing their land,
The sporting lads from Glaun.[165]

Wreck of the Iberian

Come all you gallant heroes
That dwell round Erin's shore
And likewise pay attention
To these few lines composed
It's of a jolly steamship
From Columbus she set sail
To cross the Atlantic Ocean
The Hiberian by name

When we left the Port of Boston
Our captain he did say
We'll have a speedy passage
Across the raging main
The fog it proved deceitful
Along our native shore
Which perplexed our navigator
In the rows of Carrighomes.

When the crew had landed
To Crookhaven they took their way
They telegraphed for tug steamboats
To come without delay
To take her from our ancient isle
To Liverpool in tow
But the Atlantic's foaming water
Approved their overthrow

The tugs arrived next morning
Just at the break of day
With gloomy hills and mountains
And headlands in the Bay
Into their great astonishment
She is in the rows below
With her ropes and masts and rigging
In the bows of Cuas na gno.

Thank God there is great plenty now
Along our native shore
From Brow head to sweet Cape Clear
And along to Baltimore
All the small boats in the harbour
One paddling through the bay
And they're loaded to the water's edge
And homewards with their prey.

Long life to our noble Captain
Though we can't tell his name
That he may be highly rewarded
With honour and great fame
With his pockets full of silver
Likewise of solid gold
And the blessings of the people
May be with him where he goes.[166]

Dunmanus Bay

A stroll was charming that Summer
morning,
With rod and line by the old mill stream,
It's cascade tumbling with deep note
rumbling
I often think of that fairy scene.
The flowing river going on for ever,
By grove and heather it likes to stray
In graceful ardour to kiss the harbour,
The lovely waters, Dunmanus Bay.

Some think it's pleasure, when at their
leisure,
To shoot the snipe in the moors beyond,
Or chase the hare from its secret lair,
Or drive in splendour through cities grand.
In leading races with sweetest faces,
I've seen no brace of unrivalled play,
With pleasant boating like music floating,
On your lovely waters, Dunmanus Bay

O'er the crystal tide stands with lordly
pride,
Dunmanus Castle - that ancient pile.
It's lofty dome once the chieftain's home,
When the Septs of old trod out saintly isle,
Round the balmy coves where I loved to
rove,
Those sunny shores on a holiday.
No care to fear but my boat to steer,
On your lovely waters, Dunmanus Bay.

'Twas grand to sail from this charming vale,
And to cross the Bay for that flowery glen,
Neat Ahakista with royal vista,
You're queen and mistress of Harbour's
End.
From Spain to Sweden there is no Eden,
Your groves to equal so bright and gay,
Those syllvan beauties are like the rubies,
On your lovely waters, Dunmanus Bay.

The sun is smiling on Carbery Island,
His beams are bright on Kilcrohane strand,
With rays adorning the Sabbath morning,
In rippling water, the bay is grand;
A bell is tolling its echoes rolling,
Across the ocean a magic sound,
Where'er you wonder there is nothing
grander,
Than going to Mass in the Holy Ground.

Let the Briton boast of his armed coast,
And Venice toast to old Adria's sea
While thie emerald creek crowned with
shamrock make
Outshines an emblem of sanctity.
With caves and inlets and meandering
streamlets,
And Canty's cove where the lambkins lay
Or the evening's blaze of the westring rays,
O your lovely waters, Dunmanus Bay.[167]

Collected by Michael Hegarty, Dunmanus East

DUNMANUS
History and Archaeology

Forts

There are many forts in this district. Meall-an-leasa is the nearest one to us. The forts are said to belong to the people that lived in Ireland long ago called the Danes. They made these forts on high ground so they could sight any invasion for miles around them. They were constructed in this way - they were low in the centre to a certain depth, and they formed a house and built it into the level of the surface and covered it over with some clay. There was only one opening left from the top. Then they formed a circle and dug the clay from outside till they built it about thirty feet outside and about sixteen feet from the inside. It is thought there is lots of war equipment concealed inside these forts such as battle axes, and spears. In these forts they worked from the centre of the floors inside and cut tunnels through the ground till they formed an opening about four hundred yards from the fort, these tunnels were their way of escaping. It is usual to see lights rising from the forts and going in different directions. The old people say that when a young person would die that it was the fairies used take them to nurse their children. Rathoora fort is situated south of Kiltomans school, and that townland goes by that name Rathoora, meaning fort of the axe, because it was with axes they defended themselves.

It is said that one day when a man was fowling, he saw a handle hidden in the bushes, and when he looked at it, it was a spear of the ancient times. Lissacaha means the battle fort because there was a battle fought there in olden times between the Danes and the Irish. It is said that if you stand on top of Mell-an-leasa you can see Lissacaha and Rathoora, that was how the Danes used give signals to one another when any harm threatened them.[168]

Collected by Bridie Walsh, Lissacaha, from Maurice Kennedy

Glaun

Co. Chorcaighe
Bar: Cairbre Thiar
Par: Scoil Mhuire
Scoil: Gleann
Oide: Nelly Hurley

GLAUN
Local Folklore and Stories

Fairy Forts and their Occupants

The only fairy forts in this district were situated at Rathoora and Lissacaha. Many people were supposed to be carried away by the fairies to Rathoora fort, and sometimes another person resembling the one brought away was put in his place. Those people who were sent back in exchange were called siocatáns, and they were always sick. They would eat nothing while anyone was looking at them. A woman called Mrs Menihane, a native of Rathoora, had a son who was carried away, and another person was put in his place. One cold night as she was nursing him in the bed of straw by the fire, he got up and taking up a shovel of red coals he threw them at her. Taking up the tongs she declared it was not her own son and when she tried to strike him, he ran out the door and instantly her own son walked in. He had for six weeks lived on food of the houses of neighbouring people by night. He refused to partake of the fairys' food and therefore they had to leave him home.[169]

Mrs Post, a native of Gubbeen, was another who was carried away. Each night she was beaten and made go for miles from home. Her legs were of a black and blue colour, and she used say it was the fairies who used beat her with a stick.[170]

Jacob Lannin, a native of Ardravinna, and his servant, were earthing potatoes in the field near Rathoora Fort one day. It was very warm, so they sat down on the ridge which ran very near the fort. One of them remarked how nice it would be to have a drink of buttermilk. Just then they heard the churn being made inside in the fort. When they came to the end of the next ridge after earthing it, they saw two large basins of buttermilk placed near them. They did not drink any of it because it was said that anyone who ate or drank any of the fairies' food could be carried away.[171]

There was another fort situated in Toormore, but it was not as important as the one in Rathoora. A cow belonging to Jim Coughlan used go to the fort every morning and evening to be milked. When she was brought home, she never had any milk. In order to prevent her from going to the fort, the owner kept the cow inside, but still, she would give no milk. Mr. Coughlan then killed the cow, but on the following week every one of his remaining cows died also.

One evening a man named Mr Attridge who lived in Lissacaha was milking a black cow in a field adjoining the Lissacaha fort. To his surprise he heard somebody crying inside in the fort. Curious to see who it was, he went to the fort, and saw a woman dressed in black, minding a baby who was crying. He heard her say "Do not cry, the black cow will soon be milked." The man then returned and finished milking the cow. As he was about to get up, the cow raised her leg and spilled the milk. But the strange thing was that the milk did not fall on the ground. It disappeared before it reached it. The man went back again to the fort and saw the woman and the child drinking milk.[172]

Some years ago, a woman from Muintir Bháire got married to a Driscoll man in Glaun. When she had lived in Glaun for a while she decided to go home on a visit. She and her husband, with a baby about six months old, set out with another man for Dunmanus, where they got a boat to go across the bay. When they landed on the other side she came out of the boat and walked towards her house which was about a mile distant. The men stayed behind to moor the boat. When she had gone about half-way, she met a man who had come from the opposite direction. He asked her would she come to him to nurse a baby. She replied that she did not know until she asked her husband When she arrived at her home, she told what had happened and described the man to the best of her ability. But the members of her family did not know anyone like the person she described. Having spent the day with her family the woman and her husband and child returned home and heard no more about the strange man. A few months later the Driscoll man found his wife dead outside the bed in the morning. When she was buried, he had a suspicion that the man she had met in Muinntir Bháire had taken her away. At that time, there was a woman in Dunmanway who used be "with the Fairies." The man went to her, and she told him that his wife was in Lissacaha fort. The woman knew every house in Glaun, and she was able to name the houses that the fairies used get the most food in at night. She also told him that he could get back his wife if he had the courage of going to the fort at midnight to carry out her instructions. She ordered him to take to the fort a hazel rod, and upon entering there to make a circle of holy water. He should then stand inside the circle and have a piece of steel in his hand. After a short time, he would see five horses with riders coming into the fort, and on the fifth horse he would see his wife. She would reach out her hand to him, and he should pull her off the horse, and bring her inside the circle of holy water where no harm would come to them. When the man returned home his friends would not let him go to the fort, and so his wife was never brought back.[173]

Long ago, a Newman man lived in Ardmanagh, whose daughter was said to be taken away by the fairies, and a siocatán put in her place for seven years. This siocatán whom the man did not know from his own daughter, never went to bed at night but remained in a corner by the fire. She would neither eat nor drink until the were all in bed at night. One night a knock came to the door about twelve o'clock, and a voice from outside said, "Father, get up and leave me in." The man asked who was there and a person outside said "I am your daughter." He said "You cannot be my daughter, because she is here. But if you are, you must say the prayer I taught you when you were young." She said the prayer as quickly as she could, and the man got up and let her in. When she entered, the girl that was in the corner went up the chimney saying "Cad a deanfad anois, Cad a deanfad anois. Cad a deanfad anois."[xv] The girl told her father that she was going through a field with a crowd of fairies and a bit of shamrock went between her toes and kept her there until they had gone a little distance. She had run home then as fast as she could. This girl lived to be a very old woman, and she was able to tell a great many stories about the fairies.[174]

[xv] Cad a deanfad anois – What would I do now?

GLAUN
People, Places and Property

Local Landlords

The first landlord of Gubbeen who lived about one hundred years ago, was Mr Hickson, a native of Kerry. He was a very wicked man. He made his tenants pay extremely high rents. A farm containing only fifteen acres of poor land had a rent of ten pounds yearly in Hickson's time, and its present rent is only twenty-six shillings. No tenant would be allowed admittance to his office in Bantry when they came to pay the rent, for he was afraid of being shot. The rent had to be put into the letterbox. He then sold the land to Colonel Longfield, Gubbeen and Crewe, which contains about six hundred acres, costing fourteen thousand pounds. Mr Longfield was a native of Queenstown. His agent was Savage French, a native of Kusskenny, a place near Queenstown. His first rent warner was Henry Daly, a native of Toormore, who lived in Schull, in a house occupied at present by a family called Scullys. Several times when Savage French, the agent was sick or absent, he gathered the rent. He kept some of the rent always, and then wanted the people to say they did not pay it. The people of course would not do this, and his tricks were found out by Mr French. The night he was to be arrested he committed suicide, by shooting himself in his house. The next rent warner was Simon Levis who lived in Gubbeen, in a house occupied at present by a family called Fergusons. He was a clever, tricky man, and fearing he might do the same as his predecessor, Henry Daly, he was sacked. His successor was Patrick Hurley, a native of Busheen, Schull. He was a good man and held his post until his death. His son, Denis Hurley, was the last rent warner and he died four years ago. Mr Longfield was a very good landlord. He never had an occasion to evict any person. One family called O'Roycroft, who could not pay the rent, stole off by night, and emigrated to America afterwards. Their farm was then occupied by a man called Mr Shipsey, the present doctor's grandfather. He had a dairy there and it is now occupied by the Driscolls. Mr Longfield owned Gubbeen, Crewe, Cahirleascha, Long Island and several other places. The landlord who owned Ardmanagh and Corthna was called Mr Limerick, who lived where the parish priest now lives. His agent was William O'Regan, a native of Schull. He also acted as a rent warner. Once when Mr Limerick was sick, he got medicine from a doctor in Bandon. His butler who was to give him the medicine, never gave it but prepared another medicine himself instead, and it cured him. So glad was the landlord, when the doctor's medicine cured him, as he thought, that he invited the doctor to a great feast. During the feast the doctor said, that only for the first bottle of medicine he sent, the landlord he would not be present at the feast. The butler, on hearing this, presented the doctor with the bottle of medicine. The landlord, Mr Limerick, gave some of the medicine to his dog.

No sooner had he the medicine drank, than he fell dead. The medicine was poisoned by the doctor, for to kill the landlord. The successor was Colonel Spate. He got Limerick's land by marrying his daughter. He lived near Skibbereen. His agent was Abram Jagoe, who lived in the house next to Provincial Bank, now occupied by the manager. It was Abram Jagoe who built the Grove Hotel. His son lived in it until he removed to Killarney last year. The landlord who owned Schull, etc, was called Mr Swanton, a native of "Gort na gCruach", north of Ballydehob. One of his eyes were knocked out when a shot was fired at him. He then ordered that, from Bantry north, and Skibbereen east, west to the Mizen Head, every house should pay a shilling in damages. His son, George Swanton, was a landlord also, and was more commonly known as "Yellow George". The parish priest of Schull at the time, whose name was Father Murphy, spoke very hard against the landlords at the time of the Land League. George Swanton signed a warrant for the arrest of Father Murphy. When he had the priest's name written on the warrant, he suddenly got palsy in his hand, which deprived him of the use of his hand for ever. He then sent a thousand soldiers under the command of a man called Mr Hamilton to help the peelers to arrest the priest and drive back the people who had come to defend him. When the people heard of the priest's intended arrest, they flocked from all parts, Bantry, Drimoleague, Caheragh, Lisheen, Dunbeacon - "From Caheragh and Lisheen, From Dunbeacon and Goleen." They left the turf bogs in Caheragh in "meithalls'. They received bread and porter in plenty, from the shopkeepers in Schull. Father Bernard, the curate of Ballydehob, was coming to visit Father Murphy, the day he was to be arrested. He was on horseback, and he passed the soldiers near the Woodlands, and in a miraclous manner put the soldiers, in such a position that they could not stir. In this position they remained until next day. Then they pitched tent in South Schull. An English gunboat, anchored in Schull harbour, fired shots up at the town. When the Schull peelers heard of the soldiers they fled in terror to the barrack. There were thirteen of them there and the barrack was situated where the petrol pumps now stand, opposite the Chapel. Some of the people thrust pikes through the barrack windows. Some of those who broke them were arrested. Some of those who were arrested were William Bennett of Skeagh, and John MacCarthy of Glaun, who were well known. Those who were found in the streets were arrested and sent to Cork gaol for a month or more. Father Murphy was not arrested. He was transferred to Dunmanway after. Father Bernard lived to the age of ninety-two, and was made a parish priest after this, and was living near Dunmanway. For years after this incident a number of soldiers were kept in Schull under the command of Mr Hamilton. The landlord of Glaun was Miss Clarke, a native of Bantry. She also owned land in Cork and Kerry. Her agent was William Bird, a native of Bantry, and her rent-warner was Michael Hegarty, a native of Dunmanus. Messrs Bird and Hegarty were supposed to be very wicked people. Mr Hegarty was an emergency man in East Cork. Sometimes, during evictions, he would go on the roofs of houses and break them with a sledgehammer. He is still living in Dunmanus. William Bird, the agent, was shot in his office in Bantry. A man called Tim Cadogan a native of Kerry, was hung for the crime. Several people say he was an innocent man.[175]

Glaun

The name of the townland in which I live, and in the which this school is situated, is Glaun. It is in the parish of Schull about three miles from the village, in the county of Cork, in the Barony of West Carbery. It is bounded on the north by the Glaun river, on the east by Mound Gabriel, on the south by "Fionn's Ridge" and on the west by the Lios a Cata river. There is a river in Glaun, but it is a mere stream compared with some larger rivers. Trout and salmon are fished there. There is one deep hole called 'Áth na gCaorach' from the shallow ford nearby, over which, I suppose, sheep crossed. There was once a wood growing in the slopes of Mount Gabriel - bounding Glaun. It was planted by Dr. Hicks, the landlord of Mount Gabriel who lived in Derreenatra. Only shrubs, small holly bushes and small oaks now remain along with bare stumps - to show that there once flourished a fine wood there. "Fionn's Ridge" separates Glaun from Gubbeen. It is a ridge of rock with seams resembling the furrows made by a plough and it is said that Fionn Mac Cumhail ploughed it with two rams and a wooden plough. Of course, it is only a story since the surface was torn off by masses of ice moving south to the hollow below leaving the rock bare like a ridge. Glaun is a glen between hills - Mount Gabriel on the east, Rathura mountain on the west, Shountullig mountain on the north and Glaun mountain on the south. Hence its name "Gleann" or Glaun in English.

The family name most common in Glaun at present is Sullivan. In former years McCarthy was most common. Most of the land is rather boggy and hilly, but some of the land is good also. There is up to a hundred people in Glaun and twenty-one families. The houses are mostly all slated. There are nine old people - over seventy years of age living there:

Mrs. T. Sullivan, East Glaun, Schull, Co. Cork
T. Sullivan, East Glaun, Schull, Co. Cork
D. Sweeney, East Glaun, Schull, Co. Cork

Mrs. Goggin, East Glaun, Schull, Co. Cork
F. Sullivan, East Glaun, Schull, Co. Cork
Mrs. N. Sullivan, East Glaun, Schull, Co. Cork
D. Bowen, West Glaun, Schull, Co. Cork
John Sullivan, East Glaun, Schull, Co. Cork
Mrs. Driscoll, South Glaun, Schull, Co. Cork

None of them know Irish. Some of them can tell stories. Houses were much more numerous locally in former years. There are many now in ruins. A fence on one of my father's fields bounding a road is part of a wall of an old house. An O'Driscoll family lived there. They say that an old man lived there and that he died of the famine. They say that he had only a sixpence in his pocket. There is a grave in one of Florence Sullivan's fields near which an old ruin was. I do not know who lived there but it is supposed that they died of the famine. Graves are also in fields of Patrick Lucey's - bounding Glaun. There is a little lake on the top of Mount Gabriel called Poll an Oighin. There is a saying that Fionn Mac Cumhail took a handful of rock and threw it out into the Atlantic Ocean where it is now as the Fastnet Rock or Carraig Aonair - leaving the hole of Poll an Oighin. Another saying is that if a stick was thrown into Poll an Oighin it would come out in Schull harbour. There is a kind of a "Poll Talmhan" in one of Stephen Sullivan's fields. There were families living in Glaun who emigrated, such as the Harte family who lived in one of the houses now in ruins down back of the National School. There was a Brien family living in west Glaun on a rock called Brien's Rock. The wall of the house is still to be seen. There was a Cunningham family living on the side of the Glaun hill - one of whom was a noted fenian - who emigrated. A Leahy family lived in south Glaun who emigrated to California. The houses are now in ruins. All those family names are now extinct in the townland. There were certain circular holes in rocks on the side of Mount Gabriel called the Danes' Mines. They were supposed to be cut out by the Danes in seams of copper. It was thought they used to burst the rock with lime by putting it into the hole and spilling water on it and and then covering it closely by which way the lime swelled and burst the rock and then they could extract the copper. But these were researched and blasted out by the English mining companies who found a little copper there. Stone hammers were found supposedly belonging to the Danes. There is a kind of cromlech or dolmen on the top of the Rathura mountain, formed of four stones or flags - one on each side one at the head, and supporting a large flag on top. It is about 6 or 7 feet long and about two high. The stones are in their rough state without being hammered or chiselled into shape. The bottom inside is covered with small stones. It is supposed to be some kind of grave. Glaun was renowned for music and dancing some years ago. Michael Kelleher who died some years ago was famous for dancing and music. A song was composed about him called "The Sporting Lad from Glaun", but the name Seán was given instead of his name.[176]

Gubbeen

The townland of Gubbeen is in the parish of Schull, the County of Cork, and the West Carbery Barony. It is bounded on the north by Fionn's Ridge, on the east by Ardmanagh and Corthna, and on the south by the Atlantic, and on the west by the Gubbeen River, which separates Gubbeen from Lowertown. There are about eighty residents living there, consisting of twenty-two families. All the houses of the district are slated, save one thatched one. The family name most common is Driscoll and O'Regan. There are only four old people over seventy living there. They are: William O' Brien, Gubbeen, Schull, Co. Cork; Kathleen Sweetnam, Gubbeen, Schull, Co. Cork; Mrs. Coughlan, Gubbeen, Schull, Co. Cork; William Coughlan, Gubbeen, Schull, Co. Cork. None of them can speak Irish, but they can tell fine English stories. The houses were more numerous locally in former days. In several parts of the district, streets of houses were to be seen, in which lived tinkers, weavers, and other tradesmen. There are very few ruins in Gubbeen now, the ruins of two dwelling houses, and a big corn store, being the only ones. The owner of the corn store was called Fred Brown, the Tyrant. He bought the corn from the neighbouring farmers and sold it to English traders who came for it in ships. One of the ships was called Gubbeen. Fred Brown was drowned coming from England. One of the dwelling houses was occupied by a family called Courtney who died at the time of the famine and the other house was occupied by a family called Woods. They removed from that to Corthna, and their descendants are still living there. There are sites of houses also pointed out by old people. One house was occupied by a man called Murphy who emigrated to America. Another house situated near the road to Glaun was occupied by a family called Driscolls, who died at the time of the famine. Several families emigrated to America in the famine times. Their unoccupied houses thrown down and the stones were used to build other houses. There is only one bog in Gubbeen, and there are very little hills there also, except on the north side. The land is fairly good throughout, but it is very good in the south side. There is only one river of any importance in Gubbeen, which separates Lowertown from Gubbeen. Trout, salmon, and eel are to be found in it. Gubbeen itself got its name from the mouth or inlet which is in the south side by the sea.[177]

GLAUN
Farming, Trade and Crafts

Harmful Weeds

The farmers are the constant enemies of the harmful weeds. Some weeds are harmful because they spread rapidly, grow strong quickly, and thus smother the seedlings which the farmers sow. Others impoverish the soil by using up all the manure set out for other plants to strengthen themselves. Many of such weeds are not to be found in poor soil as they require nourishment which is not to be found in poor land. I've heard my father speak of such weeds as the Praiseach Bhuidhe or Charlock, the Buachallan or Ragweed, Sponnc or Coltsfoot, the Feócadán or thistle, the Cupóg or Dock-leaf, the Cois Phréacháin or Crowsfoot, Glúineach; Clúbán; An Géasadán, Broim-fhéar, The Sheep Sorrel; Chickenweed, The Black Buttons; The Cockle Yarrow, Rib-leaf, Grounsel.

Glúineach is said to be so called because of the knots on the stem resembling knees. The Cos Préacáin or Crowsfoot is said to be so called because its leaves resemble a crow's foot. Its flower is called the Buttercup. Broim-Fhéar is regarded by the farmers as being a very bad weed. It is a kind of a grass, and its roots are like little onions. Praiseach Bhuidhe or Charlock is said to live in a field for a score years and after that time it dies. Its blossoms are yellow. Black Buttons are relished by horses. Groundsel seeds are favourites with linnets. The seeds of the dock-leaf when ripe and mixed with the horse´s food is a cure for broken wind. Seamer, wild vetches, and wild clover grow only in good soil. Seamer is a kind of grass. Ferns grow in poor soil. Sponnc or coltsfoot is so called because its leaf resembles a colt´s hoof.

Poisonous Plants

Bainne Cíoch Éan is poisonous. Its root contains a white milky fluid which is poisonous. People used it for poisoning trout in the river. It is never eaten by any animals with the exception of the goat. The goat eats it and is said to banish it. It will kill people. Red berries come on top of the Bainne Cíoch Éan in the summertime. The Leith-uisge or Butterwort kills sheep and cattle. It grows in marshy places. The leaves are covered with little hairs which are always covered with a dew-like drop which is very sticky. They say it lives on flies and insects. When the flies alight upon it the leaves close and the fly is held fast. The plant digests certain parts and then reopens and the wind blows away the indigestible parts, such as the wings and legs of the fly. It kills the sheep by sticking to the liver when it is eaten by the animal. It eats out the liver and so the animal dies. So also with the cattle. The disease given to the cattle is called fluke. The cure for the fluke is got from the male fern.[178]

GLAUN
Local Customs

Marriage Customs

Matchmaking

Domhnac Féach Suas is the first Sunday of Shrove. Shrovetime brings about matchmaking. The man who wishes to get married sends account of a match to a certain girl. We will suppose the man is Mike Murphy and the girl is Kate Driscoll. Then Mike chooses a good speaker and takes him with him to the girl's house, along with a stick and a bottle of whiskey. They generally choose a dark night for this business, so that nobody will know what they are doing until the match is made. Then the speaker asks Kate's father would he be satisfied to give his daughter to Mike in marriage. After hearing of the matter, the father makes inquiries about the stock and land and the speaker praises everything, how the boy is a good steady hard-working fellow, and producing the bottle of whiskey, gives the father and mother some now and then, to soften them as they say. The boy of course refuses any of the whiskey. Then the girl's father inquires of Mike what fortune does he want, and he gets £200 as a reply. The father then says that £200 is too much for such a small farm. Mike says he will not take less. The speaker tries to make the bargain between both parties to the best of his ability. Then he asks if £150 would satisfy him. The whiskey is again distributed, and both agree at £150. Then the speaker asks of the money which is to be given to the girl. Fortune it is called. So much money is given to her by her parents. Stock or goods are sometimes given as fortune. Then the parties visit the attorney for the assignment if both are satisfied, or to make arrangements for old or unmarried folk in the house. They get a sum of money and a room in the house while they live. Both parties make arrangements with the parish Priest. Mike pays the marriage fee before it takes place. The amount is estimated on the means of the man. The match is usually made at the girl's house or in a public house sometimes.[179]

Country Weddings

Up to about twenty years ago all country weddings in this locality took place towards the end of Shrove. Sometimes as many as nine or ten couples were married in Schull on Shrove Tuesday. Now weddings take place at any time of the year, but it is thought unlucky to marry in May. "Marry in May and you'll rue the day", says the proverb. Monday, Wednesday and Friday are the unlucky days, and nobody around here would dream of getting married on those days. Those who were eligible and did not marry during Shrove were supposed to go to the Skelligs on Shrove Tuesday night to get married. The reason being that marriages were allowed during Lent in the monastery of Skelligs. The local poets got a list of the unmarried people and linked them in the oddest order - a very proud person for instance, was coupled with someone he despised. The lists were displayed on crossroads on Ash Wednesday morning and were a source of great amusement. They are not made now. They were called "Skelligs Lists."

About sixty or seventy years ago the people used not go to the Chapel in order to get married, but the Parish Priest used come to the house at about eleven o' clock, or sometime before twelve, and perform the ceremony there. After the marriage the Priest used sometimes stay for the wedding feast. Later on, the couple went to the Chapel in the evening or about nightfall. The guests used go in sidecars, and the bride in a covered car, which was the last leaving the house and the first on the road home. On the way home the cars raced in order to get in behind the bride's car and they say that many a car came home with only the driver - having lost all passengers on the way.

The old people say that before cars were used commonly, saddled horses were in the drive, a woman riding sidesaddle behind every man. A great number of guests are invited to the wedding. The wedding feast is held at the bride's house. Many different kinds of food and drink are provided, bread, biscuits, and the wedding cake of which everyone gets a piece. The greatness of the feast long ago was reckoned on the quantity of porter and whiskey consumed. Great quantities of rice were cooked, it being one of the chief features at the wedding feast some years ago. Rice was thrown after the couple for luck, as well as old shoes. The bride must always wear:

Something old and something new
Something borrowed and something blue."

The Wren Boys

With the approach of Christmas and Saint Stephen's Day, the boys of the land begin to think of the wren. They go from house to house singing the wren song. On Christmas Day they hunt up the wren trying to catch and kill a little bird. If they fail to find a wren, hoping to kill it with sticks and stones, which they seldom do, they get a lump of moss and put it in a holly branch saying that a wren is in the nest formed of moss. They get a stick and tie a branch of holly on top of it in which is supposed to be the wren. They decorate it with ribbon and strips of coloured paper. On Saint Stephen's Day morning they meet at some place appointed and dress up with ribbons, and hats of coloured paper. One is a clown, and he blackens his face and hands with either soot or black boot polish. One carries the holly bush. When dressed they sally forth. They make a gay sight, coloured ribbons and paper floating in the breeze. The clown with his black face and dressed in brilliant colours acts half-foolishly as it were. They must also provide a moneybox. If a right one is not in their possession they get a tin box, usually a cocoa-box, and cut a slit in the cover, having already bound on the cover. They let the money drop in the slit. One of them also carries a bugle or horn. I've seen a large kind of a seashell use as a bugle, which they sounded, meaning to tell every house they were coming. A bottle is also used. They sing the wren song at every house, and they get money from the man of the house. At some houses they get tea. After the day's travelling, they divide the money among themselves, or sometimes they use it on food and other things which they take to some house and hold a dance there. By singing the wren song they earn the money.[180]

GLAUN
Local Cures

Local Cures

1. Wild Sage is a cure for pains when it is boiled and strained, and the liquid drank
2. The Lus Mór- or soft leaves in the heart of the plant out of which the "Fairy Thimbles" grow - is good for healing a cut. The little hard thread on the back of the leaf should be pulled out and the leaf heated at the fire and applied to the cut.
3. Rib-leaf and cream is good for a cut when it is ground up and applied to the cut with a little cream.
4. Camomile Root is a cure for a toothache. It should be put down on the aching tooth.
5. Penny-leaf is good for boils and chilblains when heated at the fire and applied to the sores.
6. A Foxe's Tongue will draw a thorn, or any foreign substance embedded in the flesh.
7. Cobwebs are used to stop bleeding.
8. The lining inside the shell of a raw egg is used for a burn to exclude air.
9. The Starch of Grated Potatoes and cream is good for a burn. The potatoes should be grated, and the water pressed out into a vessel. The starch from the potatoes collects and sets at the bottom. The water should be skimmed off the top and the starch mixed with cream should be applied to the burn.
10. Dandelion is good for a bad stomach when boiled in water and strained and the brewage drank.
11. Nettles are good to cure pains when boiled in water and the liquid drank.
12. Carrigeen Moss is a cure for a bad stomach when boiled with milk and strained and left thicken.
13. Onions and milk boiled together and drank are a cure for a cough.
14. Flax seed is a cure for a cough when left simmer in water by the fire for a few hours and lemon juice squeezed into it and strained and the brewage drank.
15. Buttermilk when boiled is good for a cold
16. Water cress is good for a bad stomach. It is eaten raw.
17. Leeches are good to draw the bad blood from an injured part of the body as they suck out the blood. The old people called them Súgairí.
18. Tobacco is a cure for a toothache. It should be cut small and put down on the tooth.

19. Garlic is a cure for a pain in the stomach. It should be boiled in milk and strained, and the brewage drank.
20. Blackcurrant jelly is good for a sore throat.
21. Dock-leaf is a cure for a sore lip when it is applied to it. In the head of the dock-leaf a funnel-like stem is to be got. It is white and should be opened out and applied to the lip. The stem contains a sticky white matter.
22. Black Weeds are good for pains. The weed should be dried and rubbed to the part effected.
23. Primroses are good for hoarseness. The person that would be hoarse should eat them.
24. Snails are a cure for choking in the chest. The slime of the snails is to be drunk with sugar
25. Elder and Devil's bit are a cure for Erysipelas when they are boiled together and placed on the sores.
26. Besom is a cure for rheumatism. The besom should be boiled, and strained, and its liquid drank.
27. Black Wrinkles are a cure for the liver. The wrinkles should be taken out and boiled with butter and the liquid to be then drank.
28. Heather is a cure for a cough. It should be boiled, and its liquid drank.
29. Smoke is a cure for a toothache. The person who has the toothache should put his mouth over the smoke.
30. Gold earrings are used for sore eyes. The earrings should be put up to the sore eyes.
31. Frogs are a cure for consumption. I don't know how they are used.
32. A key would stop a person's nose from bleeding. It should be put down the back of the neck.
33. Red Moss is a cure for Erysipelas, when the moss is dryed at the fire and mixed with flour.
34. Sore lips or wounds. This cure is generally used for sore or breaking-out lips. It is called by old people the scannán cure. The part of an onion called the scannán which is like tissue paper is put on the sore place together with some cream.
35. Nettle juice is a cure for rheumatism when the plant is boiled in water and strained, and the liquid drank.
36. The cure for warts is to fill a little bag of stones, a stone for every wart you have, and place the bag on the road. It is supposed that the wart will go to the person who takes up the bag. Another cure is to rub to the wart the froth of the potatoe-water when it is beginning to boil.

Also, to rub the water which is got from the pockets or crevices of a rock to the warts.

37. Whooping cough is cured by giving some milk to drink in a saucer to a ferret. Leave him drink some and give the remainder to the person who has the whooping cough. Another cure is to tie a necklace of insects called hairy Jacks around the neck of the infected person and leave them wriggling there until they die. Another cure is to run before a man riding a white horse and ask him for a cure. What ever he would say will cure it.
38. The cure for a burned tongue is to lick a lizard three times.
39. Pain in the ear is cured with the juice of an ash tree stick when burning. Then soak a piece of cotton wool in the juice and put it into the sore ear.
40. Sprains are cured by holding the sprained limb under a water shoot or immerging in running water and leave it there for a half-an-hour or more.
41. To cure vomiting, boil some yellow dandelion and peppermint in water and when strained the liquid is drank.
42. To cure toothache, redden the end of a knitting needle and put it down in the bad tooth, while still red.
43. To cure asthma, eat a live snail, not too big, or without chewing him.
44. To cure coughs, put two eggs into an airtight vessel with vinegar. Leave the eggs there until the vinegar breaks the shells. Drink some of it every morning fasting.
45. To cure sore eyes, bathe the eyes in cold black tea, or hang a green shade or leaf on the eye, or put a piece of gold up to the eye.
46. To cure a sore throat, put roasted potatoes into a piece of cloth or a stocking and put it around the sore throat.
47. Blane is a disease cured by lighting sooty straw under the animal's head. It makes the cattle hang their head down and a white matter runs from their nose.
48. Chilblains are cured by rubbing the juice of an onion to them.
49. Bad health is cured by boiling and seasoning camomile and drinking the liquid.
50. To cure stomach pains, tip the top of your toes every morning with your fingers and without bending your knees.
51. Cleas na Péiste a cure for sick cattle. It is a cure used by knotting a cord in some manner over the animal's nose.
52. Bounds' water which is found in streams separating two lands will cure almost all pains when drank.[181]

GLAUN
Songs

A Tribute to Tim Cadogan

Tim Cadogan was a farmer's son
His lawful debts he paid.
Of landlord or of bailiff
He never was afraid.
No Bird, no crow, no magpie
His spirit proud could tame,
A rough and rugged son of toil
From the Kerry hills he came.

One day he went to Bantry
'Twas in the afternoon,
As he had often done before
In Winter time and June,
A bird was winged that morning
A minion of the crown,
No loss is he to Bantry
Or to any other town.

It was Walter Dennis,
He did my cause betray,
That cursed vile informer
He swore my life away;
Before the Judge and Jury
He swore I was the man,
He saw upon the staircase
With a pistol in my hand.

The jury found him guilty
One bleak December day,
And the Judge made up his mind
To take his life away;
He was murdered in old Ireland
Far across the sea,
One thousand men like Cadogan
Would set old Ireland free,

When they took him to the prison
No danger did he fear,
He knew that he was innocent
This gallant mountaineer;
The jury thought the same of him
But some decreed it so,
Despite the perjured evidence
Of Dennis and Dukelow

The blood hounds and informers
Baffled at the sea,
Hounded, gallant, Cadogan
Which proved his destiny;
The peelers in pursuit of him
No evidence could find.
Through treachery they did conspire
To gain that hero's mind.

Another trial the jury packed
The spawn of Cromwell's breed,
To hand this gallant farmer's son
At last they did succeed;
The jury found him guilty
The Judge's charge was vile,
With gown and wig a la Norbury
A native of the soil.

And now his spirit hovers
From Cork to Bantry Bay,
For Dennis and Dukelow
Both swore his life away;
When he received his sentence
Disappointment did abound,
Among his friends and countrymen
Who gathered all around.

He faced the laws and prison walls
Like Emmet and Wolfe Tone,
Despite the judge and jury
From him there was no moan;
He knew he would be murdered
As thousands were before,
By Norbury and Lord O' Brien
Throughout old Erin's shore.

Though young in years, his spirit proud
O' Brien could not break,
He tried to cheat Norbury
And his own life take;
He knew what Wolfe Tone did
When in his youth and prime,
He tried to do the same
He thought it was no crime.

Long life to Paddy Meathe
His name will never die,
The judge and jury in the court
He boldly did defy;
He knew the trial would be a farce
Presided by O' Brien,
The Judas of the Irish race
From Cork to Ballyline.

Gilhooly, Flynn and Barry
Tried with might and main
To save the life of Cadogan
Their efforts were in vain;
The judge decreed that he should die
A traitor to the crown,
No more to see his native hills
Or visit Bantry town.

The names of Dennis and his band
Are loathsome now to hear,
They dare not visit Bantry
Their hearts are full of fear;
The grass they tread will wither
And never again will grow,
When trampled by Iscariots
Like Dennis and Dukelow.

Now like the owl that shuns the day
When darkness is around,
They creep from their hiding places
Where reptiles doth abound;
May Cadogan's spirit rest in peace
On that bright heavenly shore,
Before that court above the clouds
Where sorrow is no more.[182]

ALTAR

Co. Chorcaighe
Bar: Cairbre Thiar
Par: Kilmoe (Teampoll nam Bocht)
Scoil: Altóir, Tuar Mór, An Sciobairín
Oide: Henry Evanson
11.1937-12.1938

ALTAR
Local Folklore and Stories

How Mrs O'Donoghue's Milk was Carried Away by Witchcraft

Once upon a time there lived a wealthy family named Donoghue not far from Rathmullen, and some distance away there lived another family named Dogherty. The two families had good cows, but the Donoghues had a Kerry cow which gave more milk and better butter than the other cows. Grace Dogherty, a young girl, came one night to Mrs Donoghue's door while she was milking the Kerry cow, with the queerest request, "will you let me milk your Kerry cow?"

"And why do you ask to milk my Kerry cow, Grace?" inquired Mrs Donoghue.

"Oh, just because you are so busy, and I would like to help you."

"Thank you, Grace, but I will not let you milk my Kerry cow, for I can do my own work, and I will not trouble you to milk her."

The girl went away, but the next evening she stood at Mrs Donoghue's door with the same request. At length, Mrs Donoghue could not find any excuse to give the girl, so she let her milk the Kerry cow. Mrs Donoghue was soon very sorry for allowing Grace to milk the Kerry cow, because that cow would not give any more milk to her owner. When this terrible thing began to happen, Mrs Donoghue sent for a witch, and they told her the story. "The cow has been milked by someone with an evil spirit", said the witch. "Well, Mrs Donoghue", said the witch, "lock the door and put nine new pins that were never used before into the saucepan with a pint of the Kerry cow's milk. Put them in the fire and let them boil". The nine pins soon began to boil in the saucepan. Heavy steps were heard coming to the house, and Grace Dogherty's voice was heard.

"Let me in, Mrs Donoghue", she cried. "Take off that cruel pot and pins, for they are pricking my heart. I will never offer to touch the milk of yours again."[clxxxiii]

Collected by Thomas Hegarty, Toormore
From Mr Michael Allen, Goleen

How a Crock of Gold was Found

Once upon a time there lived a man in Skeanhannore named John Kelly. He dreamed three nights in succession if he went to London Bridge that there was money hidden there. One day he started for London, and for three days he walked to and fro on the bridge. The third day a man noticed him, and he asked him what he was looking for. He told him he dreamt that he would get money on the bridge, and the other man told him that he was a fool to believe it, that he himself dreamt that he would get money in Ireland under an elder tree, which happened to be growing near the man's house. He said nothing but came home and uprooted the tree and found a crock of gold, and he lived happily ever after.[clxxxiv]

Tom Donovan's Fright

Some years ago there lived in this district a man named Tom Donovan. People long ago had to go far away to get a suit made. There was at that time a tailor in Ballydevlin, and Tom when to him to get a suit of clothes made. The tailor told him that he would have the suit of clothes made for him if he would come about 12 o'clock the next night, so Tom said to him that he would. Then Tom went home.

When the next night came, Tom started off on his journey. There was an old road from Toormore to Ballydevlin at that time, and Tom went that way. As he was going across a field at 12 o'clock he saw a lot of boys dressed in red coats and caps and they were playing hockey. "Good," said Tom, "and where are you going?" They made him no answer. Tom asked again and they said, "We are going to the New Found Out." Then they took up their hurleys and went their way. Tom went for his suit of clothes, and you may be sure he was not willing to come out the next night, or for many a night afterwards.[clxxxv]

Collected by Nellie Allen, Goleen
From Mr Thomas Allen (aged 60 years), Goleen

How the Priest Saw the Witch

It was about one hundred years ago in the month of May that a clergy man near Rathdowney in Queen's County was awakened to attend a dying man in the parish. As it was yet dark when he left his house, the good priest hurried on his way. He journeyed on slowly and when he had gone a good part of the way, the grey dawn began to appear. When he had gone about three miles from his own house, his horse, which was a very brave animal, stopped and looked into a field. The priest also looked in and saw a little spectacle which made his blood run cold. It was the legs of a man from the hips down, without head or body, trotting up the lane at a smart pace. At last, it came to the road and stood there. "Hello, friend, and where are you going so early", said the priest. The little spectacle made no answer but uttered a fierce growl. "Why don't you speak?" said the priest again. Another growl was the reply. "Perhaps," said the good priest, "a crack of a whip might do you good", and so saying, he struck the little man a heavy blow with his whip. The little man uttered an unearthly yell, and fell onto the road, and what was the priest's astonishment when he saw the whole place running over with milk, not blood. He was struck dumb with fright. The priest's head swam, and when he recovered, the spectacle had vanished and in its stead he found stretched on the road, and half drowned in the milk, the form of Sarah Kennedy, who had been long known in that district for her witchcraft and who had turned herself to that shape, and was employed that morning in sucking the cows of the village. "Oh, father", shouted the unfortunate woman, "Can you do anything to save me? I am lost. Hell is open for me." The priest had not strength enough to reply and he went home.

The remains of Sarah Kennedy were removed to her cabin that evening. On the evening of her burial the neighbours burned her cabin to the ground. Her daughter made her escape and never after returned to that place.[clxxxvi]

Collected by Thomas Hegarty, Toormore
From Mr Michael Allen (aged 72 years), Goleen

Hay Burning

A few years ago, near Goleen, there was a man whose hayrick was burnt. His young son was looking for some nice place to light a fire. He thought it would be a nice place to have a fire near the hayrick, so he laid down the sticks and put some lighted matches to them. After a few minutes the hayrick caught fire. Mr Roycroft, who was going along the road, saw the smoke and went to tell the boy's father. After a while his father came out and he sent his son around to all the houses in the neighbourhood for help. They drew buckets of water, and poured the water on the hayrick, but it was no good, for the fire was gone too far in the rick. There was about £5 worth of hay burnt. The father was very angry with his son for burning all his hay. The son got a great fright when he knew what harm he had done.[clxxxvii]

Collected by Lucille Sweetman, Cove, Toormore

Mr Willbank's Boat Wreck

About twenty years ago, a man and his two sons went out fishing near Crookhaven harbour. The man's name was Mr Willbanks, and his son's names were Tom and George. One night, Mr Willbanks put out his nets hoping the next day to bring them in. Next day came and Mr Willbanks and his two sons went for their nets. They had a good handful of fish. Suddenly a storm rose, and Mr Willbanks tried to come to shore as fast as he could, but the storm rose so fast that the boat was upset, and one of Mr Willbank's sons was drowned. Mr Willbanks himself and his other son were caught under the boat. A man on shore saw the boat and ran quickly for help. Soon the strand was covered with people. Then the men got a hook and turned the boat right again. They found that the men who were under the capsized boat were nearly dead. They took Mr Willbanks and his son to a house nearby, where they got hot water, drinks, and dry clothing and received every possible kindness. Sad to say, poor Mr Willbanks died, but his son recovered and is living still.[clxxxviii]

Collected by Lucille Sweetman, Cove, Toormore

The Farmer and the Leprechaun

Once upon a man from Kerry was unable to pay his rent. In the early morning he went out and sat down near a lake and began to 'hulagone" [sic]. All of a sudden, a man in a blue jacket and a red cap jumped out of big bush and came towards him asking what was he "hulagoning" for. He told his story about how he would not be able to pay his rent and would be thrown out on the roadside. When the fairy heard this, he gave the man a purse of gold sovereigns and he told him to pay his rent. Then the other man went off and paid his rent, and the landlord gave him the receipt. He went home quite happy. In the evening when the landlord came to look at the payment, all he had were round pieces of tin, but he could not say a word for the other man had a receipt.[clxxxix]

Collected by Thomas Hegarty, Gurtyowen, Toormore
From Mr Michael Allen (72 years), Goleen

A Mermaid who Saved Two Men from Drowning

One day three men went out fishing. They set their nets again, and they then sat down to eat bread in the boat. As they were eating their bread, a mermaid came up to them and put her hands on the side of the boat and asked for a piece of bread. One of the men refused, but the other two gave her half of their own bread, so she ate it sitting on the water beside the boat. When she had finished, she told them to haul their nets and go home as fast as they could, for there was a terrible storm going to rise. She then sank into the water. They did not believe her, so they went father out in the sea. When they were out a good distance, a terrible storm arose. They tried to come home as quickly as they could, but it was no good. Soon a frightful wave came and overturned the boat. They all were thrown out of the boat. They began to scream, and at last the very same mermaid swam up to them and took the two men who gave her the bread by the hands, and left the other man who refused, behind. She led both of them to the shore safely. The other man was drowned, because his body was found next day on the shore after it had been washed in by the tide. This was how he was treated for his selfishness.[cxc]

Collected by Nellie Allen, Goleen
From Mr Carty (aged 62 years), Goleen

How the Fairies Carried Away John's Cow

Once upon a time there lived a little distance away from Loughleagh Lake a little man called John, and his old mother. They lived by hook and by crook in the best way that they could. They had a little bit of ground which gave them plenty, and a little red cow that gave them a drop of milk. John was a very useful little man. Every day he used to milk the red cow and cut heather on the mountain. One day he went up the mountain and the cow followed him. When he had a good bundle cut, he lay down on the grass and he went asleep. He had not long to sleep for when he woke the fairies were dancing around him. One of them hurled a ball into his eye and nearly blinded him. He closed his eyes and when he opened them again the fairies were gone away with his cow. Away went John after the fairies. Sure enough he overtook them at the fort in which they used to live, and he caught his little cow by the horn, and the fairies offered him gold and silver if he would leave them the cow, but he said that she was his mother's cow and he carried the cow home, but the minute his mother said, 'God bless the beast", the cow sank down through the ground.[cxci]

Collected by Thomas Hegarty, Toormore
From Mr Henry Allen (62 years), Goleen

The Haunted Tree

Some years ago around this district there were two men who used to frighten people as they used be coming to or going from houses at night time. There were three big trees growing on the side of the road by Cove at that time. The men used to put a blanket across the top of each tree, and then light a candle on the blanket so that when the people would be passing by, they would frighten them. The men used to stay up among the branches and make queer noises too. They succeeded in frightening a lot of people.

One night a man was going along the road and the two men made all sorts of noises. The man did not say one word only turned back and went home. Next evening about 6 o'clock the man dressed himself in white and went up on the tree. The two men, as usual, came soon afterwards up on the tree so as to be ready to frighten anyone passing, and when they saw the man dressed in white, they slipped down hurriedly with fright and ran home. This is a case where the 'bighter himself got bitten', and the two men ceased frightening people from then on.[cxcii]

The Lazy Beauty and the Fairies

There was once a poor widow woman who had a daughter that was as handsome as the day, but very lazy. The poor mother was a great hand at the spinning wheel, and she wished that her daughter would be as handy as herself. Her daughter used to get up late, eat her breakfast before she would say her prayers, and anything she used do seemed to be burning her fingers. One day her mother was scolding her daughter very hard and who should be riding by but the king's son. "My, O my", said he, "surely its not your daughter that's vexing you?"

"Not at all", said the woman, forgetting herself, "but I was scolding her for working too hard. She spins three pounds of flax every day and weaves it all into thread the next day."

"That's the very girl who will suit my mother", said the prince. "Will you get your daughter's cloak and I will carry her home. Perhaps my mother will make her her daughter-in-law in a week."

Well, the girl went away with the prince. The prince's mother was very surprised when she heard all that the girl could do. When the night came, the old queen pointed to a heap of flax and said, "You may begin as soon as you like tomorrow morning, and I will expect to see these three pounds of flax woven into nice thread the morning after." Little did the poor girl sleep that night. When the next morning came, she began to spin the flax, and though she had a nice mahogany wheel and the finest flax you ever saw, the thread was breaking every moment. At last, she pushed her chair back and burst out crying. A small old woman with very big feet came in at the same moment and said, "What ails you, you handsome colleen?"

"And haven't I been told to weave all the flax before tomorrow morning and I'll never be able to put it together."

"Well", said the Old Woman Big Foot, "if you will promise to ask me to your wedding, all your three pounds of flax will be made up into fine thred while you are taking your sleep tonight." Then the poor girl promised the Old Woman Big Foot that she would ask her to her wedding.

It was all as the Old Woman Big Foot said, for all the flax was woven into fine thread next morning. "My brave girl", said the queen when she saw all the fine threat, "you needn't do any more today, but tomorrow you may weave all this thread." The girl was more frightened than ever, and she was in great grief when she saw the second old woman come into the room. This old woman had very broad shoulders, and she told the girl that her name was Old Woman Broad Shoulders. She made the same bargain with the girl as Old Woman Big Foot did. Great was the queen's surprise next morning when she found a web as fine as the finest paper one could see. Then said the queen, 'tomorrow you must make all this into shirts, and you may give one of them to my son for a present."

The poor girl waited very patiently for a minute, and she was overjoyed to see the third old woman appear. She had a big red nose, and she told the girl that her name was Old Woman Red Nose on that account. She made up her mind to be so good to her as the others, for a dozen white shirts were lying on the table when the queen paid an early visit. Now there was nothing talked of but the wedding. The poor old mother was there with the rest.

At dinner the old queen could talk of nothing but how happy herself and the bride would be, spinning and weaving all their lives. The bridegroom did not like this, and the bride liked it less. He was going to say something when the footman came running to the bride and said, "Old Woman Big Foot asked if she could come in." The bride said she could and in came the Old Woman Big Foot and sat down. The prince asked why her foot was so big. "I was standing at the spinning wheel all my life, and that's why." After a while in came Old Woman Broad Shoulders and sat down. The prince asked her why her shoulders were so broad, and she replied, "It is owing to sitting all my life at the loom." Again, in came Old Woman Red Nose and sat down. The prince asked why her nose was so red. She replied that it was owing to being stooped down over her stitching, and all the blood ran into her nose.

Well, boys and girls. If you go about taking off the lazy beauty it won't go well with you. Besides, she had three powerful fairies to help her. This story was ended by a priest's servant about half-a-century ago.[cxciii]

Collected by Thomas Hegarty, Toormore
From Mr Michael Allen (72 years), Goleen

The Farmer, the Leprechaun, and the White Cow

Once upon a time there lived a man in Rock Island near Goleen village. He had no cow and his family were starving in want of milk. One day, the farmer was walking round his farm, and as he was doing so, he saw a funny little man sitting on a mushroom. When he saw him, he began to run away but the little man called him back. When he came back the little man asked him why he was so sad, and the farmer told him his troubles. The little man told him to wait until he came back. When he returned, he brought a pure white cow. "This cow is for you. Take her home with you and do not ever sell her no matter whether she is young or old." The farmer took her home with him and he at first got a bucket and milked the cow. She filled every bucket in the house and had twenty-four pure white calves in twenty years. The farmer's wife said to him to sell the old white cow, that they had plenty of new cows now. So, he started for the fair next morning. The old cow did not want to go at all, but the farmer beat her cruelly. She began to low until all the rest came running after her. The farmer and his wife did their best to stop the cows, but it was all no good. They were never seen or heard of anymore.

The farmer and his family died of starvation. The poor fellow brought all that misfortune and misery on himself and on his family simply because he didn't heed the leprechaun's advice.[cxciv]

Collected by Nellie Allen, Goleen
From Mr John Bohan (60 years), Goleen

Dickey's Height

Long ago, around this district, the people used to call a hill near Schull, 'Dickey's Height'. A man, whose name was Mr Dick Roycroft of Kilpatrick, was walking down that hill when suddenly he saw a lot of people standing before him. When he was passing them by, they moved to one side of the road, and when he had, he looked back immediately and they had all gone, but they left their black caps behind. No one since that night would care to pass by that place, for it was said afterwards that they were some of the 'good people' who used to appear at that particular place.[cxcv]

Collected by Lucille Sweetnam, Toormore
From Mr Luke Sweetnam (84 years), Toormore

The Milk Stealing Witch

Once there was what appeared to be a poor woman, but really a witch, and her grandson living in a tiny house on the side of a hill. They had no cows, so the woman used to change herself into a hare and go every morning and evening to the neighbours' cows and milk them in turn. The cows at that time used to be milked out in the field. This woman used churn and sell the butter in the village, and with the money she got for the butter, she and her grandson were able to live happily together. All the people were wondering why their cows used have no milk some mornings. Every morning they would see a big hare jumping into the rushes nearby, and they began to think, in fact came to the conclusion, that the hare had something to do with the cows. They decided to kill the hare. So, one day a party with hounds and horses set out to kill the hare. The poor grandson was there also, patiently waiting to see what would turn up. They came to the field, and they saw the hare. The men put the hounds after it, but it ran for its life; several times the dogs were up to its heals, so one time the grandson shouted, "Nanny, nanny, run!" The hare ran in the direction of the small house, but just as she was jumping over the gate outside the house, the hounds took a big bite out of her leg. She ran into the house but when the hunters came in, they could see nothing but an old woman sitting by the fire. They asked her did any hare come in just a few minutes ago. She said, "no". They said, "Are you sure? Perhaps it ran up into that dark corner. Would you mind getting up one minute?" When she got up, to the hunters' great surprise her leg was streaming blood. Meanwhile they had the piece which the hounds took out of the supposed hare's leg. So, when no explanation could be given by the woman as to why her leg was bleeding, they fitted the piece and came to the conclusion that it belonged to her.

Nothing is told as to what happened to the woman and her grandson, only they went away from their little home and were never seen, or heard of, anymore.[cxcvi]

Collected by Sadie Roycroft, Goleen
From Mr William Roycroft (58 years), Goleen

ALTAR
People, places and Property

Lissacaha – My Home District

I live in the townland of Lissacaha North. It is five miles from the village of Schull in the Parish of Kilmoe. The Church of Ireland divided the Parish of Kilmoe into two parts. They called the east part Altar Parish. It is in Altar Parish the townland of Lissacaha is. This division was made about the time of the famine. It is in the Barony of the west division of West Carbery. Lissacaha means 'the fort of the battle.' There are 550¼ acres in the townland of Lissacaha North. The people around here nearly always call it the Prairie. It was Captain Somerville gave it that name. He lived for some years in the prairies of North America. He called his house 'The Prairie Cottage.' He owned all the townland, so it all got the name of the Prairie. The Somervilles were the landlords of it until three years ago. There are ten families living in it, three families of Driscolls, three families of Kennedys, one family of Glanviles, one family of Hunts, one family of Walshes, and one family of Roycrofts. There are two people over seventy. Both are over eighty now. They cannot tell stories in Irish. I do not know if they can tell stories in English. The houses are all slated. Houses were more numerous formerly. There were three dwelling houses on our farm. A lot of people went to America in former years, but it is to England they emigrate now. A building in ruins is called a cabhach. The land in Lissacaha is very flat and boggy. There are no rivers or lakes or streams in it. There are no woods in it now but there must have been there long ago because there are a lot of logs in the bogs. Mr J Kennedy's house was an old R.I.C. Barrack. The prairie cottage is in ruins now. It is owned by Mr R. King. There is a Methodist church in Lissacaha North. Bishop Downes visited Schull in the year 1700, and in the description, he gave of his visit he said that there were wolves in the woods of Mount Gabriel. All the woods are cut down now. There is a lake on the top of it. It is called Poulanenine. The Fastnet Rock is supposed to be the piece of rock that was taken out of Mount Gabriel. One time there was a man standing beside the lake. He had a sore leg. There was a ship passing the Fastnet Rock. When he saw it, he exclaimed, "Don't hurt my leg."[cxcvii]

From Lilly Hunt, Toormore

Local Heroes

Over a hundred years ago there lived a man named Tom Roycroft in the townland of Ardravinna. He was known all over the district as a great jumper. He could jump over a gate about seven feet high. Another great jumper lived in the townland of The Prairie, named James Hunt. He used to sharpen a razor and holding it in his hand used to jump over it. I am sure he must have had great courage to do such a daring thing.

Over a hundred years ago, in a little thatched farmhouse near Dunmanus Pier, lived a farmer named O'Driscoll. His wife was a very thrifty woman and worked hard to bring up a large family of children. She was very quick-tempered, and when any of the children annoyed her by their pranks, she picked them up and threw them over the pier into the water. They soon learned to swim. One of the boys, called Michael, was very mischievous, so he got a ducking several times a day. Eventually he became an expert swimmer. Very often when the fishing fleet wanted to unmoor their boats, he was called to dive down and unloose the cable. When he grew up he did many a daring deed which are still told by the firesides on winter nights. One dark night, two boats were out after mackerel. They put out their nets and when about to draw them in, they found they had so many fish that the two boats could not contain them all. Michael was ordered to swim ashore (two miles) for another boat. He accomplished the journey, procured the boat, and arrived back in time to take the remaining fish. A few years later he had to emigrate to America, and he never returned to his native land.

Particulars of a Famous Local Mower

There lives a man, away out by the Mizen Head, named Elias Roycroft. He is now over seventy years of age and retired from farming, though still hale and strong. When he was a young man, over forty years ago, one fine day in June he met a neighbour, and they talked of the hay cutting, and Mr Roycroft bet that he would have his hay cut before him. So accordingly, they started off next day, after an early breakfast, with their scythes, to the hayfield. Mr Roycroft toiled, and before evening he had mown an acre and a half of hay. Next day, he was up early, and before nightfall he had mown another acre and a half, and on the third day, feeling as fresh as ever, he easily cut nearly two acres more. He easily finished mowing the last field on the fourth day, having mown six acres in all in four days. He then went over in the evening to see how his neighbour had got on, but he had only barely two acres done. So, Mr Roycroft won the bet.

Particulars of a Famous Local Dancer

Over sixty years ago there lived a man in Dunmanus named Frank Helen. He was considered a wonderful dancer. All the people in the district loved to watch him dancing. His favourite dances were 'The Irish Hornpipe' and the 'Reel and Jig'. He could dance many other dances as well as those two, and better still he could 'keep the floor warm' for a considerable time without being in the least tired. Recently foreign dances were introduced into Ireland, and for a time found favour with the Irish people, but evidently the people have now grown tired of such dances, and instead are everywhere taking up a fresh, with a new zest, the beautiful old Irish dances, with the result that the foreign dances are fast dying out, and very few, if any, of them are now to be seen in this locality.[cxcviii]

From Violet Hunt, Toormore

Mack Allen, the Storyteller

There is a great storyteller, known locally by the Irish name 'Seanchuí'. He is living in the Altar Parish. His name is Mack Allen. He is known around this locality for the great stories he can tell. You would often hear the people round the country saying, "Mack Allen has a great warrant to tell stories" (meaning that he is an adept in the art). Sometimes he tells very funny stories, one of which is as follows: -

Some ten or twelve years ago he was passing through a lonely field, when a big cross goat with two long horns followed him and attacked him. The goat stood up on her hind legs and drew in towards Mack to poke him with her horns but instead of running away with fear, Mack closed in to fight the goat. After a few bouts, Mack succeeded in getting a firm grip of the goat's horns, and knocking the goat, he fixed her horns into the ground firmly, then leaving her in that position, he resumed his journey in safety. He tells this story in such a way that any listener with a sense of humour has to laugh heartily. He acts out the story when telling it.[cxcix]

From Edith Grace Roycroft, Toormore

ALTAR
Farming, Trade and Crafts

Forges

There are three forges in our district. The owners of these forges are Jack Carthy, Jack Sullivan, and Danny Harrington. Jack Carthy's forge is situated on the main road leading from Goleen to Schull. It is about 100 yards from the crossroads leading to Dunkelly and Dunmanus. The roof is slated, the same as a country house, but there are no beams or ceilings. At one end of the house the hob is erected; it stands about two or three feet from the floor. On the left-hand side of the hob the bellows stand. They are erected so that the smith can blow with the left hand and see to his irons and make up the fire when needed with his right hand. The bellows are made of wood and leather, and of an iron pipe which is going through the hob on to the centre of the fire. The anvil is 3½ ft. from the hob, placed on a wooden block, and put on so that it can't move. This block is sunk down about two feet into the floor. At the other side of the block there is room for a horse to stand to get shod.

The implements the smith works with are the sledgehammer, shoeing hammer, tongs, pincers, knife, and rasp. He uses the sledge hammer to beat out the iron when it is hot; the tongs are used to hold the iron and to take it out of the fire; the shoeing hammer is used for driving the nails into the hoof; the knife is used for paring the hoof before the shoe is put on; the pincers are for drawing nails if they go wrong; and last of all he uses the rasp for filing the hoof when the shoe is on. The smith has a big wooden box in which he holds all his implements, and he also has a barrel for holding water to cool the hot iron. There is a local belief about this water as to its curative qualities. It is said if you had warts on your hands and if you washed them in this water that it would cure them. The smith's outside work is shoeing wheels of carts and traps; for this branch of his work he makes a big fire of turf on the ground and places a wheel in the middle of it. Then he hammers on the band while another man holds the wheel, and when the band is firmly fixed on to the wheel, he then throws on water to cool it. He also makes gates, ploughs, and pieces of harrows, outside. The smith has very strong sinewy hands from all the exercise and hammering he does every day. The smith is a great pet in our district; everyone brings him presents at Xmas such as milk, butter, potatoes, cabbage, &c.

A smith's work must be very hard in the summer, but he doesn't mind it so much in winter. It is most convenient for those who have to travel about a good deal with horses that so many forges are to be found on the wayside.[cc]

From Nellie Allen, The Elms, Goleen

ALTAR
Local Customs

All Hallows Eve

All Hallows' Eve, the vigil of All Saints Day, is the occasion of many amusements in Ireland, some of which are handed down from Pagan days. The following are some of the amusements that are practiced in the district of Altar school. All the local people assemble together and cut up cakes in which rings, rags, peas, and beans have been baked. The pieces of cake are then handed around, and it is believed that the person who gets the ring will be married during the following twelve months. Everyone tries to avoid getting the rag, as it is the omen of poverty, while the pea signifies wealth, and the bean happiness.

Another favourite game is nut burning. Two nuts are placed near the fire to represent a boy and a girl in the company, and all gather around to see the result. If one of the nuts jump away from the other the couple will not be married, but it they jump in the same direction or remain as placed, the couple will be married during the year.

Another way to tell your fortune is lead melting. Lead is melted and then poured into water or on sand and the shape it takes tells all about your future husband or wife. It sometimes gives the initial of the name and many other interesting indications as to the size and description of the person you will be married to. To tell the fortunes of the coming year the lead must be poured through the ring of a key; the ring being an ancient symbol for the circle of the year, and the key being symbolic of the door of the future.

Another ceremony is the placing of three saucers on the table; in one is salt, in the second a ring, and the third a handful of earth. Each of the company is then blindfolded, and after being led around the table three times, he places his right hand on one of the saucers. If the saucer containing the earth is touched, it brings a pious prayer to the lips of the blindfolded person, for it is a grim reminder that the time is not far off when he too will be but a handful of graveyard clay; if the saucer with the ring is touched it means that a happy marriage is in the offing; and the hand that rests upon the salt may expect to cry salt tears in the near future.

If a girl remains up until midnight and then goes out to a well and waits until the moon rises, she will see the face of the man she will be married to reflected on the surface of the water. By looking over one's shoulder at midnight one will see the face of his or her life partner in a mirror placed at one's back, for on this night the fairies have great power and wander around the earth and are only too willing to come in and warm themselves to the fire as they used to do in the days of old when the Druids rekindled the sacred fire for them. On this night, a coal of this fire was brought into every homestead to kindle a sacred fire for the fairies who used to come in and sing and dance with the company and tell them all about the future.

Halloween is known around this district as Snap-apple Night to the youngsters, for on that night a wooden cross is hung to the kitchen rafters and to each alternate point a lighted candle is attached. Then a number of apples are suspended from the cross at a height the children can conveniently reach. With their hands tied behind their backs, the youngsters try to grip the apples with their teeth, which is more easily said than done as the apples swing backwards when touched, and the cross revolves around on the string on which its suspended from the ceiling. There is many a laugh before the apples are all captured and consumed by the children. Then a big tub is placed in the kitchen floor and filled with water, into which coins are dropped. The task now before the youngsters is to plunge their heads into the tubs and bring up one of the coins between their teeth. Nerved on by versions of all the wonderful things those coins would buy, the cold water holds no terror for them and soon every alluring sixpence and three penny bit is retrieved by the youthful divers.

While the children are thus enjoying themselves, many of the elder boys and girls are engaged in apple-paring which consists of paring the skin of the apple in one continuous strip, which must remain intact from start to finish of the paring process; if it breaks it is a sign of a disappointment. This ribbon of apple skin is then passed over the head three times, and then dropped over the left shoulder on to the floor where it sometimes forms the initial of a name which is taken to be that of your future husband or wife.

By the time all those ceremonies are concluded, the old kettle that has served in the joys and sorrows of generations long gone, sings merrily on its crook over the blazing turf fire in the open hearth, and the woman of the house rises from her seat in the chimney corner to 'wet' the 'tay' in the big brown earthen-ware teapot which she places to draw on the 'griesoah' which she has drawn out of the fire. The table is then placed in the centre of the floor and the old woman produces her best tablecloth to spread over it. The young girls spring from their seats to help the woman of the house, and it is a labour of love to them to assist her for they know that the tribute of gratitude, respect, reverence, love, and admiration which they offer to the old folk was dearly bought by them in dark and evil days, when they toiled and suffered that we may have a roof over our heads 'this blessed night'. 'Many hands make light work', and before you would have time to say, 'God bless us', everything is ready for a feast fit for a prince. When the tea is over, the company sings and dances until the clock strikes midnight, when everyone prepares for home, and the old man of the house stands up and says, "God grant that we may all be living and doing well this time twelve months", and we all say "Amen". Then home they go and not one of them is idiotic enough to think that he has indulged in superstitious practices, for they fully realize the true and noble significance of the ceremonies they have assisted in. They know that they were simply observing old Celtic customs, Christian and Pagan, and forging another link to bind them to those who are gone before. Thus, a very pleasant night comes to a close with each member of the party looking forward to the following Hallows' Eve for a repetition of the observances and customs.[cci]

From Frances J. Connell, Altar

Holy Wells

For several centuries Holy Wells have been held with great respect all over Ireland. 'Holy Wells', or 'Blessed Wells', as some people call them, are in a great many cases very blessed. Some people believe they were blessed by some Saint of Ireland. Of course, there is not a sure account of that, but the Saints used baptize people in some of them. People believe that lots of those wells were made by pagan people long ago. Of course, they used worship the water and they made those deep holes in rocks, or whatever suited best to hold the water for them to worship. Those wells were also very useful, because many a boy or girl used go and take a 'rounds' around the Holy Well nearer their home and get cured from whatever disease they might have had. All people who used get cured would leave a button or rag, or a handkerchief near the well as a thank-offering.

There are some Holy Wells near Altar School, but the most important of all are the wells at Gurranes. The Holy Wells at Gurranes are situated in the side of a cliff in Mr John Shannon's field, which is about a mile from Altar School. Those three wells are close together and shaped like a horse shoe, but of course much bigger. They are about three feet deep. All the year around those wells are full up of water and it is always very bright and sparkling. All the rock around the well is covered with ivy, and one can scarcely see them without going very close to them. They are facing eastwards towards the rising sun, so this would make it clear that the pagan people long ago used worship the water and the sun, as the latter slowly sparkled into the well in the morning. Long ago the people used come very early on May morning and walk around them three times. Then they would watch the water until it gave a slight bubble, and then they would dip their hands or feet into it, or maybe if they had sore eyes, they would wash their eyes. While they would be doing this, they would be sending a silent prayer upward in honour of whatever saint they believed used it or blessed it. There is also another little well, not a Holy Well, in a rock by the sea, and it is said that the fishes come up and wash themselves in it once a day, and they also bring up their young fishes and christen them on the 7th day of every month. This well can scarcely be seen because it is in a hole in a rock, and the tide must be very far out before one can get to it.

There is another Holy Well in Tureen, about 1½ miles from Altar School. It is cut out of a rock, and the local name for it is the 'Warty Well'. This well is so called because it was famous for curing warts. It is about one foot long, one foot broad, and two feet deep. There is a flat stone placed over the well, so as to keep it clean. The people used come to this well early on Easter Sunday morning and get cured of warts. All around this well used be crowded with people on Easter morn, to be cured of warts. When they used be cured, they would cover the well with the stone over it. They would leave their handkerchiefs or buttons around it. One could easily fill a bag of handkerchiefs, rags, and buttons, left by the people as thank-offering at this well.

Everybody takes great care of Holy Wells because they believe if they harmed or polluted them in any way that some misfortune would happen to them soon afterwards. Indeed, some people go so far as to say that it was a blessing from God that those Holy Wells were available to the people because when there were very few doctors in the country, the sick or sore could get cure by means of Holy Wells instead. Anybody would not take the water of those Holy Wells for house use, because they believe it is unlucky to use it in that way. It has been told of a woman who lived in Tureen, and who took water out of the Warty Well, and used it in her house, that she or her children never had a bit of luck for five years. This story goes to prove that the people have grounds for their fears.[ccii]

From Lillian Jermyn, Toormore

Matchmaking and Weddings

Many years ago, young folk around were not allowed much freedom, especially girls. It was considered highly improper for a girl to be seen out along after nightfall unless accompanied by her parents or brothers. It was considered incorrect for a girl to be seen walking with a young man, even in broad daylight. So, there was no chance of lovemaking whatever.

The father of a young girl met a neighbour at a fair. They both went into a public house and after a few bottles of stout each, the girl's father would suggest that he thought the other man's son would be a good match for his daughter. They would then begin bargaining about how much fortune should be paid, and after a few hours arguing, the match was generally made. When they would return home, they would both mention to the parties concerned that they should get married on a certain day, without consulting their wishes in the matter at all. In many cases indeed, the young pair had never spoken to each other until they were really married. I am thankful to say that this old customary matchmaking as above described is now entirely altered, and nowadays young people choose for themselves, and would brook no interference. It was only thought lucky to marry in Shrove, i.e. from Epiphany to Ash Wednesday.

Weddings in those days were entirely different to what they are now. The brides were usually dressed in blue with a white hat trimmed with ostrich feathers, and they always wore a white veil over their faces. They usually drove to the church in a covered car drawn by one or two horses.

In country places, all the relatives and neighbours were invited, usually making a large party, even as many as a hundred guests sometimes. They met at the bride's home in the morning, and after refreshments were served, they would all accompany the bride to the church in different conveyances, some in carts, others on horseback. After the ceremony, the bride's car leading, they usually went for a drive, and then back again to the bride's home for dinner. In the afternoon, the bride was taken to her future home, attended by the guests. This was called the drag home, when a jolly night's feasting and dancing followed. A wedding was a great event then.

Now, in most cases, there are only a few near friends present at the church ceremony, followed by a breakfast, and the happy couple start off on their honeymoon. At the present time, marriages take place at all times during the year, but Easter seems to be favoured by the majority.[cciii]

From Violet Hunt, Toormore

ALTAR
History and Archaeology

Forts

There are quite a number of underground hiding places in this district which are usually called forts. Very little is known about the greater part of these, but there are a few which have been explored by the older people of the district. One fort is situated right above the sea overlooking Toor Dock in Mr Wilkinson's field about 12 miles west of Altar School. Mr Wilkinson's father was supposed at one time to have removed a large stone which covered the entrance to this fort, intending to explore it, when he fell sick. When his people found out he had interfered with the stone, they pulled herbs and gave them to him as a cure, believing that his interference with the fort was the cause of his sickness. The herbs cured him, however, and taught him a lesson also, that he should not interfere with any of those mysterious old ruins which are to be found here and there through the country. There is another in Mr Allen's field in Toor which nothing is known about. There is an underground connection between this fort and Mr Wilkinson's. On the side of a hill in Mr Roycrofts ground is another one of these hiding places. It is covered with furze, so nothing is known about it.

At the foot of Cahar Hill, right across the plain, there is another fort in Mr Regan's field which is said to have been explored by men some time ago. This fort is said to contain several large rooms, one about 15 feet long and about 12 broad; two more are round and flagged overhead. The largest room was a lake owing to the passage being foul. There is a road over this leading to Cahar houses, which also are built over this fort. A few years ago, this road broke down, and a man putting down a fishing rod into the breach on end, was unable to find firm ground. At the mouth of this there is a huge mound with a lot of stones filling it. There is a connection between this fort and the one about half-mile distant in Mr Sullivan's ground, Lissagriffin, Goleen. Long ago when the field in which the fort is found was being ploughed, the stone which covered the mouth of this fort fell in and was never disturbed since. This being left so, a certain man, anxious to see the inside, brought from his home a reel of cotton wool, a candle, and some matches, and on arriving at the fort he tied one end of the thread to a stick at the mouth of the fort, he then lit his candle and went in, letting the reel unravel as he went along. All went well until he came to the third apartment, and then unfortunately his candle quenched in want of air; he then tried to light his matches but of course they would not light. He then wound his reel as quickly as possible and came home rather disappointed as he did not see the interior of the fort with its contents. A few weeks later two women were coming home from a wake, and while passing beside this fort they heard people counting money, and the also heard some falling. They got such a fright that they ran as quickly as possible home and they never passed that way home again.

Another fort is situated in Mr Sheehan's field near Goleen, but it has never been explored. When the field was being tilled the owner of this field blasted the stone which lay on the mouth of the fort. Then he drew the stone by cart to the roadside and left them there to help repair the road. Next morning, he went to the field to continue his ploughing. But to his surprise there lay the same stone on the mouth of the fort.

He went to the roadside where the stones were put but there was no trace of them there. This taught him a lesson, so he never touched it again. It is thought that there is a connection between this and the fort in Mr Hegarty's ground near Goleen. This one has been partly explored. It contains several large rooms, oblong in shape. An interesting, if sad little story is told in connection with this fort. It is as follows:

> Once there were two men mowing corn in the field in which this fort is. One said he would like to have a drink of buttermilk, the other said he was not thirsty at all. After a conversation like this, to their surprise there stood a lady dressed in white in front of them with a pail of buttermilk. She offered a drink to the man who said he was thirsty, but he refused it. She then offered it to the other man, and he took it and said it was the nicest he had ever taken. The fairy then disappeared. After a short while, sad to say, the man who said he was thirsty and then refused the drink died. It is strongly believed that his refusal of the milk was the direct cause of his death. Since that man's death people believe that they hear that lady making butter and they also hear her singing.

There is another fort in Dunmanus, a townland about two miles north of Altar School. A huge mound, about from 20 to 30 feet high appears right over this fort. In this mound is a round hole about 5 inches in diameter which is supposed to have acted as a chimney. This fort is built wonderfully well; it is supposed to have been built by the Tuatha de Danann, a race of people who came to Ireland about 1,000 B.C. and who were supposed to understand magic. It has been partly explored and found to contain several large rooms, among which there is one room shut away from the rest which contained, according to legend, several casks of money. There is another larger room containing a stone table, and some stone squares which were probably used for chairs; in the same rooms there is a large fireplace, which at the time is said to have been always full of fir, ready to be lit. The following little legend goes with this fort:

> A girl who was supposed at one time to have been stolen from Dúnmanús by the fairies was heard singing an Irish song, and people say that sometimes she is still seen by passers, at the door of this fort.

There is also a fort in Lisacaha, a townland situated about three miles north of Altar School, from which Lisacaha has got its name. Nothing particular however seems to be known about this one. There is supposed to be still another fort in Toormore, a townland about ¼ mile west of Altar School, but there are doubts and contradictions about this as to whether it is there or not. Some people say it is only an underground passage about 4 feet wide leading from Toormore to a strand called Toormore Strand, about one-furlong distance southwards. Others say that the remains of the fort are there, and there are numerous stories in connection with it, but anyone never seems to tell them. Of all these forts, Dúnmanús fort is the most important. Some of the forts are very interesting, and others are not quite so interesting. Any boy or girl who is interested in their local history should try to seek as much information as possible about these mysterious old hiding places. They are monuments which go to show the skill and art of the olden people. It would be a shame to misuse them by putting turf or hay or any such things into them.[cciv]

Collected by Sadie J. Roycroft, Goleen

The Old Altar Ruin

There are several historic ruins in these districts around Altar School such as altars, castles, and forts, but the most ancient and important is the old altar ruin. It is situated in the townland of Altar in a nice green field overlooking the sea about ¼ of a mile south of Altar School, and midway between Schull and Goleen. This altar consists of five large stones, four are standing on edge, and the remaining one rests flat on top which gives the ruin the appearance of a large table. It is about 9 feet long, 4 feet broad, and 3 feet high. This old ruin is covered over with grey moss so no one can gather that it is very ancient. People say that it has been there for hundreds of years before the time of St Patrick. There are several different beliefs among the people as to by whom this altar was built. Some say it was built there by the pagans long ago for purposes of worship because there is a hole cut in the flat stone laid on top, and they believe that the pagan idolators used to worship the water in that hole just as it fell into it from heaven to them. It is also believed that they used to worship the sun, because the altar is slightly slanting towards the east, as if they were interested in the sun. Others say that it was put there to mark the burial place of an old Irish chieftain who lived in Lowertown, a place about three miles from Altar school. Of course, he was a heathen, and when he died, they burnt his body, putting his ashes in a small box, and burying it in the ground. They then put this altar to mark it. Others again say it was a druidical altar and that the druids used offer sacrifices to their gods off it. Long ago the pagan people used think of their chieftains as some kind of gods, and when the chieftains used die, they would burn them and bury their ashes in the ground. They would then build an altar around them to protect that piece of holy ground, as they thought. They used come every day to those altars wherever they might be and worship them and offer a sacrifice to the chieftain. Many people believe that they used to do the same at the old altar of this district, but, of course, anybody is not sure about that, out of all the general beliefs among the people. Everybody takes great care of this old altar, because they believe it would be unlucky to stir it or even take a stone of it for any use.[ccv]

Collected by Lilian Jermyn, Toormore

Figure 18. The Altar wedge tomb, Toormore
(looking to the southwest (top) and west (bottom)).

Figure 19. The Altar wedge tomb, Toormore
(looking to the north-east (top) and east (bottom)).

Castles

In this locality there are four castles, the Three Castles being the most important. Those castles are situated in a valley near a lough by Three-Castle-Head, which is about thirteen miles west of Altar School and about eight and a half miles west of Goleen. The Three Castles are built in a line running east and west, about 36 yards distant from one another. They are three stories high, each one being a different height. The east is about 40 feet in height, the middle about 35 feet, and the west one 30 feet. There are two doorways and three windows in each castle. There is a doorway in the bottom storey but there is no entrance from the bottom storey to the main body of the castle. There is another doorway in the second storey which is connected by a staircase winding all-round the castle wall to the top storey. The doors were arranged in this manner so that the castle might more easily be defended from within. When an enemy used to be spied, the defenders used to gather into the top storeys and shoot out through the small windows, usual in castles in olden days. The windows appear small from the outside, but they let in sufficient light, as they are splayed inwards to a great extent. There are small holes in the top of the castle walls put above the roof which are supposed to have been for resting guns on when shooting down at their enemies. From the tops of the castles, signals used to be given in time of invasion to a section of the clan which lived in Dúnmanús Castle. The Three Castles were built by the O'Mahony clann about the year 1207. The people of the clanns in most places obtained their livelihood by making the inhabitants of the locality pay them tribute. It was different, however, with the O'Mahony Clann. They made their living by charging a fixed rate to anyone hunting in the neighbourhood of the castles, or fishing in the lake nearby. The second of the clann which lived in Dúnmanús Castle obtained their livelihood by charging what was called a toll to anyone who would fish in Dúnmanús Bay. The Three Castles are built in a different way from other castles, as they are built in a valley, and most of the other castles are built on top of hills commanding a view of several miles all around. In those days, the head of the Dublin clann used to come for his holidays in the summer to the Three Castles. The Three Castles were very important in olden days for the above reasons. Indeed, it would appear that they were considered the most important in the whole island. They are now in ruins but yet they are very interesting. In summer, many tourists visit those old castles, and some take snaps of the castle, lakes, and the immediate surroundings.

Dúnmanús Castle is built in the same style as the Three Castles, but it is built on a rock, whereas the Three Castles are built in a valley. It is in a very good state of preservation. There is a green patch, somewhat like a very small garden, in the top storey. It is very remarkable how this garden ever got there. Most people believe that the wind brought some grass seed, and it grew in the earth of the fallen ruins. Of course, in those days all houses were built with earth, and it is not strange that some earth was also used in the building of castles at that time. Though those castles were built partly with earth, yet none of the tradesmen of today can build as sound a building, even with modern invention. This castle is reckoned to be quite as important and as nice by the people of Dúnmanús, as are the Three Castles. People of the district take great care of Dúnmanús Castle and that is partly the reason of its being in such a good state of preservation at present. If one wanted to get to the top, one would have to climb up the walls on the outside, and the trouble of doing so would then be well rewarded by the beautiful picture of mountains and sea which spreads out to the view. One could see Dúnmanús Bay, and the castle in Múntir a Máire at the other side of Dúnmanús Bay.[xvi] Lots of people come to see Dúnmanús Castle and many agree that it is just as interesting and nice as the Three Castles. Every Irish boy and girl should know, if at all possible, the history connected with the castles in their several localities, for such knowledge would form an excellent basis for fuller study of the history of their native land.[ccvi]

Collected by Frances Connell, Altar

[xvi] Presumably the writer is referring to Mhúntir a Bháire here, the Sheep's Head.

Figure 20. O'Mahoney castles, Three Castles Head

Castles

There are several castles in the district near Altar School. Although there is not anybody living in them, some people still used them by keeping sheep or calves in them by night. The nearest castles to Altar School are Dúnmanús and Larne Castle. Dúnmanús Castle gets its name from a man called Manús who lived there. Dún means fort or fortification, so the word Dúnmanús probably means the fort of Manús. It is about three miles north of Altar School. It is situated on the side of a rock overlooking Dúnmanús Bay. Dúnmanús Castle is rectangular in shape. It is about sixty feet high, twenty feet long, and about fifteen feet broad. It is very difficult to make out the colour of this castle because it is so old that it is all covered with grey moss. There are three storeys in this castle and several little rooms and apartments in each storey. Strange to say there is only one window in each room or apartment. The windows are splayed inwards so as to show great light. Of course, there is a doorway level with the ground floor, but remarkably enough, the staircase is not level with the floor as is usual nowadays, but it is leading up from the second storey. This is erected so because in times of trouble or invasion the enemy cannot rush in on them. There are not any remains of a chimney in the castle, or anything likely to have been used for a chimney. The only hole of any kind is the 'blood hole' which some people say was used for throwing away any waste. Other people say it was for throwing prisoners down if they caught any enemy, or if between the inhabitants themselves any disturbances arose, they would throw one another down. Of course, this castle was roofed, but it is so old the wind has blown it off. There is what appears to be a nice green garden in one room in the top storey. Several people come to see Dúnmanús Castle and get to the top either by ladder or by climbing. There is such a wonderful view from Dúnmanús Castle that it very well repays anybody who takes the trouble of getting to the top. Dúnmanús Castle is in a very good state of preservation, even more so than any of the other castles in districts near Altar School.

Larne Castle is situated about 1½ miles south of Altar School. This castle is also situated on a rock overlooking the sea. It is rectangular in shape. It is about 40 feet high, 15 feet long, and 10 feet broad. Larne Castle is ever so old because it is all covered over with grey moss, far more so than Dúnmanús Castle. There are only two storeys in Larne Castle and two windows in each storey. The windows are splayed inwards as is usually found in all old castles. The door is level with the floor, but the staircase is in the second storey. People say there is a chimney in Larne Castle. Of course, there is not much difference in the style of the castles of West Cork because they all belonged to the O'Mahonys and were built somewhat in the same way (early in the 13th century). Some people say when one could see light right through the castle by means of two windows, which are opposite each other, from Toormore Cross, that it is the sign of fine weather. Lots of people came to see this castle also, and many agree that Dúnmanús Castle is far nicer and more interesting than Larne Castle.

Dunbeacon Castle is another famous old castle. It is about 4½ miles north of Altar School. The castle is situated on a rock right down by the sea, far nearer the sea than the other castles of the district are. It is about fifty feet high, fifteen feet long, and about ten feet broad. It is rectangular in shape like the other castles. Dunbeacon Castle is so called probably because the inhabitants used to light a fire, called the 'beacon fire', on a high hill just behind the castle as a signal to their friends in Múintír Mháire of an approaching attack by enemies. Of course, it may not have been from that source that it got its name, but it does seem likely because 'dûn' means a fort or fortification, so Dunbeacon would mean the fort of the beacon fires. This castle is not as exposed as other castles, because it is closed in by a hill on the north and northwest, and by the sea on the south. It is rather remarkable that this castle was built so low down near the sea, so unlike all other castles. Some people believe it was built so, because if the inhabitants saw an enemy approaching by land, they could escape by boat across Dunmanus Bay to Múintír Mháire and return again when they would suppose the enemy had gone. Other people say it was so built because if the enemy was approaching by sea, they need not let them come up the shore at all. The former reason, however, would appear to be the more correct one. Dunbeacon Castle is not in a good state of preservation; indeed, it seems to be very fast falling into ruins. There is a huge hole in one of its walls, which makes it appear very old and dilapidated looking. People say there was a certain man long ago who committed some great wrong for which he was to be hanged; but he got a chance, that if he would be able to knock a piece of the castle with a shot, he could live. So, of course, the man took his chance and shot the castle, tearing a big hole in the west wall, and so succeeded in saving his life. Everybody does not agree on that matter. Some think it is just falling from old age. Others think that the rent in the wall was caused by a thunderbolt, or lightning. The latter seems more likely to be true and is more believed.

If these old castles could speak, they could tell some wonderful tales, which would fill several books.[ccvii]

Collected by Lilian Jermyn, Toormore

Lowertown

Co. Chorcaighe
Bar: Cairbre Thiar
Par: An Góilin
Scoil: Lubhghortán
Oide: Máire Bean Uí Mhathúna
25.10.1937 – 16.3.1938

LOWERTOWN
Local Folklore and Stories

The Mermaid, the Boy, the Rook, and the Hound

Long, long ago there lived in Hare Island a very poor fisherman. He hadn't any way of supporting himself and his wife but by fishing. He fished day and night but caught no fish. One day he went out fishing but caught none, and when the evening came, he said that the best thing he could do was to drown himself. He spoke it out loud and suddenly, a mermaid rose out of the water and spoke to him. He told her his story, and she told him to come again the following day and that he would catch a salmon. She also told him that a son would be born to them but that she would claim him at the age of twenty-one. Everything happened just as she had said, and when the son was growing up everyone told him what was to happen to him. When he was nearing twenty-one years, he resolved to run away. He took leave of his parents and started inland. He was walking through a wood and he met a dead sheep, and a rook and a hound were arguing. They asked the boy to divide the sheep between them. He did so, and as a reward for his kindness the rook pulled a feather, and the hound pulled a hair off his tail. They said that if he was ever in trouble these would help him. He struck himself with the feather and he turned himself into a rook and flew off to Cork. All the people were amazed to see a rook perch upon the windows, and they tried to catch him but failed. A rich lady opened the highest window in her house and laid crumbs on the window stool. When the bird saw the bread and found the window was open, he went in. No sooner did he touch the floor than he turned into a man again. He remained two days with the lady until the fox chase, which was to be held near the city, was at hand. He and the lady were at the window looking at the chase when he saw the fox go by. He was anxious to chase him, so he struck himself with the hair and turned himself into a hound and ran off after him. The fox ran towards the cliff and swung himself around a briar and into his den. The hound missed him and fell into the sea into the arms of the mermaid. There he had to remain with her. The people came every day to see would he appear, but he didn't. After a long time, he asked the mermaid to let him put his head above the water to see his friends. She agreed, and he next asked her to let him stand on her shoulders so that his father could see him more plainly. She did so, and he struck himself with the feather which changed him into a rook, and he flew back to the lady in the city. The two got married and he brought his father and mother to live in their grand house where they lived very happily until their death.[ccviii]

Collected by Annie Donovan, Schull
From Mr John Murphy (aged 80), Schull

Mr Hull and the Fairies

Long ago, many people met fairies or people from the other world. There was a man in Gunpoint named Mikie Callaghan and he often met Mr Hull riding a white horse. One day he was at stations and a conversation arose between himself and the priest about Mr Hull. The priest said that he had fine times while he was here on earth. The man said that he had finer times now than ever he had. The priest asked him how he knew, and he said that he meets him very often around the green gate riding a white horse. "Do you think he has fine times?" said the priest. "I do", said the man. Then the priest asked him did he think he would ever see him again and he said he would. He told him to catch his bridle, but Mr O'Callaghan said that he would be afraid to do that. The priest gave him some blessed thing and the man promised him that he would tell him what happened. A few nights later he met Hull again at the green gate, riding the white horse. He caught the bridle and as soon as he did the whole thing went up in a blaze, Mr O'Callaghan's hand was burned, and he was blind for a good while. When he recovered he told the priest. The priest told him that he now knew if Mr Hull had fine times. [ccix]

From Michael Holland, Schull

Pushed by the Good People

Long ago it was a common thing for people to be with fairies. There was a man in Dunkelly whose right name was John Downey but who was called Johney Moisín (probably Mauirisín). People say that he was with the fairies. One day a girl from Dunmanus, named Annie Driscoll, was visiting her friend's house in Dunkelly, and in the evening they sent her to Goleen for messages and a bottle of whiskey. She took a near way home through a big meadow where some invisible person pushed her. She fell but before she did someone else caught her and held her back. She got a terrible fright, but she made her mind not to tell anybody. She went back with her messages and then went home. That night Mr Downey, who often paid them a visit, came in. The girl started joking him about being out so late. He said that it was a bad night for her to say anything to himself because when the fairies wanted to get the whiskey in the evening, he saved it for her. [ccx]

Collected by Kathleen McCarthy
From Mrs Catherine O'Driscoll (aged 93), Schull

Scrumping Apples

Another time a man called Thade Minihane went with another man to steal apples out of Hull's orchard. When they had the bag full, they went to the gate. They walked beyond the gate out over the wall. Then they walked another bit to get a place to come out. When they came back to where the bag was, every apple was chewed like a pig would chew them in the bag.[ccxi]

Rocking the Cradle

Before this school was built, there was a school in Rathoora, and there was a little girl from Lowertown who used to go to school every day. On her way she had to pass the fort and every morning an old woman came out of the fort and carried her in. She kept her all day rocking a cradle and when it was time to be going home from school, she left her home. After a long time, her parents found it out and they asked the advice of an old woman in the neighbourhood. She told them to wash the child with the water of many different kinds of herbs. They did and the child never met the old woman after.[ccxii]

From Thomas McCarthy, Schull

The Clothes of a Dead Man

Where Mr O'Donovan lives in Schull now, there once lived a man called Mr O'Sullivan. On Sunday he always wore a blue suit and a white shirt. The man died, and sometime after his wife, who was poor, sold his coat. Once evening when it was getting dark, a woman next door, named Mrs Goggin, was spreading clothes on a tree and when she turned round the man was standing behind her wearing blue pants and vest and a white shirt. She got a fright because she knew him. The man did not speak but disappeared at once. When she went in, she told the story and another woman told her that she saw him also. It is said that it is wrong for people to sell the clothes of their dead friends.[ccxiii]

From Mrs Goggin, Schull

Johny Downy and the Fairies

There was a man once living in Letter called Johny Downy. He was supposed to be going with the fairies. One day some people were going out fishing and he bargained some nuts for a share of the catch. They got a lot of fish but when they came ashore, they made up a plan to keep it all for themselves. Johny, who was about two miles away in his bed said, "Oh! The thieves robbing the poor man of his fish." When the people came up to the house the brother asked them was that what they made up and they said it was. It seems he had some power above nature.

Johny met a man one day and gave him a stick and told him not to let it go till he went inside his own door. The rest of the men joked about the stick, so he threw it over the fence. In the morning, he found himself in an old ruin about a mile away from his own house. It is said that the fairies kept him walking all night. Johny knew that in the morning, and he knew the place where he threw the stick.

When my uncle got a cut on his head, no one was allowed to see it but his father and the doctor from Cork. Johny said that there was no need to get the doctor. He said that the fairies carried him into the room and opened the bandages and showed him where the cut was. It is the truth I suppose for he was able to show the exact place where the cut was to another man.

Once, the protestant minister told Johny to become a protestant. He gave him new clothes and a donkey. Johny said that his donkey had no grass, so the minister gave him some and told him to go to church every Sunday ever more. He did not go next Sunday saying that the people were tormenting him, so he asked him for a gun, and Johny did not go next Sunday either, so the minister came to him and asked him why. Johny held up his gun and said, "I have a gun now to defend myself," and the minister ran for his life. Johny remained a catholic for the rest of his life.

It is said that Johny never used to drink milk. He always used to drink black tea.[ccxiv]

Collected by Maurice Anthony
From Florence O'Mahony, retold by John Downy, who died aged 80

Lowertown
People, places and Property

Local Heroes

When my grandfather was a young man long ago, a travelling man came to Schull every fair day and he offered a sum of money to anyone that would break a stone on his breast. Everyone there tried, but anyone couldn't do it. A man from Larne named Denis Mahony caught the sledge and with all his strength he gave the stone a blow and broke it. He was a strong man. There was another man named Jerry Callaghan living in Ballybrack long ago. One morning he went to the south side of the land to look for a wreck. He saw a big baulk[xvii] inside in a small strand, and he went down to tie a rope to it to pull it up. A big wave came in and carried him and the baulk off the rock into the sea. He couldn't swim, so he clung on to it and the next wave threw the two of them up on the rock again. He clung to the rock and brought the baulk with him and was saved. Another stormy night, a sailing ship came around the Mizen Head. Her sails were broken by the wind and her steering gear broken down, so she drifted along until she came to the Dollar Rocks. There she was smashed among the rocks and the people were dying on the rocks with the cold. The people from Gunpoint and Ballybrack got a boat and rowed up to them. When they got up there, they couldn't get near them because the sea was covered with wreckage, so some of the boat men tied ropes round their bodies and walked along until they came to the rock which the people were on. They picked up as many of the unconscious men as they could see and brought them to their boat. They rowed homed and when they came ashore in Gunpoint, they divided the men between the three houses in the eastern end of Gunpoint. Each man had five men and when they carried them to their houses, they fed them with oat-meal porridge, because that was the food was used by the people at that time. The men that came to Jerry Callaghan's house couldn't talk English very good, and when one of them had his plate of porridge eaten, he began to call for "more mungee".[xviii] Anyone of the people of the house didn't understand him, so one of the boys who was in the house said that perhaps he wanted more food so he filled another bowl of the porridge and gave it to him. He finished it and was satisfied. They then knew that it was food he wanted. The man that gave him the food was called "mungee" from that time until the day of his death.

The coast guards who were in Schull heard about them and they sent a car for them to Gunpoint.

[xvii] Baulk – a large square timber.

[xviii] It's likely that the sailors were French, 'mangee' being a phonetic representation of manger – to eat; the man wanted more to eat.

When they were leaving, they cried, and they shook hands with the people who saved them from the sea, and they said "Good Mothers" to the women that fed them. The crew that saved the men were:- John Donovan, Gunpoint, who was the captain; Jeremiah Donovan, captain's son, who was then sixteen years of age; Denis and Mike Callaghan, Gunpoint (brothers); Jim Callaghan, Gunpoint; Jim Sullivan, Ballybrack; and Denis Burke, Ballybrack.[ccxv]

Collected by Annie Donovan, Schull
From Mr Jeremiah Donavan (aged 97), Schull

Henry Sweetman – The Landlord

The landlords that were living in these districts were Hull and his followers, and Henry Sweetman and his followers. They were very hard on the people. It was then the road outside there and other roads were made. They had the men working for them, and eight pence a day each got, or a gallon of yellow meal. He [the worker] carried home the meal, and his wife, himself, and his children made yellow meal gruel out of it. That is all they had to rear them, and a lot of them died with hunger. Hull's descendants are all gone, but Henry Sweetman's are remaining. They are called Luke's, and they are living in Cove.

One day a little boy went eating green stalks and potatoes out of a field in Henry's with hunger. Henry caught him and cracked his legs and threw him into a drain. The name of the boy was Cronin. He was inside in the drain there roaring until Bill John heard him. He was carrying butter to the market for John Joe Daily when he saw him. Bill John reported him, and he was put to jail. He should learn the child shoemaking and start a shoe-maker's house for him. He had to buy him leather for him first until he was able to buy it himself. The child grew up, but his legs were twisted. He made a good living in shoemaking after that. When Henry came out of jail, he had like to kill Bill John for telling on him. Henry was put into jail again. When he was let free, he held no other chance, and if he ever again was caught, he would be hung. I tell you he kept quiet after that then until the day he died. He was an agent for Fisher.[ccxvi]

Collected by James Anthony Hayes, Schull
From Mr Timothy Hayes (aged 68), Schull

James McCarthy - Agent

Where George McCormick lived in Goleen there once lived an agent. His name was James McCarthy. His brother Florence was agent for this district, and he was living where the dispensary is now. Any time they wanted to do anything they sent for five or six men and they should go. At the time for digging potatoes, James sent for some men from his district. One man that went was Tom Leary who was living where Charles McCarthy is living now in Gurranes. He was only sixteen years at that time, and he was not able to keep up to the rest of the men digging. In his hurry he left one stalk after him. Old James saw it and he sent Tom back to dig it. He said somebody would want what was under it before the year was out. Tom did, and when he turned around after digging it old James was dead behind it.[ccxvii]

Collected by Kathleen McCarthy, Schull
From Thomas McCarthy (aged 64), Schull

Lahorn Townland

Lahorn is situated southwest of Leimcon. There are only two families living there and the number of people is eleven. Some of the present people that are living there call it Castlepoint on account of the castle being situated on the western point of it. In that district also there is a blessed well. In olden days a priest came visiting to that place, he blessed that well and said that from that day on, anyone who had anything wrong with them if they used the water would get cured. The old people, if they had a pain in their backs or any other illness, would go to the well and rub the water to the part of them that wasn't well, or sometimes they would drink the water. They would then tie a bit of rag to the briars that are growing around the well. They would come to the well then, a certain number of days after, and do the same thing. Some people say that the water in the well wouldn't boil at all.

In the western side of that townland also there is a castle. Some people say that it was built by robbers and whatever they plundered they stored it up there. More say it was built by the O'Mahoneys to keep a watch on the coast for they were afraid the English would land there.[ccxviii]

Collected by Timothy Regan
From Mrs Mahony (aged 78), Schull

Hidden Treasure

People say that there is copper hidden in Ballybrack. There lived in Ballybrack once a man named James Donovan. When he heard that the copper was hidden there, he got a candle because there was not any electric lights then, and he went down into the hole. When he was a good way down, he found stone steps and he carried on walking on the steps for a while. Some people say that a man was below, and he quenched the candle. Others say that the candle quenched in want of air. When it quenched, he had to grope his way back again. Anymore attempts were not made to get at the copper. There is a small field there and when the same man was ploughing that field, he found rows of stones all along the field and he stopped ploughing because he thought that there were coffins there. The old people saw the leprechaun there long ago. The old people say that a passage is going under the ground west to the castle, and they say that there is wine hidden in the cellars under the castle. The people that lived in the castle long ago got wine and fruits in from foreign lands and they hid them from the English under the castle.

There is another deep hole with a flat stone over it near the passage in Ballybrack and long-ago young boys threw stones into it. They heard the stones falling down for a long time. That is covered now fearing anyone would fall in there. Another day, two boys named Jerry Brien and John Hosford were minding cows near the hole. They threw big stones into the hole. A big white cat about as big as a dog came up and followed them nearly to their houses.[ccxix]

Collected by Annie Donovan, Schull
From Mrs John Donavan (aged 88), Schull

Lowertown

The meaning of Lowertown is the townland where the herbs grow. There is very good land in it. There is a river in it called the Lowertown river which flows beyond the school east and flows into Croagh harbour. There are a number of Protestant families in it. Three Levis's, two Pyburns, one King, and a Roycroft. A Barnett and a Driscoll family and two Daly families live by the sea. There are two other catholic families in it; a Moynihan and a Roycroft family.

In years gone by there was a post office. This was done away with when our native government came into existence. This place is in complete ruins now. There is only one gable standing now. There is a school in it too.

It is a two-teacher school. About a quarter of a mile away from the school the teacher's residence was. There is an old fort in Mr Levis's land. Not far from this there is a cill. Lots of people were buried here in the famine times. Some families are still buried there; Graham's, Lucey's and a Callaghan family.

At the south side of the land there is an old building which was a wheat store in olden times when the farmers sold their wheat to pay the rent. It was kept there for exportation. In the famine times it was turned into a workhouse for the poor people who were dying with the fever.

This townland was part of the Hull estate and was bought out by one of the early land acts. The priest in Goleen held several meetings in Lowertown school which catholics and protestants attended. He was chiefly instrumental in having the land bought out. His name was Father O'Callaghan.

There is only one old lady in it who can tell old stories of incidents that occurred in the district. Her name is Miss Daly.[ccxx]

Collected by Mary P. O. Mahony, Schull
From Miss Daly (aged 70), Lowertown

Croagh: My Home District

The name of my townland is Croagh. Some say it got its name from a horseshoe for its shape is like a horseshoe. It is a peninsula. The sea lies north, west, and east of it. There are only three farms in it, Mr O'Driscoll's, Mr Kingston's, and Mr O'Mahony's. Mr O'Mahony's farm is the biggest farm in it. On the south side near the strand there are numerous old ruins. Around every one of these ruins there is a small garden but all the other fields in the farm are very large. This looks like these were houses of workmen and the garden was the plot they got. Mr O'Mahony was the first catholic owner of this place. The land is supposed to be very good there. Wheat was grown extensively there in olden times.

At the south side there is a Cill. Not far from that there was a coast guard station long ago. There is none of that now. Near Mr O'Mahony's house there is a fort. It is an earthen one. There is only one wall around it. There is a doorway in the eastern side. This fort is very near the sea and from that Mr O'Mahony's house is called 'Seafort'. There is a pier in the north side. From this pier a lot of wheat was exported in days gone by. The wheat was dried in a Kill convenient to the pier. The ruins of this are still to be seen. Mr Brown was the name of the man who owned the land and bought the wheat exportation. It is said that a priest once visited his house to enquire about a catholic workman he had, and that Mr Brown slammed the door in his face.

The priest wiped his feet on the mat outside the door and said, "that before long Croagh would be seen without Brown." He was true for there is no 'Brown' there now. There are only two people living in Mr O'Driscoll's house, himself and his sister. There are six people in Mr Kingston's house, four children, the man, and his wife. There are no old people in the townland. A river separates Croagh from Gubbeen.[ccxxi]

Collected by Mary P. O'Mahony
From Mr O'Mahony (aged 40), Schull

Leimcon: My Home District

The name of the townland in which I live is Leimcon. They say that it got that name on account of the jump of the hound. They say that in olden days a hound gave a jump from Cenn Conn, a mile to the east, to Leimcon. In olden days the old people called that townland Carraig a Leim. The cause of them giving it that name was on account of a flight of steps that is going down a hill, west of our house. There are six families here; two Callaghans, one Donovan, one Cowhig, one O'Regan. There are two old people. One is seventy-three years and the older seventy-four years. It is English they speak, and they can tell stories in English. The man, named Mr Cowhig, is living in the residence where Mr Hull the landlord lived, and we are living in the house where Mr Hull's agent lived. His name was Mr Sweetman. That was the second biggest farm in Leimcon. The other three people were from Gunpoint and they bought the ground in which they live from Mr Hull. The old people say that he went out hunting one morning with his horse and hound. The first thing he started was a hare. The hound kept after the hare around the field the whole day. When nightfall came the hare broke out on the road and the hound kept after him east the road, each of them were so worn out that neither of them could not make any odds on the other. In that way the hare escaped. Before the hound reached home, he fell dead, and that was what Mr Hull had by his day's hunting. When the people that have it now bought it, they had to ditch it and divide it up between them.[ccxxii]

Collected by Timothy Regan
From Mr William Regan, Schull

Ardravinna: My Home District

The name of the district in which I live is "Ardravinna". This portion of land is elevated and at either side of it is a bog, and this is how it got its name. There are twenty families living in it, and each family bears a different name. There are eleven catholic families and nine protestant families in it. There are seventy-three people living there altogether, forty-four protestants and twenty-nine catholics. There are very few old people there. The only people over eighty are John Roycroft and his brother Edward, and Mrs O'Driscoll. None of these people can speak Irish but they can tell stories in English. The majority of the houses are slated and cemented on the outside. There are two iron covered houses and two thatched houses in the townland. Mr Ferguson has a shop there also. There are a few old ruins to be seen still, and this proves to us that there were more people living there long ago than there is now. There are four ruins in Mr Wilcox's ground. There is an old ruin in Robert King's ground, and one in Miss Hegarty's ground also. It is said that a man called Collins lived there. There is an old ruin in front of our house and a man called "Gorman" lived there. He lived alone and he owned half the farm that we own now. When he was getting old, he sold his farm and went to live with his brother in Tipperary. My Grandfather bought the land then. Nearly all the old people that live in Ardravinna were in America. Until emigration was stopped, one is as much as would stay in any house. They all went to America and then sent home money to help their parents. The land in Ardravinna is very bad, all bogs and rocks. No one there can grow wheat. In the penal times when the people paid their rent with wheat, they had to pay with money. They nearly all got that money from their people in America.

Long ago there were many craftsmen living in Ardravinna, and some of them are still living. There was a forge where John Wilcox is living now. There was a thatcher there whose name was Baker and there was a carpenter whose name was Baker also. Where Mr Bowen is living now there once lived a lady whose name was Coppinger. She always kept a good supply of whiskey. All the neighbours went there every night playing cards, and if they took her anything such as potatoes or anything, she would give them whiskey. One night they took her potatoes and gave out three half pints of whiskey. They drank the whiskey and then went playing cards. About twelve o'clock they fell out over the cards, and they beat each other. It was about one o'clock when they left the house. One man whose way to come home would be to come beyond the chapel was afraid to pass the chapel so late in the night on account of the row. So, he came down the road and went up the old road. When he was near the place where the mass rock, was he met a man. He told him that he was not fit to meet the people that were coming, on account of the row he had, and he told him to go inside the fence for a while. The man did and he said that the biggest funeral he ever saw passed. Ever since the field is called "the field of the dead".[ccxxiii]

Collected by Kathleen McCarthy
From Thomas McCarthy (aged 64), Schull

Dreenane Townland

That townland is so called because every ditch in it is covered with blackthorn trees, both sloes and haws. There are only three families now. Tim Mahony owns most of the land lives there with his wife and four children. Andrew Donoghue lives alone and is aged seventy-two years, and Maggie Mahony lives with her mother who is aged ninety-two years. In Mr Hull's time there were twenty families. The people were very poor tthen and Mr Hull went beyond his limit in generosity. He went to a merchant in Cork and ordered clothes and food for them. He gave it to them several times, but when the merchant wanted his money, Mr Hull hadn't money to pay him. He sent his deputy to Dreenane to all the people who got the goods to go to Schull to sign a document to pay fifty pounds between every three houses. They dared not refuse, or if they did, they were put out of their homes. They all signed and paid what they could, but some gave up in despair and went off to America. Then Fr Holland came to Goleen. When he saw the state the Catholics were in, he went to Cork and interceded with the merchant and brought the balance down to thirty-six pounds each, and the remaining people paid that.

If Mr Hull wanted an urgent message, he was sure to rely on the Dreenane people because that was his nearest place, and Dreenane was persecuted by him. He would order them to go to Skibbereen or Bantry in the middle of the night for a message. My great-grandfather, Denis Mahony, who was living in Dreenan at that time, was sowing wheat one day. In the evening the sky looked rainy, and he was trying to sow the wheat as quick as he could. Who should come into the field to him but Mr Hull's deputy called "Dan the nailer" to tell him to go off to Skibbereen on a message. The man said that he couldn't go that day at all. The deputy said, "very well" and went away and told Mr Hull his story. Next day Denis Mahony got a notice to be out of his home and land in three day's time. He went down to Lemcon to Mr Hull to ask pardon for offending him, and he had to go down on his two knees before him and make a resolution not to offend him again. The people of Dreenane also had to sow the crops and dig them for him, cut the turf and draw it home to the door for him, and cut the weeds and furze for him without any pay or food. When he was dead and gone, the people of Dreenane weren't sorry for him.

At dusk one summer's evening when the women were driving out their cows, they heard as they thought a baby's cry coming from the northeast to them. Next it changed to a young donkey braying, and next it changed to a lion's roar. Everyone ran for their houses, and barred the doors, and the men stood at the doors with pikes in their hands to defend themselves. They thought it was a lion that escaped from a menagerie that was visiting Schull at that time. They saw nothing and the roaring continued and passed them by, until it reached Lemcon lake where it plunged in and wasn't seen or heard of since, and the Dreenane people said that it was Mr Hull's spirit was coming back to be doomed for ever in his own lake for the punishment he gave them. The menagerie in Schull was traced up and there wasn't any animal missing.

The old people in Dreenane were educated because they had hedge schools in the penal times. Two hedge schools were in Tim Mahony's two fields in top of Ceann Conn called "Finne". Another was in later years in a house in Dreenane which his now used as a cow house by Tim Mahony. A man named Bourke was a teacher in that school. There is also another relic of the penal days in Andrew Donoghue's field. It is the mass rock where the priests said mass on long ago when they couldn't say it anywhere else because they would be put to death by the protestants.

Dreenane is also famous for its tower which visitors visit every summer to see from it all the coast around. They were as signals along the coast. That tower could signal to three towers along the coast – Sheep's Head tower, Malabhóg tower in Crookhaven, and Baltimore tower – when they saw any enemy coming.

In winter, when the ground was covered with snow, the rooks Mr Hull had couldn't get any food, so he ordered the people of the surrounding district to strip their pits of potatoes so that the rooks could eat them. He had no thought whatsoever of what themselves would have for the year, although the potato was the only food, they had for themselves. There was one man in Dreenane named Charles MacCarthy and he had ten baskets of carpink potatoes once,[xix] and he didn't want to let them go to the rooks so he buried them all level with the ground, and anyone wouldn't know that there would be anything under the ground. But alas when he went for them, they were all rotten and he hadn't any potato then.[ccxxiv]

Collected by Annie Donovan
From Mrs John Donovan (aged 88), Schull

[xix] Carpink potatoes - probably Kerr pink potatoes.

Ballybrack Townland

Some people say that that townland got its name from all the houses that were in it long ago, and others say that it was from the white rocks that are there. In that land there were once twelve families, but there is but one descendant of them there now whose name is Timmie Breen. There lived there a Driscoll man and a Cadogan man, both from Cape Clear. There was a family named Brien, a family named Hosford, a family named Brown, and a family named Driscoll, and the remaining families were all Donovans. They had very little land because there were so many families there and the townland was small. They were very poor and when the young people grew up, they went to America to earn money, and the old people died. The Gunpoint people bought the land, and the farmers there now have bigger farms because there are only three farmers there now. They are Dan Hegarty, James Murphy, and Timothy Sullivan. There is a passage underground in one field there which was owned by Micky Donovan. Once he lit a candle and went down the passage. He found stone steps going down, and all of a sudden, he imagined that a man stood before him. His light quenched. He took to his heels, and no one entered in there since.

In olden times the people of Ballybrack made their living by fishing. They were fishing in the Cape Clear boats and in the Long Island boats.[ccxxv]

Collected by Annie Donovan
From Mr Jeremiah Donovan (aged 97), Schull

My Home District – Gunpoint

The name of my townland is Gunpoint. It is so called because in Mr Hull's time, when he was the owner of this district, he mounted two great guns at the eastern point. In it there are six families; two Donovan families, two Callaghan families, one Sullivan family and one Murphy family. All the old people can speak a little Irish and can tell good English stories. The oldest person there is Jeremiah Donovan who is aged ninety-seven years. The next oldest is Mrs Callaghan who is his sister and is aged ninety-six years. The next oldest is Mrs John Donovan who is aged eighty-one years, followed by John Murphy who is seventy-eight years. The last person is Kerry Callaghan who is aged seventy-one years. All the houses are big, white, and slated now. But long ago the houses were small and had straw roofs on them. Those houses are used for animals. Long ago there was a lot more people in Gunpoint. But now a big number of them are gone to America, and others are gone to other parts of the country. There are only thirty-six people now between young and old. The land is dry and suitable for crops such as wheat, oats, barley, and potatoes. Every farmer can keep over six cows and a horse. Long ago the people there were poor and it was by fishing they made their living. It is out of the land they are making their living now because there isn't any fish in the coast around them.

Long ago a man was drowned at Croagh. He was missing over a week and was found in a strand in the middle of Gunpoint by a man named Mike Callaghan. It was late in the evening, so they wrapped him in a white sheet and buried him in the field opposite the strand where he was found. His people came for him, but they wouldn't give him for they said that if a dead person was found in a strand that he should be buried opposite that strand and not carried out of that townland, or if he was, three people would die out of it that year. There is a stone over his grave which is still to be seen, and the Callaghans would be afraid to pass that in the night, fearing they would meet him as they didn't give him to his owners.[ccxxvi]

Collected by Annie Donovan
From Mr Jeremiah Donovan (aged 97), Schull

Local Place Names

Páirċ fada:	Because it is a long narrow field.[xx]
Gan na carraige:	Because there are not rocks or stones on it.[xxi]
Poll:	Because it is a rich sunken field.[xxii]
Páirċ an tobar:	Because there is a well in that field.[xxiii]
Poll a lín:	Because it was there the flax was bogged long ago.[xxiv]
Páirċ garb:	Because it is a rough field with little rocks.[xxv]
Acre:	Because there is an acre of ground in it.
Páirċhín Cunningham:	Because a man named Cunningham lived there.
Cnocán Mór:	Because there is a big cnocán in it.[xxvi]
Cúl staighre:	Because it is rising up like a stairs.[xxvii]
Breakeen:	Because there is furze growing in it.[xxviii]
Páirċhín na gcloch:	Because there is a lot of big stones sunk in it.[xxix]
Daniel Haye's Garden:	Because a man named Daniel Hayes lived.
Páirċ na loc:	Because that's where Lemcon Lake is situated.[xxx]
Boathouse field:	Because it was there Mr Hull had his boat long ago.
Forge field:	Because there was a forge there long ago.
Dead man's field:	Because long ago there were races in that field, and a man was running down the hill that is in it. He fell and was killed in the spot.
Dick's Island:	Long ago the people of the castle went out, and any pirate they caught they brought them and kept them in the castle. They brought one person whom they didn't like, so they put him into that Island and left him to die there.
Ceann Conn:	Because long ago, when Fionn MacCuail came to this district hunting, he came as far as Ceann Conn. He had a lot of hounds and one of them couldn't see any

[xx] *Páirċ fada* – long fields.
[xxi] *Gan na carriage* – without the rock.
[xxii] *Poll* – hole.
[xxiii] *Páirċ an tobar* - Fields of the well.
[xxiv] *Poll a lín* – flax hole.
[xxv] *Páirċ garb[h]* – rough fields.
[xxvi] *Cnocán Mór* – big hillock.
[xxvii] *Cúl [possibly Cúil] staighre* – stair corner or nook.
[xxviii] *Breakeen [probably Beakeen (An Béicín)]* – translation unclear.
[xxix] *Páirċín na gcloċ [cloch]* - Stone fields.
[xxx] *Páirċ na loc* – Lake fields.

	way to go, so he gave a big jump and stopped at Lemcon Lake.
Cúl tráig:	Because it is a lone strand in among the rocks away from every other strand.[xxxi]
Cuas a' púca:	Because it is said that the fairies are there.[xxxii]
Cuas mór:	Because there is a big cliff over it.[xxxiii]
Cuas gorm:	Because the water below in it is blue.[xxxiv]
Cuas a' dá béal:	Because there are two openings or mouths in it.[xxxv]
Faill na briadac:	Because the black raven sits on the rock there.
Cuas a' capall:	Because a dead horse came in there long ago.
Cuas dgainm:	Because there is sand below in it.
Castle cuas:	Because the castle is built on that cuas.[ccxxvii]
Pairce an play:	In olden times that was a field where sports and games were played.
Barrack field:	An English barrack was built in that field.
Mick's hill:	An old man named Mick grew early potatoes there.
Outclitts:	These are long strips of fields, that you would see when you would go to the Lahorn castle over the sea.
Tráig na Cearcín:	The water hen is supposed to be seen in that strand.
Poll a mharcarg:[xxxvi]	A horseman and his horse fell down that hole and were killed.
Cathaoir: [xxxvii]	That is a rock in Dunleary, the shape of a chair in which the people sit when they are fishing the fish called conners.
Poinnte Reamhar: [xxxviii]	That is a thick chunk of land that is sticking out in the sea at Castlepoint. [ccxxviii]
Dreenane:	Where the Draighean (the black thorn) grows.
Lemcon:	The leap of the hound. Fionn's hound is supposed to have made leap over this place.
Ballybrack:	Where numerous little houses were long ago.
Gubbeen:	point or bill of land sticking out like a bird's beak.

[xxxi] *Cúl tráig* – Back strand
[xxxii] Cuas a' púca – Fairy cove.
[xxxiii] Cuas mór – Big cove.
[xxxiv] Cuas gorm – Blue cove.
[xxxv] Cuas a' dá béal – cove with two mouths
[xxxvi] *Poll a mharcarg* – Carcass hole.
[xxxvii] *Cathaoir* – Chair.
[xxxviii] *Poinnte Reamhar* – Thick-part point.

Lowertown:	the herb garden where numerous herbs grow used for cures.
Caheravirane:	'Cathair', a stone fort of Uí Bhriarain.
Knoc, 'Cnon':	a hilly town land.
Caher caska:	the stone fort that was burned.
Derryleary:	the oak wood of Leary.
Larne:	half a town land.
Lissacaha, 'Liosachatha':	The fort where the battle was fought.
The Cill field:	a field where an old graveyard is.
The fort field:	a field where an old house of the Irish was.
Gáirdín na uball:	where there was an orchard long ago.
Gáirdín na mealla:	the field where the hives were kept long ago.
Gort an uisce:	a wet field.
Trág nanama:	where a person was drowned.
Kilpatrick:	Patrick's little church.
Gort na móna:	the field where the turf was got.
Glaun:	a glen between two mountains.
Toormore, 'Tuar mór':	a big sheltry field where cattle are kept at night.
Rathura, 'Rath tuara':	a big sheltry field where a fort was.
Tooreen, 'Tuairín':	a small sheltry field where cattle are kept at night.[ccxxix]
Black field:	So called because when the blackberry time comes the berries are always plentiful in that field.
The ivy cliff:	because there is a rock in the middle of the field and it's covered with ivy.
The menineachs:	because it is all cliffs.
The currac:	It's a marshy field.
The coulach field:	because there is an old ruin in it. [ccxxx]

Collected by Annie Donovan, Timothy Regan,
Mary P. O'Mahony, and Eileen McCarthy, Schull

LOWERTOWN

Farming, Trade and Crafts

The Linen Industry

In Ireland long ago there was several industries carried on in the homesteads. They helped home industry and helped to give the Irish people a living instead of the foreigner. The stuff made in Ireland was a lot more durable and lasting than that from foreign countries. Only one of the industries carried on in this district was the linen industry. There were several people engaged in this industry in this locality, but the one I heard about was a woman named Mrs Hayes Beaheen. She and her family used grow the flax in the same class of ground as you would sow wheat, rich fertile ground. They sowed the seed in spring. In the end of July or the first of August the flax would blossom. The colour of the blossom was blue. When the blossoms would fall off, the flax was ripe and fit for cutting. As soon as they had the flax cut, they made it into thaweens or bundles. They then carried them to a bog, and put them into the bog hole, and laid stone on top of them to make the flax tough. It was taken out then and dried. After that they took it up and carried it home. They pounded it then with a thurgeen. It was then hackled to get off the fibres with a hackle. After this it was made smooth and clear with a chiloes. It was then made into skeins and put in the end of a stick. The thread on the end of the stick was then attached to the spinning wheel. The spindle was then put on in which the thread must go round. The wheel was then twisted with the right hand and the thread was drawn back with the left hand. It was then made into spools. After that it was warped. How that was done was to have two sticks and twist the thread around whatever length you'd want the piece of linen to be. The thread was then ready to send to the weaver. He used to make tablecloths, sheets, towels, and shirts, or whatever they would want out of it. The name of the weaver then was a man named Mr Crosston from Durrus.[ccxxxi]

Collected by Timothy C. Regan, Schull
From William Regan (aged 56), Schull
(Information received from his father, Thomas Regan, deceased)

Nail Making

There wasn't any nails made in Ireland long ago, and so the smiths of the locality made them themselves. The man who made them for this district was Mac Donell. He had a small forge in Schull near where Mr Whitley lives now. He had a number of different shapes, one for horseshoe nails, one for boat nails, and one for iron nails and many other shapes. Whatever kind of nails a person wanted, he heated a piece of iron in the fire, and put it into the shape, and beat it until he had it into whatever shape he wanted.[ccxxxii]

Collected by Annie Donovan, Schull
From Mrs John Donavan (aged 88), Schull

Skiff Making

In this district long ago skiff making was done very much. The first they used do was to get a bundle of green twigs and out of that bundle they would pick the two thickest rods. Then they would fasten one rod on to the other and make them round. They used put it near the fire then for a week until it hardened, and they used to call that part of the skiff the bowgh. The next thing they'd do is to put twigs from one end of the bowgh to the other, and they call them the ribs of the skiff. Then they get thin little twigs, and they put those in and out between the ribs and they continue that until the skiff is made. It is very few that can make skiffs now. They aren't used at all. Long ago they got a lot of money for those skiffs. The man that used to make those skiffs most in this district was John Murphy and he lives in Gunpoint. Those skiffs were used for holding potatoes long ago. They were in boats too, for holding fish. The old people would never give those skiffs to anybody for nothing because they considered it unlucky. Those twigs are very scarce now because people make no used of them and they grew into thick sticks and no use can be made out of them.[ccxxxiii]

Collected by Mary K. Sullivan, Schull
From John Sullivan (aged 56), Schull

Basket Making

Basket making isn't done hardly now at all. The first thing they do is to stand four twigs on the ground. Then they get three rods and wind them around those four twigs. They call that part of the basket the buinnes. Then they get eighteen twigs and wind in them in threes around the four rods until it is made, and they call that window making of the basket. Before they finish it off, they get three thick twigs to put around the top of it and they call that the buinne too. The one that had made these baskets most in this district was Tom Sullivan and he lived in Ballybrack. They used carry those baskets on their backs with heavy loads in them, such as potatoes, mangolds, turnips, and grass. The old people used always keep four or five of these baskets in their houses, because they considered them very useful.[ccxxxiv]

From John Sullivan (aged 56), Schull

Candle Making

Long ago there wasn't any candles made in Ireland, and so the people had to make candles themselves. When the people killed a sow, or if a sow died, they took out all her fat and melted it in a pan. When it was melted, they picked out all the lumps of fat that wouldn't melt and kept them for some other use. They had a long round piece of iron, empty in the middle, called the mould. They plugged one end and fastened the wick to it by a nail. They pulled the wick out the other side of it and kept it in the centre of the mould by supporting it with a stick across the centre of the mouth of it. The wick was made by platting three linen threats together. When all was fixed, they filled the mould with the melted lard out of the pipe of a tea pot. They let it set for a day or two, and then they heated the mould to the fire, and the candle slipped out. The only difference in those candles was that they were a yellower colour than the candles that are selling now.[ccxxxv]

Collected by Annie Donovan, Schull
From Mrs John Donavan (aged 88), Schull

Wooden Vessels

Long ago the people hadn't any cups, only timber ones. There was a man called the Turner, living in Dreenane, who made them for all the district around. He made vessels that would hold two quarts, with one handle in it. They were call 'Piggins' and they were used for drawing water and milking. He made timber cups, saucers, plates, and jugs, and everyone's dresser at that time was full of timber vessels. These vessels were called mórnáns. They were very hard to keep clean. There isn't any of those to be seen now. [ccxxxvi]

Collected by Annie Donovan
From Mrs John Donovan (aged 88), Schull

Thatching

Forty or fifty years ago there were no slated or iron covered houses in this district. It was all thatch, so thatchers were kept busy. Every house should be thatched every winter so that all during the winter the thatcher would be busy working and earning money. The houses were thatched with straw or sometimes with rushes. A thatcher always had two ladders, a long one and a short one. The long one is from the ground up to the roof and the short one is always used up on the roof. He has a thatching muddle and thread and thin cord to fasten the straw to the rafters inside. The needle is used to put the threat through the straw which is worked up and down from the bottom of the rood to the top. When he has one baye finished, he comes down and moves the ladder on to the next baye. The only thatcher who is still living in this district is George Baker. He does not get much work to do now because there are only a few thatched houses in this district.[ccxxxvii]

Collected by Kathleen McCarthy
From George Baker (aged 68), Schull

Churning

Long ago the people had a different way of making butter from what they have now. They had a small churn, wide at the bottom and narrowing at the top. There was a cover in the top, and a hole in the middle of it. There was a stick inside in the hole, and when the cream was put in, they turned the stick around and that would beat the cream, and in that way make their butter. The old people had charms also. Some people say that they would carry the butter from their neighbours. In May morning if they wanted to take butter from anyone, they went out and milked their cows. They also had special prayers to say on that occasion. They had pisógs also, and they wouldn't give anything to another belonging to their cows. Once my grandfather went to a man in Larne called Denis Mahony for a bundle of plants. He forgot to carry a rope, so Denis Mahony gave him one and it was the spancel[xxxix] he had for tying the cows. When he went to milk his cows, he missed the rope and he ran after my grandfather until he overtook him on the way, gave him another rope, and took back the spancel for fear he would carry away his milk. They had more pisógs also that when a person was making butter, if any person came in, he should say "God bless your work: and catch the handle and twist it a few times.

There was a woman living in Ballybrack once named Mrs Daly. She couldn't make any butter. There was another woman living near her, and she had plenty, so she thought that the other woman was taking hers. One day she was picking sticks, and in the field in which she was there was a big pool. Who should be there but the other woman, and she had the spancel that she stole from Mrs Daly. She had it caught at each end, and she was gumping up and down in the water, and splashing the water on herself, and repeating over and over again, seó, seó bóiricín.[xl] Then she knew that it was she was carrying the butter and that they were the words she had.

There was another woman in Dunmanus named Mrs Goggin. She didn't make any butter for three years. She had all the blame on her neighbour, because she knew that she was carrying the butter, and she couldn't stop her. One day there was a priest passing the field in which the cows of that women were in. He saw her neighbour milking one of the cows. He listened and he heard her repeating strange words. He went on his journey without molesting her. Weeks went on and Mrs Goggin couldn't make any butter, so she went to the priest. He remembered the other woman and the words she said. He said

---

[xxxix] Spancel – a noosed rope.

[xl] Seó, seó bóiricín literally translates as 'show, show, bow-legged person'.

those words again and when the woman went home, she made her butter, and she had a pile of it. In a few weeks after, the other woman went to the priest with the complaint that she couldn't make any butter. The priest said that he would be going to her house soon as it was, she was going to have the stations and that he would settle between them. The day of the stations he blessed each of their cows, and from that day on, each person her own lot of butter.[ccxxxviii]

Collected by Annie Donovan
From Mr Jeremiah Donovan (aged 97), Schull

It often happened long ago that some people could make no butter. There was an agent living in Goleen whose name was McCarthy. He had a lot of cows and yet he could make no butter. There was another woman living in Dunkelly and she had only three cows, but she had an enormous amount of butter. One day, an unknown man came into the agent's house and he told him that every night at twelve o'clock there was a woman in his dairy taking his milk, and every day at twelve o'clock she was in the field with the cows. Next day he went to watch, and at twelve o'clock the woman came. She walked around the field and put her hand on every cow. After that she went away. That night the unknown man visited the agent again. He told him to go away and get a big white stone and to put it in the middle of the field, and to go and sit there at twelve o'clock the following day. He also told him some magic which he should say when he saw the woman coming. The woman came and she said the same words as the man said. Then she took a ball of thread out of her pocket. She caught the end of the ball and left the rest of it fly away with the wind. The unknown man told that agent that if he could catch the thread without moving from where he was, he would be able to make his own butter from that day out. He also told him that if he did not catch the thread that day, he could not go again until that day the following year. But, if he caught the thread that day, the woman would be compelled to pay back what she had got through the devil. The women spent about two hours in the field throwing out the thread and winding if back again. In the end the man caught the thread. When the woman wound up the ball again, the man kept the end caught until he was quite near her. Then she confessed that it was she who had been taking his butter all along and in payment gave him two of her cows.[ccxxxix]

Collected by Kathleen McCarthy
From John O'Driscoll (deceased 1887m aged 90), Dunmanus

There was a parish priest in Caheragh once called Father Wall. He was going to the stations one May morning and as they were not far off, he went across the fields. As he approached the fence of one field, he saw an old woman, a farmer's wife and heard her talk. He stood behind the fence to listen and heard her incantations re her neighbour's butter. To satisfy himself if she would get it, he said to himself that "I may get half of it." A year passed by, and he called the stations for the neighbour whose butter was looked for. At the breakfast table he asked the woman of the house about how much butter she made during the year, and she said she made nothing in comparison with what she made the previous year, that everything went against her. He asked this woman in the morning to ask her neighbour to have breakfast with them, so she was listening to the conversation. He asked the neighbour about how much butter she had. She was able to boast how much more she made that year than the previous year. The increase in his own corresponded with the increase of the neighbour and he arranged there and then, in the presence of the culprit, to pay the woman what he gained out of her butter, and the culprit had to do likewise.[ccxl]

Collected by Mary P. O'Mahony, Schull
From Jeremiah Hegarty (deceased 1934, aged 78), Lowertown

LOWERTOWN
Local Customs

Sheebeens

Long ago the old people bought tobacco and whiskey, and sold it again to make profit. There were four of these people in this area. One of them whose name was Mary Regan lived in Gunpoint in an old house, now owned by Mike Donovan. She sold whiskey without any license, and all the old people bought it as they all liked whiskey, and she made a little money in that way to keep herself. There was another one in Ballybrack who sold tobacco and made a little money on that also. His name was Paul Bourke. There was a third in Beakeen named Paul Coursey. He also sold tobacco without a license, and he made a little profit on it. The was another old woman living in Lowertown in a small little house, and she also sold tobacco. There were a big number of young lads in Dreenane and Lowertown during that time, and they were all eager for a smoke. They hadn't any money to buy tobacco from this old woman, and so when they went for the tobacco, they always carried potatoes or something to her, and it pleased her. One day they met the old woman coming home from Schull with tobacco, and they said to her that they would go to her house that night and carry a half bag of potatoes for tobacco. She told them to go, and they all went that night. They thought of a plan, to put one of the boys into a bag and close the mouth of it. The boy went in, and when they went to the house, they put the bag up in the corner to the old woman. She was delighted to get all the potatoes and she gave them plenty of tobacco all night. When the time came to go home, they gave the signal to the lad in the bag and he gave a jump up and down the floor, for he knew she would strike him with something. When she saw him and knew what she had, she caught a big slat that was near the fire and threw it at him. He just escaped it, and if it hit him it would kill him dead. They all ran and left her alone scolding. The rest of the lads didn't give him any of the tobacco and they had a row on the way home about it. The houses in which the tobacco and whisky were sold were called Shebeens.[ccxli]

Collected by Annie Donovan
From Mr Jeremiah Donovan (aged 97), Schull

Lowertown
Local Cures

Local Cures

Toothache:	The person who got a toothache had to search until they found a dead frog, and they rubbed the dead frog on the tooth, and it was cured. Another cure for toothache is to take a pinch of grass off a grave and rub it to the tooth.
Consumption:	Garlic was picked and boiled, and the water was given to the person who had consumption, and he was cured. Garlic grew wild and it was very plentiful around here, but now it can hardly be found at all.
Bad stomach:	Everybody who had a bad stomach went to a man in Dunmanus called Patrick Dennis and he cured them. He boiled the blossoms of a tree with tobacco and the roots of garlic and gave the water to the people who went to him to drink. Many other people tried this but failed and the old people say that he mixed some other unknown stuff in the drink also.
Rheumatism:	Mrs Camier's son in Lissacaha once got crippled with rheumatism and he was only eight years of age. She went to a man in Gortnamona called John Leahy. He told her to get a meal bag and to fill it with blades of grass, flowers, blossoms of furze, leaves of trees, and briars, and a part of everything, and when she got home to boil them, and then to wash the child with the water and in three days he would be alright. She did this and in three days the child was alright. Another cure for rheumatism was to boil wild sage and to drink the water.
Headache:	In olden days people usually went to holy wells to cure a headache. One of these was in Rathoora and there was another in Larne.
Warts:	A great cure for these was to wash them in water that would be on a fresh cowdung on a summer's morning.
Corns:	Corns were drawn out by laying penny leaves down on them and leaving them for two nights.[ccxlii]

Collected by Kathleen McCarthy, Schull
From Thomas McCarthy, Schull

Pains or broken ribs:	Boil wild sage and dandelion and drink the juice that would come out of them.
Thrush or a sore throat:	They say that snails were to be got fastened to the walls of the Lahorn castle, and if you picked them with a pin the sticky stuff would come out of them would cure thrush or a sore throat.
Whooping cough:	Cut off the roots of the burddocks and boil the roots and drink the liquid that would come out of them.
Burns:	Rub the oil that would come out of skate to the burns.
Warts:	Rub the white milky stuff that would come out of the stem of the bannackaien to the warts, and it would drive them away.
Boils and corns:	Search for the penny leaves that grow in the side of a fence, heat them to the fire, and then place them against the boil or the corn, and it would prevent them from spreading.[ccxliii]

Collected by Timothy Regan, Schull
From Mrs Mahony, Schull

Boils:	Marsh mallow was put in a poultice and put up to them to break them and to draw them. Penny leaves were also used for the same purpose.
Consumption:	Chamomile was pulled and put into the person's stockings under his shoes. It was said to be a good cure.
Cancer:	The roots of dandelion boiled and the water drank is a cure for that.
Thrush:	A child that would have thrush; the old cure was for a child whose father was dead before he was born to breathe on the child's mouth each morning for three mornings.
Burn:	A cure for a burn was to catch an eascúlúacea[xli] and lick his belly, and then lick your burn. That was often done, and they considered it a great cure.

[xli] A lizard.

Road blisters:	Anyone having road blisters, a cure was to break up a snail and rub the broken parts to the blister.
Poison:	If a child or a big person took poison, the only cure was to drink soot. That was the cure for it because it would make the person vomit the poison again.
Toothache:	Any person having toothache, they put frog jelly on the tooth, and it stopped the pain. [ccxliv]

Collected by Annie Donovan, Schull
From Jeremiah Donovan, Schull

Cattle were cured of certain diseases by giving them water from a bound's ditch. The people would not speak a word to anybody when they were going or coming with water, and they would go early in the morning or late at night so they would not meet any person.

Agrimony:	to boil it in water and drink the water is a cure for heart disease.
Dandelion:	is a cure for liver disease and cancer also.
Chamomile:	is a cure for biliousness.
Violet leaves:	boiled is a cure for cancer.
Burdock roots:	cures kidney disease.
Nettles:	rubbed well is a cure for rheumatism.
Chicken weed:	is a cure for a toothache.
Ash tree:	a small piece of ash tree was put on the fire and the juices out of it put in the ear for earache.
Seaside dandelion:	was a cure for a bad stomach.
Goose grease:	was a cure for sore throat.
Honey and beeswax:	was a cure for thrush.
Woodbine:	cured a sore mouth.
Dock leaves:	were used to cure a nettle sting.
Cow dung:	were supposed to cure a cut.
Clean cobwebs:	were used to stop blood.
Celery:	was used as a cure for pains. [ccxlv]

Collected by Mary P. O'Mahony and Patricia Sheehan, Schull
From Denis O'Mahony (aged 70) and Mrs Hegarty (aged 77) Schull, Cork

A sore eye:	the white of an egg laid on Good Friday would cure it.
Whooping cough:	drink donkey's milk.
Stomach pain:	drink pickle.
Twisted guts:	drink a basin of suds.
A burn:	seal's oil.
Kidney trouble:	a sheep's liver eaten raw.
Rheumatism:	rabbit soup.

A seventh son was called the doctor, and he was supposed to have a cure. Some say if he cured anyone he himself would die.[ccxlvi]

Collected by Jerry Donovan, Schull
From Jeremiah Donovan (aged 97), Schull

Measles

Burdock was used to put out measles. The root of it was first got, the skin was taken off of it then, and the root was boiled until all the juice left it. Sugar candy used to be boiled with the juice to put a sweet taste in it. The froth on the top of the milk when it was milked from the cow was used to cure sore eyes. Black tea was to draw thorns out of the tops of fingers.

The woman who made those cures lived in a small house in Corthna. She was named Mrs Post. She used to go out every morning before sunrise and get the herbs she wanted, but if she happened to meet anybody on the journey she would go back home and would pick no herbs that day. She sometimes took money for the cure but it was not often.

A well which cured 'warts' was in Gurranes in Jack Shannon's field. It consisted of three small wells similar to the shape of a horse's hoof. [ccxlvii]

Collected by Mary Kate Sullivan, Schull
From Mrs Timothy Sullivan (aged 60), Schull

Lowertown
The Natural World and Weather Lore

A Great Storm of Former Times

In the year nineteen hundred a great storm took place. It was not expected. The night blew a gale and heavy rain fell. It was pitch dark. On that night an English ship laden with all kinds of fish was on her way home to England. She was a sailing ship because there were not any engine driven boats at the time. The wind tore her sails and broke her propeller, and she was driven by the wind down between two dangerous rocks called the Dollar Rocks and the Barrel Rocks. If she touched any of those rocks she would be broken, but she didn't, she came safe, and when they were below Goat Island they threw out their anchors and remained there until next morning. About ten o'clock the next morning when the storm ceased, four of the crew came in a small boat ashore in Gunpoint. They went up to Jerry Callaghan's house and told them their story. Mike Callaghan went to Schull to tell the coastguards. A crew of men from Gunpoint, namely Mike Callaghan, Jeremiah Donovan, Daniel Donovan, and John Donovan went in two boats to the ship. Another crew of people came from Long Island to her. When the coastguards arrived, they all got tea from the captain. Then the sailors put up what sails they had, and with the help of the coastguard's big boat they all towed the vessel to Schull harbour, where she remained until a British tug came from England to carry them home and to tow the ship. The people who towed them to Schull got five shillings each, and five ling fish and tobacco from the captain. Mike Callaghan got ten shillings because he went to Schull to tell the coastguards. All the crew were very thankful to the men who towed them. Anyone of the crew weren't lost. They all were English. [ccxlviii]

Collected by Annie Donovan, Schull
From Mr Jeremiah Donavan (aged 97), Schull

The Worst Gale

On Wednesday the twenty first of August in the year nineteen hundred, another gale, the worst gale that ever came, occurred. The day was a fine day, and all the people were reaping their corn. In the evening, the sky got black, and thunder and flashes were going. In the night at about ten o'clock, any person couldn't count two between the thunders. Hailstones about as big as a small apple fell, and a heavy storm arose. All the people thought that the end of the world was coming. The gale, lightening, thunder, and hailstones remained until morning. When the people got up in the morning, every bit of the corn, which they had reaped, was slung to the ground with the hailstones. The people that their own cows at that time. John Donovan's people, who were living in Lemcon at that time, had their cows out, and when they got up in the morning, three of their cows were inside the bog dead because they ran from the storm and got stuck there. All the hay ricks and straw ricks were knocked down and carried away. There were two people in Glaun who were going home from scureacting,[xlii] and they were found dead near a cliff in the morning.[ccxlix]

[xlii] Scureacting - storytelling

Lowertown
Sea and Shipwrecks

Local Happenings

One stormy night in the year eighteen forty five, a ship named Lady Charlotte, who was on her way from Lima, was thrown on the Barrel Rocks. She contained seeds, hides, wool, bark, tallow, gold dust, and silver ore. When she reached the Barrel Rocks, the gale broke her sails and tossed her against the rocks in the darkness of the night. All the people were lost, only one man, who lay on the rock, survived, and the waves rushed over him until morning. A big crowd of people gathered to the shore to try to rescue him from danger, but the waves lashed, any boat that would go out would be lost. At about ten o'clock the next morning, the storm ceased and five coastguards from Broagh went towards him, to take him off the rocks. He was nearly dead with the cold and hunger when they reached him. They brought him to the shore in their boat. They took him to Schull where he remained a few days until he got strong again. The names of the coastguards who rescued him were Tom Beasley, Andy Beasley, a man named Lynch, and another man named Grady. Strahen was a man who was over the four men. The Broagh coastguards carried up a boat, and gathered all the gold and dollars, and all the stuff that the ship contained. Some of the gold went down with the ship, but some big chests were thrown up on the rocks by the storm, and these were full of gold dollars. The people could not take anything out of the ship because the coastguards were minding her all the day. All the gold and other stuffs were sent over to England in a big ship.

There is a song made about the Lady Charlotte telling when she was wrecked, the five men who saved, the only man left, and how he was taken to Schull and clad there. He got a birth in a ship called the Chance which took him to England, his native country.[ccl]

Collected by Annie Donovan, Schull
From Mr Jeremiah Donavan (aged 97), Schull

The Wrecking of the Bohemian

The Bohemian was wrecked near Bird Islands in Dunmanus Bay in August 1898. She was an American boat loaded with copper. She sailed from Galveston in Texas in August 1898 and was wrecked on the 21st of August. The ship was to land in England but on account of the terrible bad weather she was driven all the way into Dunmanus Bay. The ship was not sunk. Two boats went out from Dunmanus, one belonged to John Driscoll and his two sons Timothy and Patrick, Patrick Ellis, Denis McGrath, and Jeremiah Murray. The other boat belonged to Timothy Driscoll. The people in that boat were Timothy Driscoll, Daniel McCarthy, Patrick Shanahan, Florence Driscoll, and James McGrath from Knockeens. They went to the place where the ship was and loaded their boats with copper. They brought it back and buried it quite near the pier. After about a month, missioners came to Goleen and they said that everybody that had copper out of that ship should give it back or that it would do them no good. So, these two Dunmanus boats gave back all they took. John Driscoll had up to fifty pounds worth of copper, and he gave it all back. It is said that one of the missioners cursed anyone that kept the copper, but a man from Gortdub kept all what he took in a small house near his dwelling house. One morning when he went to the house all the copper was turned into snails and flies and he could not go near it. He got oil and matches, and he sprinkled the house with oil and set fire to it. It is also said that everywhere he would go after nightfall while he had the copper, he would meet some dead person belonging to himself. There were seven sailors in the ship. For of them were saved by a man named Michael Goggin from Scart. The three other sailors were drowned. The body of one of them was found and buried in Bird Island. The other two were never heard of since.[ccli]

Collected by Kathleen McCarthy, Schull
From Thomas McCarthy (aged 64), Schull

The Wrecking of the Iberian

A ship called the Iberian was wrecked in Dunmanus in about 1877. She was a French boat full of wine, oil, and oranges, and was on her way to the west of Ireland, but a storm arose at sea and she tried to put in at Dunmanus Bay, but struck a rock, and she was broken in pieces. There were seven sailors on board. Timothy Driscoll and his father John Driscoll, Patrick Ellis and Denis McCarthy, went out in a boat and saved two sailors. The others drowned. After two or three days the bodies of two men were washed up by Dunmanus pier. It is said that Denis McGrath buried one of these men in the field next to the castle, and that the other one was let go out with the tide. There were cases of oranges, wine, and casks of oil thrown up on the strand, and many people from Dunmanus took them. One of the men who rescued the sailors got as much oil as did him for ten years. Another went around to Dunmanus in his boat and brought oil, cases of oranges, and wine and a lot of timber home with him. A man from Ardravinna brought a cart of thyme and a case of oranges. It is said that he also brought a case of wine, but with all of the rough handling some part of the case got broken and when he came home it was empty.[cclii]

Collected by Kathleen McCarthy, Schull
From Thomas McCarthy (aged 64) Schull

WESTERN DAILY PRESS

[23 November 1885, p.8]

Wreck of an Atlantic steamer

Intelligence reached Skibbereen on Saturday afternoon that the Leyland Line steamer Iberian had gone ashore on Dunmanus Bay. She was bound for Boston and is a sister ship of the Illyrian and Bohemian, which were wrecked near the same spot some time ago. All hands have been saved. A telegram reached Queenstown last night stating that the Leyland Line Steamer Iberian is now a total wreck. Yesterday morning she listed over and sank in deep water. The Queenstown tug Mount Etna had been at the scene of the wreck since midnight on Saturday, and there is no doubt all on board the Iberian were saved.

The Wrecking of the Queen's More

A ship called the Queen's More was wrecked near Bird Island in Dunmanus Bay on the 15th November 1897. She was an American boat full of flour, beautiful meat, and dishes, and cases of apples. Nobody knew how many sailors were on board or nobody knew that she wrecked until the next day. Michael Goggin from Scart and John Driscoll from Dunmanus were the two first people to arrive there. They had two boats, and nobody knew how much flour, meat, dishes and apples they took home. They buried all these things under the floors of their houses because the coastguards were out looking for what was taken out of the ship. They heard that these two men had everything. They searched the houses of the two men but got nothing. Every boat from Gunpoint went round to Dunmanus and brought flour, meat, and a lot of timber home with them. Daniel MacCarthy and Dick King from Ardravinna went for two carts of timber, and when they had their carts loaded, they set off for home. They had not gone far when they met two coastguards. They took down their names and told them to take back the timber again. They turned round to go back and went back halfway, but when the coastguards were gone out of their sight, they turned back and came home. It is also said that they gave the wrong names to the coastguards. The people from Dunmanus got a lot of wine out of that ship and they afterwards sold it to the shopkeepers and made a lot of money on it.[ccliii]

Collected by Kathleen McCarthy, Schull
From Catherine Driscoll (aged 93), Schull

LOWERTOWN
Local Songs

The Hiberian Steamer

My neighbour, I pray pay attention,
I hope you'll attend to my song.
And if you only listen, indeed
I'll not keep you too long.
Concerning the Hiberian Steamer,
that crossed the Atlantic foam,
And struck her stem up in Bird Island,
and landed her crew in the shore.

Chorus
Long life to the crew and the captain,
that steered her across the rough main.
Now we are eating fine flower cakes and apples,
and stealing the wreck all away

If you happened to be there that morning,
it would fill up your heart with surprise,
To behold these wild bullocks roaring,
the noise it would reach to the skies.
They swam from the Three Castle Head to the Mizen,
and over again to Sheep's Head,
Right down to the Carbury's Island,
indeed, before they were dead.

Chorus

The women of Carbury West,
they are roasting and baking away.
For providence lately had sent them,
and Neptune the god of the sea,
Fine apples exported in barrels,
for Liverpool market were they,
The Hiberian Steamer had carried,
and battled along through the sea.

Chorus

Those sister steamers are gone now,
no sorrow for them, I dare say.
One of them south in Fiallacarn,
and the two more in Dunmanus Bay.
Big wealthy merchants of England,
they thought very hard for to say,
When they would purchase those
hams out from Boston,
that we could have roasting today.
Its right they should pay our expenses,
to those tyrant and racketeer landlords,
Its many a penny we pay.

Chorus

The farmers out in Massachetts
are shooting those pigs now again.
West Carbury women get ready,
and temper your teeth for the game.
And Mr O'Neill near the harbour,
and Benjamin Roycroft too,
Edward and William O'Goggin,
and Florence MacCarthy tis true.

Chorus

The two little boys from Long Island,
went to see the Hiberian that day,
with Paddy Óg, the grey badger,
the miser who lives at the quay.
He was smuggling the meat, flour, and
apples, and stealing the wreck all away.[254]

Collected by Annie Donovan
From Jeremiah Callaghan (aged 70), Schull

The Amalgamation of the Workhouse

Joe Helen who was a porter in the workhouse wrote the following song on "The Amalgamation of the Workhouse". He was a native of Gortnamona and is still living.

'Twas early on a summer's dawn,
Perched on a tree in the workhouse lawn,
The birds all met by the morning air,
And they asked the cuckoo would he take the chair.

With a queenly air on a branch she sat,
And spoke her thanks to this feathered lot,
As your head and chairman I'm placed to act,
And your great convention is not rigged or packed.

Here a jackdaw rose and with fluent bill,
He made a speech of great power and skill,
He asked his colleagues the gull and crow,
"Can you tell me friends will the workhouse go?"

Said a stately raven "my feathered chums,
We have dined for years on the choicest crumbs,
And I need not tell you what ye all know,
That you'll miss the crumbs should the workhouse go".

The tale of woe did the sparrow tell,
"I'll finish soon, don't I know it well,
When winter comes and snow showers fall,
I won't pick up crumbs in the dining hall."

Said a shrude old thrush with a thoughtful brow,
"None hate the workhouse, all love it now,
It has of late quite a host of friends,
Who for past abuse ought to make amends?"

Here a seagull rose and with plumes so white,
"'Tis against officials to norish spite,
They begrudge them food or an honest fee,
And would drown each one with a spoon of tea."

"One moment please" said a sleepy owl,
"In Ballydehob you could hear folks growl,
Against the scheme which they deem unwise,
For the workhouse contract to make great noise."

"Round the town of Schull" said a blood-stained hawk,
"There has been for years quite a lot of talk,
Of unseen confabs and prolonged debate,
Of an empty workhouse to lower the rates".

Said a tiny wren "Ah then don't you know,
It serves folks ends that they all should go,
You bet the inmates could go to Mars,
If the yankee Ford came here making cars."

Said the corncrake "now permit a word,
Have you seen the eagle, Pat Sheehy's bird?
As on its columns I saw last night,
I read a letter that may ease your plight."

Here a blackbird rose saying "your brains are dense.
You silly fool may God give you sense,
You know right well though no name was signed,
That the author had his own axe to grind."

And people say "it's a sin and crime,
To send the poor from their local clime,
To meet strange faces in distant wards,
And lay their bones in a strange churchyard."[255]

Collected by Kathleen McCarthy
From Robert Baker (aged 69), Schull, Co. Cork

The Destruction of Schull Workhouse

In 1956, Richard Collins of Rock Island, Goleen, told the Bureau of Military History how Schull Workhouse came to be destroyed. Collins, born in 1893, was educated at Goleen National School until he was 14 when he went to work on his parents' farm. In 1912 he was appointed as a temporary light-keeper at the Fastnet lighthouse and was still working there when he joined the Goleen company of the Irish Volunteers in 1918. His knowledge of the Fastnet would play an important part in the destruction of Schull Workhouse.

> 'Early in 1921, I was called to a meeting at Coomhola where I met Liam Deasy (Brigade O/C). He gave me special instructions to return to my area and to establish an "all around the clock" watch along the coast in the district for a ship which was expected to land a supply of arms from Italy. Should the vessel arrive, it was proposed to land the arms in Dunmanus Bay. I was engaged whole time on ensuring that a regular rota of watchers were on this duty in the period from early May to mid-June 1921. The ship did not arrive. While I was engaged on the organisation of the watch for the arms ship, I was asked by the battalion O.C. (Sean Lehane) to prepare a plan of the layout of the lighthouse on the Fastnet Road as it was proposed to raid it in order to obtain a stock of guncotton which was stored there. I supplied all details including instructions as to landing on the rock, whereabouts of the material sought and general layout of the position of the lightkeepers at specified times. The raid was carried out by a party under Sean Lehane and about 30-cwt of guncotton with a supply of detonators was obtained. I did not take part on this operation as I was engaged on the watch for the arms ship. When the watch for the arms ship was called off, I rejoined the battalion column in Schull area. Within a few days, orders were received from Brigade H.Q. to destroy Schull Workhouse which was due to be occupied by fresh enemy forces which were being drafted into the area. The work of destruction was allocated to the men of Schull Company under Charlie Cotter. In order to divert attention from the operation, the battalion column was to carry out an attack on the Marine State while the operation was in progress.' The column and the men of the local company assembled at "The Gap: on the Schull-Bantry road about 10 p.m., we were just about to move off to our selected positions when a messenger arrived from Ballydehob Company to say that a strong force of British military were encamped at Drealomane National

School. Sean Lehane had been expecting a round-up by the enemy following the Fastnet raid and he decided to send the locals home and to evacuate the column from the area. I withdrew with the column to Dunmanus Pier where boats were available to take us across the bay to Muintrevara. When we landed there we were informed that the whole peninsula – Skibbereen to Mizen Head – had been sealed off by the enemy. We remained across the bay all next day and watched the enemy searching for us. When they had withdrawn, we returned to Schull area that night and attacked the Marine Station while the men of Schull Company, under Charlie Cotter, destroyed the Workhouse. This was, I think, the night of 27th June 1921.'

Statement by Richard Collins, Activities of Schull Battalion, Irish Volunteers, Co. Cork, 1918-1921, Bureau of Military History, 1913-21, 7th December 1956

Figure 21. The remains of Schull Workhouse.

Thomas Joseph

Ye mariners and fisherman
Come listen to my woe
My lines are sad and mournful
They'll cause your tears to flow
It's of the boat Thomas Joseph
Gone down, no more to sail
With six found souls,
their loving friends for ever more to wail

The owner being John Daly
From the island of Cape Clear
He steered her o'er to Baltimore
To get aboard new gear
Her engine it being ready
And nothing then seemed dull
So, he next proposed to steer her
o'er on a trial trip to Schull

Returning home with merry hearts,
and every face aglow
They never thought their end was near
Till Neptune proved their foe
The stars bright face, had hid a pace
And her engine kicked a while
On that very night they met their fate
On the rock called "Sandy Isle"

When she struck the rock that night
Young Daly cried in vain
He shouted to his comrades
"We'll shove her off again"
But as he stood upon the deck
And watched the ebbing tide
The cruel waves, they swept him down
Now sleeping by her side

It was sad to die, so far from home
When none could hear their call
But every soul worked for himself
And god above for all
Now o'er the island of Cape Clear
Dark sadness seems to reign
For the six found souls
That now lie cold beneath the watery main.

The bravest deed aboard that boat
For death, he had no fear
Was done by young John Daly
The boat-man's engineer
When he saw his loved companions
That they were doomed to die
He proudly stood above them
And prayed to God on high

O god, he prayed, if it be thou
Who call us all to thee
I pray that thou will send us aid
upon this cruel sea
And I pray today that thou
will sooth my mother's care and woe
For I know it's for her absent son
Some bitter tears will flow

Miss Collins and Miss Shipsey
Though lovely maidens, fair
In youth and bloom they met their doom
Along with the engineer
From their home they now must roam
Where none can hear their call
Where every man is for himself
And god above for all

When the diver found young Daly
And brought home his remains
To see his widowed mother
tears did fall like rain
Likewise, his loving brothers
And to all that held him dear
For sadness grew to the birds that flew
O'er the island of Cape Clear

Now on a glorious summer's night
When all is bright and fair
A motorboat with colours grand
Glides around Cape Clear
And from the deck of that frail barque
You can hear the sound of prayer
For I knew it was the humming of
The brave young engineer.[256]

The Island of Cape Clear

The composer of this song was Dan Mahony, nicknamed "Dan the fiddler", who lived in Cáirtne where Mr Bennett lives now.

Proud England boasts of her cities long and her famous seaport towns
The French man thinks that Paris is admired by the world around
But it's off the coast of Ireland there's a spot, to me, most dear
I love it too, with all my heart, it's the island of Cape Clear

In bygone days it was fine to gaze all out upon the sea
When all those ships commerce were not propelled by steam
The summer's sun is sinking now, not a ripple do appear
And ships from every nation lay all around Cape Clear

The Chinese junk and the Turkish craft, and the Austrian too are there
A yankee ship with her colours flying, for a pilot to appear
She is standing in with her mainsail,
clued for a pilot from Cape Clear

And lo, from out south harbour, a pilot boat do glide
With a pilot flag in her mizzen mast a flying in the breeze
With a little cool, she travels fast, for a stately ship she steers
She is now hoved too with main-yards backed,
for a pilot from Cape Clear.

See how the pilot hails her and gently throws a line
He glides on to her quarterdeck, and loudly cries he
"Let go your sheets for Queenstown boys,
for its welcome there we'll be"

We natives of this island are the true-bred Irish race
No mixture of the Sassenach flows through our Irish race
We are but simple fishermen but we love our island dear
Likewise, our homes and sweethearts,
in the island of Cape Clear. [257]

LOWERTOWN
History and Archaeology

Penal Times

The punishment of the Catholics in this district was terrible. Everything they had was taken. They were so poor that they could not pay their rent, and as soon as the Landlord or his agent came, they were thrown out on the side of the road. A man named Thomas Walsh who is now living in Schull had a small farm once in Cove. He was unable to pay the rent and the agent threw himself and all his brothers on the roadside and burned the house. The same thing happened to a man named John Goggin in Scart.

There was no chapel in this district at that time. There is a rock called the mass rock a small bit to the north of the creamery, and it was there all the Catholics heard mass. The priest often hid in a hole which is now a well at the eastern side of the new road above the creamery. It is said that soldiers followed him but were attacked by wild cats who tore every bit of their faces. There is another mass rock in the glen in Glaun. Once soldiers followed the priest as far as Durrus. There he met a protestant farmer and his three sons sowing wheat. They were going into their dinner when the priest came their way. The priest asked the farmer to hide him from the soldiers, and he said he would. Then they all went in for dinner. The farmer said that he would have to stay in the field to keep the rooks away from the wheat, but the priest said that no rook would go near the corn while himself was in the house. They all went in, and were eating when the soldiers came in. They told the man that they heard the priest was hiding in his house. The farmer said he was not. They searched the house and went away satisfied. It is said that the priest stood by the fireplace and stretched out his hand, and the soldiers never saw him. He then thanked the farmer and went away, and it is said that when the farmer went out after his dinner the wheat was green in the field.[258]

Collected by Kathleen McCarthy, Schull
From Michael Holland (aged 50), Schull

In the year 1850, the penal days took place in this district. It was a very hard period on the Catholics, because they were crushed by the Protestants. If the priests were caught saying mass they would be put to death, and so they had to go around the district dressed in plain clothes trying to say mass in the lonely places among the rocks. There is a stone which is said to be the mass rock in Dreenane between Johnny Barnett's and Andrew Donoghue's farms. It is said that the priests said mass on that rock every Sunday. There is another place in this district called Kill Patrick, and it is said that the priest hid there and said mass there.

It was the protestant had all the best of the land and the best of everything. The Catholics had only poverty and hunger, and that year the blight carried whatever patch of potatoes they had sown, and the little wheat they had they had to sell to make money to pay the rent. If they hadn't the rent at the appointed day, they got a notice to be out of their houses the next day. That year was the worst year they met because they had nothing to eat. At that time there lived in England a rich, pious Land Lady named Miss Coote. She had pity for the poor of every country, and she had so much money that she couldn't count it, so she gave money to every country. She gave money, nets, and fishing boats to the people of Baltimore and Cape Clear. She came over to Ireland once and she came to Skibbereen. The people there laid out carpets for her to walk on until she went to the hotel. There she was entertained highly, and she bought a cloak and took off her bonnet and put on the cloak to make herself more Irish. She then marched to Baltimore, and it was said she founded Baltimore fishery school. She was also to send flour and blankets to Goleen parish. Father Holland was parish priest at that time in Goleen, and Fisher was parish minister. Each of them settled to send for blankets and flour to that lady. They had to sign papers because both Catholics and Protestants were to get the goods. Fisher signed himself parish priest and it was to him all the goods came. When the priest heard that, he wouldn't take the goods, and he warned the Catholics not to take them or if they did "that they would burn around them." The Catholics were frightened, so they took the blankets back to Fisher again. It is said that after returning the blankets the priest cursed them. Some poor people took more blankets instead because they thought the priest had not cursed the new ones that were in Fisher's house. Anything didn't happen to them.

Fisher gathered all the orphans in his own religion. He gave meat, soup and other things to anyone that would go to his church. Nearly all the Toormore Catholics went and they were called "Soupers" since. But a big number of them turned to their own religion again. There was one man who had a cow and he had no grass for her. One day Fisher met him and told him if he went to his own church, he would give him grass. The man said that he would, and every Sunday he went to church and stood outside the door. Fisher noticed him and he asked him why he didn't go in. The man answered, "I come to church to feed my cow and I go to mass to feed my soul." His cow was driven out and he got no more grass or food.[259]

Collected by Annie Donovan, Schull
From Mrs John Donovan (aged 88), Schull

Figure 22. Teampol na bocht, Church of the Poor, Toormore.

The Famine Times

A man, named Mr Cotter from Coosheen was dying of starvation. He crawled on his hands to Schull for food. When he arrived, all he could get was a hard crust of bread. He then started for home but when he was about a mile from the town he died. It was the hard crust of bread that choked him.

This is another story about a man who was dying on the roadside. There was a man going around with a horse and car taking up the dead bodies. He came to the dying man, and thinking he was dead, threw him into the car. When he was burying the bodies, he hit them with a shovel to pack them in, the dying man groaned. The man then took him out of the grave and took him to the workhouse, and he recovered in a few months but was lame in one leg. The man hit him on the leg with the shovel and broke it. This man is only about twenty years dead. He was an inhabitant of Long Island, but I do not know his name. When the famine was nearly over, a workhouse was built to the east of Schull and all people who were dying went in there. To the back of the workhouse there is a graveyard where the people who died were buried. The graves can still be seen. [260]

In this district people died in hundreds with the fever which accompanied the famine. There was a graveyard in Lowertown call the Cill where numerous people were buried coffinless. Another graveyard is in Croagh. It was the people from the Island were buried there and still unbaptised babies are buried there. All these people were buried coffinless. One man from Coosheen buried seven of his children. The eldest girl was seventeen years of age. He carried each child on his back in a basket to the Schull graveyard and buried them coffinless. No one would help him, afraid they would get the fever too, so he had to dig the hole himself. A family living in a small house in Lowertown all died and were buried in the Cill in Lowertown.

There is an old store at the edge of the water in Lowertown where corn was stored before the famine. During the famine it was used as a workhouse. It is said that two poor people were very hungry, and they went out to the strand to pick limpets, and when the man who was in charge came out and found them there, he began to whip them.[261]

It was at that time that the main road from Schull to Goleen was created and all the people around that place were working at it. The payment a person got that was working there was a gallon of meal and that was supposed to rear his wife and himself and his family. [262]

Collected by John McFarlane, Mary P. O'Mahony and Timothy Regan

SCHULL

Co. Chorcaighe
Bar: Cairbre Thiar
Par: Scoil Mhuire
Scoil: Scoil Mhuire (B.)
Oide: Liam Ó'Raghallaigh
27 October 1937 – 11 January 1938

Schull
Local Folklore and Stories

Hidden Treasure

There is a very interesting old story about hidden treasure told in this district. Once a man dreamed three nights in succession that there was treasure buried in the Lady Charlotte strand which lies south of Schull Pier. He also dreamed that in a field near the strand he would find a bunch of keys to open the chest which contained the treasure. The man went to the field and found the keys. Then he went to the strand, dug a hole there, and found the chest, but when he went to open it, he heard a splash in the sea near him, and, turning around, he saw a man sitting with his face muffled up. He immediately shut the hole and ran away. It is said that this treasure came off the ship called the Lady Charlotte which was wrecked on the Barrel Rocks to the west of Goat Island.[263]

Gunpoint Hidden Treasure

In the townland of Gunpoint there is said to be buried treasure. It is supposed to be buried in the strand. This treasure was buried by the captain of a Norse ship. No attempt was ever made to recover the treasure. The captain of the ship buried the treasure in the strand, and he asked a man who was on board the ship to come ashore with him. When they had the treasure buried, the captain shot the man and buried him with the treasure. The captain did this so that no one would know where he had the treasure buried. It is said that the treasure is hidden near a rock in the strand. The treasure consists of a chest of silver and gold.[264]

Hidden Treasure

In many places in Ireland, there are, especially among the older people, stories which tell of hidden treasure. A very interesting story is told in this townland about a treasure which is supposed to be buried in Colla, a district about two miles from Schull. The buried treasure is supposed to be hidden in a sloping piece of land called 'Hayes Leaca', near the sea.

It is related in the story that a pirate ship landed in Colla one night long ago. The ship was a Spanish one, and on board was a great treasure. The captain and a black man came ashore to bury it. When the hole was dug, the captain shot the black man and buried him with the treasure. When his task was complete, he returned to his ship. Some years later he returned to get the treasure, but he failed to discover the place.

Since then, two other attempts have been made to find the treasure. The first attempt was made by a man named John O'Driscoll and some other, but alas it was unsuccessful. The second attempt was made by Mr Barry. He had a water divining rod which he had proved would turn in his hand if he stood over the gold. Although the rod turned several times in his hand, and the men dug each time, all were disappointed when instead of beautiful sparkling gold, only the dark surface of water met their gaze. In recent years no attempt has been made to find the treasure, whether it lies hidden there or not is a mystery which very likely will remain unsolved.[265]

A Mixed Family

A widow and a widower once got married. Both had a family by their first marriages and in the course of time they had another family. All the families lived happily in a country house. One day all the children were playing outside when the woman and her husband heard cries of distress. The man said to his wife, "Go quickly and see what is wrong." She went, and when she returned said, "Your children and my children are beating our children."[266]

Burke and the Foxy Sergeant

Some years ago, there lived in South Schull a man named John Burke, who was locally known as 'Jack Tricks.' One fair morning he was in Schull, and he got drunk. He was causing a great disturbance to the public, when a sergeant with foxy hair arrested him. This sergeant was known as 'the foxy sergeant.' As the sergeant was taking him to the barrack, Burke said, "Look out neighbours, the fox has his prey."[267]

Announcing a lost pig

Once upon a time a man lost a pig and he published his loss in the newspapers. He also asked the priest to publish it from the altar. When the priest was publishing the loss, the man went up to the altar and said to him, "Don't forget to say, Father, that he had a black spot on his belly."[268]

The Watch and the Cow thieves

Two men were imprisoned, one for stealing a cow and the other for stealing a watch. One day the man that stole the cow said to the other man, "What time is it?" The man that stole the watch said, "It is milking time."[269]

A True Story

There is an old story told in this district about a vault found in an old church which is built in the Schull cemetery. One day there were two men digging a grave in the church. When they were down about two feet the ground gave way under them and to their astonishment, they found they were standing on the body of a priest in a vault. They at once shut up the grave and told no one about it. Lately the son of one of the gravediggers told about this vault.[270]

Lowertown Fort

There is a fort in Lowertown known as the Lowertown Fort. The old people tell a very interesting story about it. Once a man was going home late at night and he heard talk in the fort. He listened and he heard voices talking about men. All of a sudden, he heard one say, "What about the man outside the fort?" When he heard this, he ran home as quick as he could.[271]

Will Joe and the Fox

Once a man named Will Joe lived in the townland of Dunmanus. One summer's morning very early he was soling a pair of gutta percha shoes. His attention was attracted by the noise of his fowl. He ran out taking the ball of gutta percha with him. He saw a fox coming along the path with two or three hens thrown over his shoulder. He threw the ball of gutta percha at the fox and hit him on the forehead. The fox went back, and on the same path he met another fox coming in the opposite direction. The two foxes struck their foreheads together and the ball of gutta percha held them together until the man came and killed them.[272]

The Mermaid, the Fisherman, and the Boy

Once upon a time, there was a very poor fisherman living near the shore. One day he went out fishing, but he caught no fish. In the evening as he was preparing to return home, a mermaid put her head above the water and said that he would get fish tomorrow. The next day the man went out fishing again and he caught a great deal of fish. The mermaid gave him a young boy to take home, and she told him to bring him back when he was seven years old. The man did so, and the mermaid gave him some money to rear the boy until he was twenty-one years old, and told him to bring him back again then. The boy refused to go back to the mermaid when he was twenty-one years old, and he decided to go and seek his fortune.

On his way he met a crow, a tiger, and a greyhound, fighting over a dead carcass. When they saw him coming, they asked him to divide it between them. He gave the eyes to the crow, the bones to the hound, and the flesh to the tiger. They were very pleased with the division, so they said they would reward him. The tiger gave him a strip of skin off his back and told him that when he put it around him, he would be the strongest man in the world. The hound gave him a bone out of his breast and told him that when he put it up to his breast, he would be the finest hound in the world. The crow gave him a feather and told him that when he put it up to his breast, he would be the finest crow in the world.

He continued his journey again and he tried the feathers, the bone, and the strip of skin to see if they would act as promised. He flew away to a big tree which was growing in front of a house. Soon afterwards a lady came out, caught him and took him into the house. Soon afterwards a coursing match was going to be held, and the boy took the feather off his breast and put the bone up to it, so he was then a hound. The lady took him to the coursing match, and he began to run. He followed the hare until he came to the sea and fell in, and the mermaid caught him again.[273]

The Minister and the Man

In Ireland at the time of the famine, there lived a man in the parish of Goleen who met a minister, and the minister offered to give him a bag of potatoes if he would become a protestant. The man said he would, but he did not go to church very often and when the minister asked him why he did not go to church, he said, "I go to church for the good of my body, and go to mass for the good of my soul."[274]

Meenevane Fort

In the townland of Meenvane there is an old fort. This fort is situated in a field belonging to Michael O'Leary. It is said that there is an underground passage running from the fort to the shore. Some years ago, Patrick Brien was making a pit of mangolds. The pit went down, and he saw a passage running towards the shore in the direction of the fort. It is said that long ago some person went into the fort. When he went in, he saw a foxy woman sitting down in a lovely chair. The table was laden with lovely ware.[275]

The Buried Treasure of McCarthy's Island

Truth is sometimes stranger than fiction, and if the following episode is true, enormous wealth lies buried in one of our isle in the form of bullion. About the year 1749 a full-rigged ship lost her rudder mid-Atlantic, and she was driven by the westerly winds on the rugged coast of McCarthy's Island. The ship was laden with maize and was bound from Melbourne to Southampton. She had also on board twelve cases of gold bullion, stolen by the captain. The crew of the ship shifted the cases and buried them somewhere along the coast of the island, which is all of a sandy nature. When all was secreted safely away, the story says that the captain drew his pistol and shot the seven members of his crew. In the hope of being sometime rescued from this prison, the captain was traversing the island when fate took a hand, and he was dashed to his doom off a precipice at the south side, burying forever the secret of the exact whereabouts of his hidden treasure. There the story would have ended were it not for a metal documents case picked up from the wreckage which lay scattered along the shore. One of the contents of the case was a letter from the captain to his brother in Valencia, which he intended to post on arriving at his destination, in which he stated what his intention would be concerning the treasure, and also how he intended to rid himself of the crew when he had safely carried out his plans. Thus, the story leaked out. Residents from other islands buried the bodies of the captain and the other sailors, and the mounds which rise over their graves can be seen to the present day. Several attempts have been made by local fishermen to find the treasure, but they were unsuccessful.[276]

Collected by Daniel Regan, Schull
From John J. Sullivan (aged 30), Schull

SCHULL
People, Places and Property

Curly Driscoll

At one time there lived in Cape Clear Island a man of mighty strength named Curly Driscoll. His height was eight feet and seven inches, and his strength was in proportion to his size. Once O'Driscoll was in Cork. One day he saw eight men on a steamer trying to pull aboard an anchor by means of a winch which had got caught in the bottom of the harbour. He went aboard and catching the anchor-chain with one hand, he pulled the anchor aboard.

At another time when a storm threatened, O'Driscoll went to the strand where he kept his four-oared boat and he carried her home on his back. One day there was a ton of salt on the pier for O'Driscoll. He got a sail, put the salt into it, and brought the whole lot home on his back.

One time twenty-four soldiers landed on the island, and they began to make the women kill cows for them. All the men of the island, except O'Driscoll, were out fishing. The women came to O'Driscoll and asked him to help them. He got a rope, tied the soldiers together, put them on his back, and then went to a cliff and threw them over it. This cliff had ever since been known as the Bullane.[277]

James Sullivan

Long ago there lived in the townland of Caherlaska a strong man named James Sullivan. He was locally known as Big Jamesy on account of his great strength. He had a small farm on which he and his wife and children lived. They were very poor.

One day Big Jamesy was drawing bags of meal from a steamer on Schull pier. Each bag contained 2½ cwt. During the day he was lamenting to his friends, who were also discharging the steamer, about his wife and children at home who had nothing to eat. One of his friends told him to hide a bag of meal and to take it home during the night. When the men stopped work Big Jamesy went home. During the night he returned to Schull and took home the 20 stone bag of meal on his back. The distance from his house to Schull is two miles.[278]

Collected by John Newman, Schull
From Mrs Newman (aged 54), Schull

Will Joe

An old resident in the townland of Dunmanus was noted for his strength. It is said he threw a stone five yards and that the stone weighed fifteen hundredweight. This man was known as Will Joe. Several men attempted to lift this stone, but they failed. It is said that Will Joe was the strongest man in the district.[279]

Jim the Painter

There is a painter in this district known as "Jim the Painter". He is very witty and clever. One day he was painting a shop front in Goleen. As he was painting, a doctor came the way and said, "Putty and paint cover a lot of your mistakes, Jim!" Jim at once retorted, "The spade and shovel cover a lot of yours."[280]

An Old School

In the workhouse grounds there are the ruins of an old school. It was at the right-hand side of the gate leading into the workhouse. The school was burned down about eighteen years ago. This year the ruins were knocked down for the purpose of building the hospital at Schull. The children were taught by Miss O'Donovan who now resides in Skibbereen. There was a special apartment in the workhouse where the children used to sleep. There were a good many children attending the school.[281]

Collected by John Newman, Schull
From Mrs Newman (aged 54), Schull

Corrydorigan

Corrydorigan lies about a quarter of a mile to the east of Schull. The meaning of this name is not known locally. The population of this townland is about 85. The most common name is Sheehan. Most of the land in this townland is fertile. All the holdings are small. The greater number of the houses are slated. There are only three old men and two old women in this townland now. Only one old man, who formerly came from Cape Clear, can speak Irish. These old people do not tell stories either in English or Irish.[282]

Local Place Names

In Mr P O'Regan's farm in south Schull there is a field called the 'Canard'. This field got this name because it is a good deal higher than the field below it. In the same farm there is a field called the 'Creagh'. This field had this name because it was originally boggy and wet. In William Regan's farm in the same townland there is a field called "Helen's Garden". This field gets its name from its former owner whose name was Helen.

In John Whooley's farm in south Schull there is a field near the seashore called "Lae Oilean". This field gets its name from the little island which lies in front of it. In Mr J. Coughlan's farm in the same townland there is a field called "Gort na Uranner", which means the tillage field. In Mr W Attridge's farm in south Schull there is a field called the "Cottage Field". Long ago there was a cottage built in this field. In the same farm there is a field which used to be called the "Butter Field". Long ago the people used to gather a butter-like substance from the plants growing in this field. This substance was used for pains. In south Schull there is a little inlet called "Cuas na gcorp". Long ago some bodies out of the graveyard, which lies nearby, were washed down into that inlet in a great flood.

In Mr J O'Brien's farm in south Schull there is a field called "Pairc Frank" which means Frank's field. In the same farm there is a hill called "Conac Rua" which means the Red Hill.[xliii] In Mr O'Regan's farm in Colla there is a bog called "Crock na bpoll". It is so called because there are a great many holes in it. In Mr Collins's farm in Caherlaska there is a bog called "Crack Jones," which means Jones' Bog. In the same farm there is a field called the "Poll Talman Field," which means the field of the Poll Talman. In Mr Regan's farm in Gubbeen there is a field called the Fort Field. There is an old fort in this field. In Mr Ferguson's farm there is a field called "Corthna." The local people do not know the meaning of this name. In Mr Wilcox's farm in the same townland there is a field called "Pairc Tige".[xliv] It is so called because there was a house built there long ago. In Mr Dempsey's farm in Corthna there is a field called "The Tennis Field". There was a tennis court in this field some time ago. The field to the west of Schull Pier is called "The Limekiln Field." Long ago there was a limekiln in this field. In the farm occupied by Micheal O'Leary in Meenevane there is a field called "Tobar an

---

[xliii] Conac is a literal pronunciation of cnoc, variously spelt cnoic, meaning hill. This is now commonly anglicised to knock – the meaning remains the same though the pronunciation varies from knock to conac.

[xliv] Tige is probably a local spelling of the word 'teach', meaning house.

gort a cill." It is so called because there is a holy well in this field. In olden days there was a church in this field. In the same townland there are bogs called the "Flax Bogs." Long ago the people used to steep their flax in these bogs. In Mr O'Leary's farm in Corrydorigan there are fields known as "The Hospital Fields." They are so called because long ago there was a hospital there. In the same farm there is a field called "The Bridge Field" because it is situated near a bridge over the Corrydorigan river. In Mr O'Driscoll's farm in Coosheen there is a field called "Pairc Larry" which means Larry's field. In Mr Leahy's farm in the same townland there is a field called "Cowhan." The meaning of this name is not known.[283]

Names of Old Roads

The road through Corrydorigan from the Skibbereen road to the Bantry road is known as "Garb Botar," which means the Rough Road. Another road crosses the Corrydorigan road and leads to a field with a big white stone in the centre of it known as 'The White Stone.' This road is called 'Cnoc Rua Botairín.' A road leading from the Bantry road to Skeagh is called 'Botairín a bloc.' It is so called because there were a great many large flag stones on the road. There is an old road in the Woodlands called "The Old Road." It is so called because it was used before the present road was made. A road which leads to Derryconnell is called 'Botairín Ban' which means the 'White Road.' A road which leads to Dreenatra is called 'The Wood Road' because it passes a wood. The 'Workhouse Road' leads to the townland of Rathcoole. It is so called because an old workhouse is built at one side of it. 'The Mine Road' is so called because some years ago a barytes mine was worked near it. This road leads to Glaun.

The road which leads to Ardmanna is called 'The Captain's Road.' It is so called because years ago a military captain lived in a house near this road. There is a road in South Schull called 'Bill Barry's Road,' because some years ago an old man named Bill Barry lived in a small house at the side of this road. There is another road in South Schull which leads to Mr Thomas O'Brien's farm, known as the 'Quarry Road.' This road is so called because it passes by a quarry.[284]

The Workhouse Graveyard

In the townland of Rathcoole there is an old graveyard. This graveyard was attached to the old workhouse. The graveyard is situated to the east of the workhouse. This year there was a fence put around the graveyard to prevent the cattle from wandering over it. The graveyard was drained also. Before the drain was made the whole graveyard was swamped with water, and from that it was called the 'Bog of Allen". There are about twelve headstones in the graveyard. Only the people who died in the workhouse were buried there. Many people who are still living remember seeing people buried there.[285]

Collected by John Newman, Schull
From Mrs Newman (aged 54), Schull

White Castle

The townland of White Castle is situated about two miles to the east of Schull. It is so called because there is a castle there which was of a white colour when it was first built. This castle belonged to the O'Mahony Clan. The population of White Castle is about 26. The most common name is O'Donovan. There are five houses in the townland, and these are all slated. All the people in this townland are engaged in farming. The land is very fertile and is level.[286]

Gubbeen

The townland of Gubbeen lies about two miles to the west of Schull. The population of this townland is about 80. There are fifteen families in the townland. All the people are engaged in farming. The houses are all slated. There is a small harbour running into the townland and near it there is an old ruin called 'The Stores.' Long ago ships used come in there for cargoes of wheat which was kept in those stores.[287]

Fionn Mac Cumhaill's Ridge

There is a curious formation of rock at the western side of Mount Gabriel. It resembles a furrow ploughed into the rock. It is called Fionn's Ridge. The people of the locality say that it was Fionn Mac Cumhaill ploughed this furrow with two goats.[288]

Figure 23. Schull (c1865-1914) Robert French (1821-1917),
call nos. L_CAB_05214 and L_ROY_10215.
Images Courtesy of the National Library of Ireland.

Figure 24. Schull Station (top) call no. ODEA 7/58.
Rail line to harbour (bottom) ref. L_CAB_10217. Photos by Ro
French. Images Courtesy of the National Library of Ireland.

South Schull

The townland of South Schull lies about a quarter of a mile to the south of the village of Schull. It got this name from an old school which was built on the farm now occupied by Mr Patrick O'Regan. There is a hay shed belonging to this man built on the place where the old school stood. This school was working at the time when Ireland was called 'The Island of Saints and Scholars.' The population of South Schull is 72. There are 17 families in the townland, all being farmers except four. The most common name is McCarthy. All the houses are slated except one which is thatched. Although most of the land in South Schull is hilly, there is also a great deal of very fertile land. There are several quarries of very hard stone in this townland. A great deal of this stone was used in the steamrolling of the road from Ballydehob to Goleen. There is also a great deal of red, white, and green sandstone in this townland.[289]

Castle Island

The O'Mahonys had a stronghold in Castle Island, which is known as the Middle Island. It is situated about three miles from the beautiful village of Schull, which lies by the harbour of the same name. Situated amid picturesque and varied scenery, nestling at the foot of Gabriel's rough defiles, and fronting the wild Atlantic, it is a charming spot. It was anciently called Scoil Mhuire (Mary's School) and in medieval documents it is designated 'Santa Maria de Scholia'. This school is said to have been founded by the 'University of Rosse' (i.e. St Fachtna's Monastery, Carbery). However this may be, I doubt it. The parish is mentioned as Scol in the Papal Letters of Pope Innocent III (1199 A.D.). 'The school', says Westropp, 'is said to have lain to the east of the harbour opposite the ruined church.' Canon O'Mahony says its site has been identified in South Schull. At all events, Ardmanagh (Monk's Hill), on which part of Schull is built, attests the presence of cenobites in the district. We are told that in 1598 John Mullbrian of Schull held the castle, and 'the mine and old Schull'. There is no trace of a tradition of a castle at Schull, so far as I know. The castle referred to may be either Ardintenant or Leamcon, both of which are near Schull and in the vicinity of copper mines.[290]

The Fastnet

The Fastnet Rock, with its lighthouse, is Ireland's last lonely outpost in the Atlantic. The great ocean liners, and the tramp-steamers which hug our own southern shores on their way to North America and Canadian ports only say goodbye to Ireland and to Europe when the Fastnet light sinks winking under the horizon. It is "the last glimpse of Éire" seen by many poor Irish emigrants, and it is the first welcoming beam which greets many of them when they return once more to their native land.

The first lighthouse erected for the direction of steamers in this region was built on Cape Clear in 1823, but as this was about four miles inside the Fastnet Rock, it sometimes proved a misleading guide. To remedy matters, and thereby to secure assistance for passing ships, it was decided to erect a lighthouse on the Fastnet Rock itself; this idea was put into execution in 1870, when an iron structure was fixed on the very pinnacle of the rock. It usually swayed alarmingly when buffeted by the winter storms. Work on the present lighthouse was commenced as the last century was coming to its close. It took several years to construct it, because the foundations could only be laid in very calm weather and during spring tides. Four or five years elapsed before any appreciable headway was made.

The tower stands 160 feet above sea level, and during winter gales the keepers are entirely isolated as gigantic seas break continuously right over the very top of the tower. It is built of Cornish granite; this material was first transported to Crookhaven, and in order to make certain that the granite sets were fashioned to fit perfectly, the tower was actually erected on Rock Island. Subsequently it was dismantled, and the sets were then laid on the Rock with infinite labour, because on several occasions large quantities of the prepared stones and materials were washed away, and duplicates had to be kept in readiness.

The entrance to the tower is by a narrow gun-metal door which weighs over half-a-ton, and which seals the tower hermetically. All windows are double, having glass several inches thick. Even on the calmest day, landing on the rock is difficult. In recent years, more than months once elapsed before a relief landing could be made.[291]

Figure 25. The old Fastnet Lighthouse. Photo by Robert French, ref. L_ROY_06669
Image used with the kind permission of The National Library of Ireland.

Figure 26. Construction of the Fastnet lighthouse. Image used with the kind permission of the National Library of Ireland, ref. NPA CIL145.

SCHULL

Farming, Trade and Crafts

Grinding Corn

Years ago there was a pair of quern stones in nearly every farmhouse in this district. These stones were circular in shape, and they were made out of very hard stone. Each stone was about two inches in thickness and about eighteen inches in diameter. In the centre of the bottom stone a hole was bored into which a round piece of wood about six inches long was driven tightly. In the centre of the top stone there was a hole which was larger than the hole in the bottom stone. A wooden handle was also fixed in the top stone.

When wheat was to be ground the bottom stone was laid on a clean sheet, and the top stone was laid on top of this, the piece of wood in the former going through the hole in the latter and acting as a spindle. The wheat was then poured in through the hole in the top stone, which was revolved by the handle. The flour then came out at the sides and fell on the sheet. This flour was sometimes mixed with milk and sugar, and this mixture was called 'reboon'. Before being ground the wheat was well dried.[292]

Farm Animals

The principal animals kept by the local farmers are cows. Some farmers keep sheep but only those who have grazing rights on the hills. Nearly every farmer keeps a horse. The small farmer keeps a pony or a donkey. When people are driving cows, they say "how how." If the cows are inclined to trespass, they say "Rowish" or "Ceartuig". When cows are driven into a cow house to be milked, they are secured in the stalls, or tied to the wall with ropes. Nearly every cow has a name such as Summer, Daisy, Primrose, Bluebell, Small, Kerry, Magpie, and Dandy. A farmer would never lend a churn on a May morning because he believes that if he did so, he would have no butter for the rest of the year.[293]

The Potato Crop

In this district potatoes are usually planted in ridges. It is said that sounder and better potatoes are got out of ridges than out of drills. If the weather permits, the main crop is sown from the end of February to the middle of March. The potatoes are usually planted in a grazing field. The manure is first drawn out and scattered evenly over the field. The field is then ploughed into ridges about four feet wide. The ridges are then well hacked with an adze-like implement called a 'griffaun.' The potatoes intended for planting are cut into pieces, each piece having two or more eyes. These pieces are then planted in the following manner: the spade is driven into the ground, the handle is shoved forward, and the seed is dropped into the hole behind the spade. The distance between each seed is about the length of a man's boot, but Irish Queen potatoes are planted closer to each other. The holes are then shut by striking them with a pike, or with an implement called a 'folaheen.' Sometime afterwards the trenches are ploughed, and the earth is scattered over the ridges. This is called 'first earthing.' 'Second earthing' is given when the stalks are about two inches high. The potatoes need no more care until they are sprayed. This takes place when the stalks are about a foot high. The spray used is made from a solution of bluestone and washing soda.

In September and October, the potatoes are dug, and they are then put into pits in the field, but some time afterwards they are drawn out and stored in a house. The potatoes grown in this district are British and Irish Queens, Kerr's Pink, Arran Banners, Lancers, and Yankee Learys. Yankee Leary potatoes are one of the most popular potatoes grown in this district. There were first brought to this district from America by a man named Leary. The women of this district make two kinds of cakes from potato cakes and 'stampy.' Potato cakes are made from a mixture of flour, boiled potatoes and milk. This mixture is baked in a pan over the fire. 'Stampy is made in the following manner: raw potatoes are first grated, and the water is then squeezed out of them. Flour and cream are then mixed with the grated potatoes, and this mixture is baked.[294]

Candle Making

Long ago the people of this district made their own candles. One method of making them was to peel the green skins off rushes and use the inner white part as a wick. This wick was then dipped into melted tallow. It was then drawn out and the tallow on the wick was left to dry. The wick was dipped in the tallow and drawn out again in the same manner until the candle was the required thickness. Some people had moulds for making candles.[295]

Weaving

Weaving was carried on extensively in this district long ago. Many women were employed in spinning the wool. First the wool was washed and then spun into thread by spinning wheels. Then it was made up in balls and made up into skeins. It was then taken to the weaver to be made into cloth. Then it was taken to the mill to be tucked and washed and was then spread out to dry. Afterwards it was made up into rolls and pressed by weights. There was a weaver called "Denis the Weaver" living near the road leading to Coosheen where it meets the main road. There is an old weaver still living in Schull named Mr J. Cole, but he has not practiced his trade in some years.[296]

Basket Making

One of the old crafts carried out in this district long ago was the making of baskets. This craft is carried out to the present day but to such a large extent as in former days. Baskets are made as follows. Green twigs are gathered and about eight hazel sticks. The hazel sticks are stood in the ground, and then the twigs are woven around the sticks. The bottom of the basket is made by putting about four hazel sticks parallel to each other, and thus the bottom is secured to the top of the basket by means of woven twigs. Basket making is not carried on extensively in this district at present. Some people make baskets and they sell them at the fairs. Baskets are sold principally in the months of October and November. The price of a basket is from 2^{d} to 2/6^{d}.[297]

SCHULL
Local Customs

Local Fairs

There are two fairs held in Schull every month. The pig fair is held on the second Thursday and the cattle fair on the following Friday. When the farmer is satisfied with the price given by the buyer, they both strike hands. The buyer marks cattle with a colour of red or blue, and pigs by a scratch made with a knife on the back. The buyer gets luck money from the farmers. Pigs are usually brought to the fair in cars, and the cattle are walked.[298]

St John's Eve

In this district fires are lit in the potato fields on St John's eve. Withered bushes are gathered together, and they are so placed that when lit, the wind blows the smoke over the crop. The people say that the lighting of these fires brings a blessing on the crops. This custom has been carried out in this district as long as people can remember.[299]

St Stephen's Day

On St Stephen's Day boys decorate their clothes with coloured ribbons and go singing the wren song. They take with them a long pole on the top of which they tie a big bunch of holly and ivy. The practice of tying a dead wren on to the bunch of holly has now died out. There are different versions of the song, but they all begin with the following words:

The wren, the wren, the king of all birds,
St Stephen's Day he was caught in the furze,
Although he's little his family's great,
Rise up old lady and give us our treat.

In this district, wren is pronounced 'wran', and treat 'trate'. The money received is divided among the boys, but sometimes a 'wren dance' is held with the money.[300]

Old Customs

The old people would never build a house on an old pathway, or cross the road or a stream to build a new house because they said it was unlucky. They would never go into a new house on a Friday or in the month of May. They would always go out the same door of a house as they came in, because they said if they went out a different door, they would take the luck out of the house. They would never lend anything on May morning. No person would go out after dark on May eve or November eve.

If a person died, the body would not be taken to the church if the cemetery would be passed on the way. When a corpse was brought out of a house, everything in the house was washed and the chairs turned upside down. When a person is brought to Schull cemetery to be buried, the coffin is brought all around the old church. This custom originated in penal times when the priest was forbidden to read the service at the graveside, so the coffin was brought around the church while the priest read the service inside.

In this district candles are lit in the windows on Christmas eve and Christmas night, New Year's Eve and New Year's night, eve of the epiphany and the night of the epiphany. The candles are lit by the youngest person in the house. The Christmas candle is lit and quenched by the oldest person.

On Shrove Tuesday pancakes are made for supper. Years ago, bonfires were lit in the street, and the Skelig List was written. This was a list of poetries written about the bachelors in the place. On November eve the hallow 'een cake is made in every house, and then apples are eaten. On Easter Sunday morning everybody eats a great deal of eggs for their breakfast. On Good Friday the people pick limpets and periwinkles. These are boiled and eaten. On St John's eve bushes are lit near the potatoes so that the smoke is blown over them.[301]

Schull
Local Cures

Old Cures

The people of this district had a great many cures for different ailments. Most of these cures were got from the herbs. The most commonly used herb by the old people was wild sage. This herb was boiled in water and then strained. This water was said to be very good for stomach trouble or broken bones. It was said that it would make the bones mend quickly. The milk left over by a ferret was said to be a very good cure for whooping cough or measles. Wormwood was used as a cure for people suffering with worms. This plant was boiled, and the water was then drank by the person who wanted to get cured.

If a horse or another animal got a bad cut, cobwebs or pig dung was always put to the cut to stop the bleeding. The old people used to say that nothing else was effective in stopping the bleeding. Boiled nettles were considered to be a very good blood purifier. The leaves of a certain kind of buttercup were used as a cure for a whitlow. The leaves were first bruised well, and then put on the whitlow as a poultice. Watercress was used as a cure for a cold. For a bad wound the people used to make ointment out of a mixture of ribleaf and cream. A pink flower found growing on wet land was used as a cure for ringworm. This flower was boiled, and the water was then rubbed to the ringworm.

The old people would always prick a blister with a gooseberry thorn. The old people said that if a boy who was very dull was put sleeping in a house with sheep that he would become more intelligent. A butter-like substance found on the stems of plants growing in certain fields was used as a cure for pains. This substance was rubbed on the part of the body affected. If a person got a sting from a nettle, bruised dock leaves were rubbed to the affected part to deaden the pain.[302]

SCHULL

The Natural World and Weather lore

Weather Lore

The people of this district have been always particularly good at predicting the weather, but for some years back they cannot predict the weather with the same certainty. For some reason the signs by which they predicted the weather do not hold good now. The following are regarded by the people of this district as signs of wet weather.

A halo around the moon.
A certain kind of fog on Mount Gabriel.
Swallows flying low.
The dust on the road blown up in clouds by the wind.
A dog eating grass.
The rooks flying around and perching on the hills.
Cows gathering together in a field.
A great many cobwebs on the bushes.
The hills and island looking near.
A white frost three nights in succession.
Soot falling.
When the light of the Fastnet can be seen far over land.
When a person's toes are itching.
The flame of the fire a blue colour.
One cow licking another.

The following are regarded as signs of fine weather.

A calm sea.
Swallows flying high.
The hills and island looking far away.
A certain kind of fog on the hills.
The wind following the sun around.
A dry-looking moon.
Smoke going straight out of a chimney.
A red sky at sunset.

Seagulls flying inland, and the seals uttering cries are regarded as signs of stormy weather. Twinkling stars are a sign of frost.[303]

Schull
Sea and Shipwrecks

The Wrecking of the Memphis

At one time there traded between the British Isle and other countries a ship called the Memphis. The Memphis left Montreal one fine summer's day with a cargo of cattle, butter, bacon, and eggs. She was bound for Liverpool. On the south coast of Cork she ran into a fog which sent her to her doom. She was wrecked on the ragged rocks of Dunlough Bay. All the crew except the captain were drowned. He was saved by getting on a bullock's back which swam with him safely to the shore. For a long time afterwards, the shores around here were strewn with the wreckage of the Memphis.[304]

The Wreck of the Lady Charlotte

Many years ago a ship named the Lady Charlotte left Lima in Peru with a cargo of hides, seeds, tallow, gold, and silver. She was bound for Liverpool. All went well with the ship until, nearing the Irish coast, a gale blew up and she was driven on the Barrel Rocks which lie a little to the west of Goat Island. Four local men named Tom and Andy Beasley, and Lynch and Brady went to the rescue. When they arrived at the place of the wreck there was only one survivor, and they rescued him. It is said that along with the cargo, the ship also had on board the figures of a sow and twelve bonhams in gold, and that these, with other gold, still lie at the bottom of the sea where the ship was wrecked. There is a strand a little to the south of Schull Pier called the Lady Charlotte Strand, and it so called because some wreckage of the ship was washed there.[305]

SCHULL
History and Archaeology

A Holy Well

There is only one holy well in this district. That one is situated in the fifth field west of Meenvane Bridge at the north side of the stream. Long ago people used to go to this well to be cured of certain ailments, but no one goes there now. The water was supposed to be a very good cure for warts. At the side of the well there is a stone with a hollow on top, into which people who visited the well put a coin, a rag, a button, or some other article. The name of this well is 'Tobar na gort a cill' which means the well of the field of the church. There is no trace of a church or other building in this field now. This field is never ploughed but cattle graze upon it. It is not known with what saint this well is connected.[306]

Saint Kieran's Well

There is a well in Cape Clear which is known as St Kieran's well. It is so called because it was connected with St Kieran. It is a holy well. This well is situated a little above the pier in the island. The well is covered with a stone and when the tide comes in it covers the well. When the tide goes out the water becomes fresh again. Long ago people who had certain diseases used to go to the well to be cured. For a good many years now, no one has gone to this well to be cured.[307]

The Poll Talmans

In this district there are curious underground chambers called poll talmans. These chambers are about three feet high and shapes like a beehive. The chambers are connected by passages about a foot and a half high. Nobody knows who made these, but evidently, they were made in pre-historic times.[308]

Old Monuments

In a strand west of Colla there is a stone about the size of a small boat. Its circumference is about 20 feet. In this stone there are five holes looking as if they were made by sticking five fingers into it. It is said that one day a giant was working in a field near the strand when the stone fell on him. He, being angry, caught the stone and flung it into the strand.

In the middle of a field belonging to Mr Wilcox of Glaun there are two stones standing upright. It is said that two men were buried here long ago. In Mr O'Sullivan's farm in South Schull there are two stones standing upright in a field. It is said that people were buried there long ago and that the graves were marked with those stones. It is said that it is unlucky to plough that field, so it is always left under grass. In the same farm there is a stone standing upright in a field which is said to mark the burial place of a giant.

In a field belonging to Mr Edward Sweeny of Rathcool there are two stones standing about two and a half feet apart. It is said that long ago they were used as goal posts for playing football. In a field belonging to Mr Patrick Sheehan of Corrydorigan there is a flat stone near a fence. It is about six feet long, four feet wide, and two feet high. It is said that in the penal days mass was celebrated on that stone.

In the townland of Toormore there are two stones standing in a field, and another stone resting on them. These stones are called 'The Altar.' It is said that mass was said on these stone in the penal days. Another stone which stands on Mount Gabriel is called 'The White Lady.' It is said that a giant threw this stone from Lemcon, jumped on it, and stuck it into the rock. Then he painted the stone with white paint.

In Mrs Hall's farm in Gubbeen there is a stone about 2½ feet long and 2 feet wide. It is said that mass was said on this rock long ago during penal days. In another field in the same far there are two big stones which resemble two furrows turned by a plough.[309]

Leamcon Castle

Leamcon signifies the hound's leap. The castle is sometimes called the Black Castle. It is built on a small promontory surrounded by water and is accessible only by a narrow arch over a collapsed cave. This arch is hardly a yard wide. Leamcon was built probably on some older residence late in the fifteenth century. Conor Cabaice, the Chieftain of Ivahagh died in 1473. He built Leamcon for his second son, Fineen Caol (slender), ancestor of the O'Mahony Caol sliocht, who are still proud to trace their descent from Finghin of Leamcon.

In 1602, Carew reported that Captain Henry had captured Leamcon and six other castles, strongly seated on rocks, and nests of smuggling, and had their shares of the spoil. In 1612 the representatives of Conor O'Mahony who migrated, leased certain ploughlands to Hull. This shows that the O'Mahony's still held a portion of their ancient inheritance. In 1631 Fineen MacConnor O'Mahony held Leamcon Castle. Fineen MacConnor died in 1627 and his son sold Leamcon to Hull. The latter took part in the rising of 1641. He was indignant at the conduct of the Irish robbers, forgetting that he was an arch-robber himself. The castle and town of Crookhaven were besieged and the goods of the townsmen were taken. The rebels further plundered the fish sellers at Dunbeacon, Dunmanus, and Leamcon, and took 800 barrels of salt. They looted also big supplies of timber, pitch, malt, and ammunition.

A fine stone house with a garden near Leamcon Castle shows that the modern residence was in existence in Sir William Petty's time. In 1562 Donal son of Conor, the owner of Rossbrin, was tried for felony and executed at Cork. The castle was given to O'Mahony Finn and his son Cornelius. Among the chieftains who left for Spain in 1602 we find Conor O'Mahony of Leamcon; Conor, son of Sir Fineen O'Driscoll; O'Sullivan Bere's son from Berehaven; and Colla McSwiny of Carbery. In the list of forces of West Cork we find that O'Mahony of Ivahagh had twenty horses and 120 kerns;[xlv] O'Mahony of Rossbrin had 46 warhorses and 100 kerns; O'Driscoll of Collymore has six horses and 200 kerns; O'Sullivan Bere had ten horses and 100 kerns.[310]

[xlv] Kern – a light-armed foot soldier.

Rossbrin Castle

Most of the O'Mahony's castles were built on headland or near inlets of the sea. The object was, no doubt, to protect the coastal fisheries from poachers. These chieftains drew princely revenue from their fishing rights. Foreigners in large number came from Spain, Portugal, France, and elsewhere, in search of the fish that abounded along the southwestern littoral of Cork County. Here I may say that the western O'Mahonys maintained a fleet, which rendered great help to Brian Boru in some of his campaigns.

There is an extensive liss near Schull.[xlvi] It is surrounded by two ramparts and a fosse.[xlvii] It is called Lissacaha. It must have been the residence of some powerful chief and probably was the scene of a battle. One of the earliest chieftains of a western O'Mahonys was called Donnchadh Ratha Dreoain. Many years ago, I heard that that place referred to was Rathruane or Rathrovane, where there is an old stone fort.

The most easterly of the O'Mahonys castle was Rossbrin, which stands on a little headland that juts into the sea near Ballydehob. Rossbrin signifies the headland of Bran or Bron – a named found in the O'Mahony pedigree. Not far away there is a townland called Kilbronoge. The castle is best known as the residence of Fineen O'Mahony of Rossbrin, a famous Irish scholar who lived there when he was tanist of Ivahagh. He died in 1496.[311]

[xlvi] Lis – a fort.

[xlvii] Fosse – a long narrow fortification trench.

Figure 27. Rossbrin Castle.

ROSSBRIN

Co. Chorcaighe
Bar: Cairbre Thiar
Par: Scoil Mhuire
Scoil: Rossbrin
Oide: Cormac MacCarthaigh
December 1938

ROSSBRIN
Local Folklore and Stories

An Old Story

I heard a story about the naming of Stouke graveyard. The Irish name for this graveyard is Kiel-Aspig Owen. It is said that during the Catholic persecution in Ireland, a bishop by the name of Bishop Owen was administering the sacrament of confirmation in the church when himself and four hundred children were killed by the English soldiers. They were buried where we have Stouke graveyard now. This graveyard is supposed to be about four hundred years in use. So this must have occurred in fifteenth century. People go to the graveyard on St. Johns Eve for to make a rounds at the tomb of Fathers John and James Barry who were buried there.[312]

A Story

Once upon a time there lived a certain family who were told by a woman who used to be in company with the fairies, that they used not get the full produce of their milk. Not far from where they lived, an old woman lived alone in a hut. She had the power of changing herself into a hare, which no one except herself knew. One May, as the owner of the cows was driving them in, he noticed a hare with them. He was very surprised to see it there, so he sent his hound after it. The hound tore a piece of the hare's side just as it was disappearing through a hole in the door of the old woman's house. A few days afterwards it was learned that the old woman was dead. The people that owned the cows got the produce of their milk ever afterwards.[313]

A Story

Once upon a time there lived a woman who could steal butter by magic. She lived in Stouke. One day as another woman who also lived in Stouke was churning, she was churning for a long time and still the butter wasn't coming. It happened that a beggar man came in. He said that the butter was stolen and that if holy water was put into the churn the butter would come back. He also said that the thief would be at the door next morning. The woman got the holy water and put it into the churn. The butter came back, and the thief was at the door next morning confessing that she stole the butter.[314]

ROSSBRIN

People, Places and Property

Travelling Folk

I see a great many travelling folk. Some of them have big caravans or houses in which they sleep and live. Those in the caravan's are not so badly off. They sell chairs, nice tables, and many other things around the country. They also sell donkeys and goats. I see tinkers that mend tins and umbrellas and other things also. I also see chimney sweeps that sweep chimneys, and fortune tellers who pretend to tell fortunes. Some of the tinker class are very cross. They would want things and if you did not give them to them, they would get very angry and scold you. There are very poor old people that come, and you would always try and give them something. They have a very hard life travelling around in the wet and cold and very often they are hungry.[315]

Rossbrin National Schools

Rossbrin National School was built in the year 1909. It is situated near the public road and is surrounded by a low stone wall. Previous to this there was a school at the northeastern end of the plot in an old, thatched dwelling owned by a McCarthy family. When this family left, it was transformed into a school. This school was taught by a McSweeny man who had the use of one hand only. It was quill pens that were in use and he had to make pens for the pupils. There was not much pay given to teachers by the Board of Education at that time so that each child had to pay fees, and also in the winter season each child had to bring a sod of turf for the fire. When this school began to crumble, the Manager thought it necessary to erect a new school. There is a local story told in connection with the erection of that school. The Ballycumisk mines were in use at the time, and the Manager, whose name was Pope, had stones drawn to a place called the crosseen for the erection of mine houses. A dispute arose about the site of these houses with the result that the stones lay there for a considerable time. So, on a certain morning the people of the townland assembled to draw the stones for the erection of a school. The Curate of the parish was present. Pope objected to the stones being taken and he came forward with a loaded revolver and said that "the first man who handled a stone would fall", so the priest persuaded them to go home. Some time after Pope was passing on his horse, and just where he aimed his revolver he was thrown from his horse and was killed. This school was situated parallel to the present one and was taught by Brown ODriscoll, Tucker, O'Donovan, and Lyons. Some time after a new school was built south of it for the girls, and these schools remained so until our present building was erected.[316]

Rossbrin Mensal Land

Rossbrin is one of the Mensal townlands which number eleven. It is called the Rossbrin Manor estate. It is situated about three miles southwest of the village of Ballydehob. It is a fairly large townland. It has an ancient Castle which was one of the dwelling places of the O'Mahonys. This castle is situated near the sea. It is said that there is an underground channel connecting it with the sea. It is said that the O'Mahonys were pirates and that some of them were buried north of the Castle, because bones were unearthed there. Some time after that, Carew blew the west side off it as he was passing from Kinsale to Dunboy, from near the Fastnet. In the year 1432 this castle was erected. It is situated on the top of a high rock. The top of the Castle is about ninety feet above sea-level. Finean O'Mahony was one of the tenants of Rossbrin. It is said he was accused of piracy and hanged in Cork. Conor O'Mahony was the writer of the Psalter of Rossbrin'. Many of these books were lost and cannot be found. The chief of the O'Mahonys lived at Ardantenant, about two miles from Rossbrin. Some time after that Rossbrin Manor Estate was sold. It was bought from the Cages by Edinburgh Life Insurance Company. In the year nineteen hundred and three the tenants bought back the land.[317]

Local Place Names

There are a great many ancient names around here; the following are some of them: Páirc an Tobair, Páirc-na Scráicí, Páircín Desmond, Palíasí, Páirc-Fliuch, Pairc-an-Druma, Páircín-Dóire, Páirc-Amhain, Páircín-Seanntaillog, Páirc-an-Tulahán, Páirc-Gréine, Páirc-na-Bréochaoán, Páirc-na-Raichnig, Pairc-na-Carairs, Páirc-an-Dóthair, Garrarhoglas, Garrarhoréal, Garrarhonúch, Lacha-Mhór Claisín-Fharoa, Dreen-na-Gréine, Clash, Crioch-Achairn, Cnoch-na-Sríana Croch, Cuiliheen, Scráin-Gairrith, Muinlighe, Conaca-n-arhmavo, Cras-na-lían, Clarhoean-Avann.[318]

Graveyards

There are several Graveyards in this locality. There is one situated about a mile south of the village of Schull. In it stands an old ruin which was very famous in ancient days. The name of this school was Sancta-maria-de-scholia which means school of Mary. It was from this old school that the village of Schull got its name. The Graveyard slopes towards the east. The catholics who lived in this locality are buried outside this old ruin, and the Protestants are buried within its walls. At the burial of some Catholic, a person was generally paid to "caoin" along the way. At the time of the Reformation the Protestants took possession of this old church and used it as a house of Worship. It was supposed that with this "caoining" the Protestants were unable to hold services. So, they removed farther north and there they erected a church of their own. While building this church the Protestants wanted to draw the stones of this old ruin to the building. It is said that whatever they carried north from this old Church was put back there again by night. About a mile South-west of the village of Ballydehob is situated another Graveyard called Kil-aspa-eoghan, which means Church of Bishop Eoghan. It slopes towards the east. It is said that there was an old ruin there also. There is a priest buried there whose name is Rev. John Barry. Every year on St John's Eve some of the people of the locality go to his grave to pray. There is another graveyard situated in Baunakane about a mile and a half north of the village of Ballydehob. Baunakane means an enclosed hillock. The graveyard slopes towards the east. It is thought that there was a religious house there also. There is also what is called Kiels in this parish, or unused graveyards. They are situated in the following townlands: Cusheen, Kilbronogue and Coolagh. They slope towards the east. It is thought that it was unbaptised children were buried in the Kilbronogue Kiel. And it is supposed that it was children were buried in the Cusheen and Coolagh Kiels.[319]

Local Roads

The roads of the locality are known as the New Road, the Mine Road, the Green Boreen, the Shanava Road and the Rainbow Road. The Green Boreen is the oldest of these roads. It was the Board of Works that got it made some time after the Famine. It starts at the cove of Rossbrin and it passes through the townlands of Ballycumisk and Cappanacalee, through to Barna-Gaoithe, and from there to Bantry and through Priest's Leap near the border of Cork and Kerry, and it ends at Kenmare. In some places it is rough and choked with briars, and therefore it is almost useless for traffic. In some places it is used as a path. This old road is not cared for at all now as no one is responsible for its repair. In the winter the roads are wet and muddy, but in the summer they are dry and very dusty. The road known as the Rainbow Road is also very old. It is in the townland of Ballycumisk. It is an old Board of Works road. It was made after the Famine. It is not used as a road at all now but as a path. It is covered with grass. Nobody is responsible for its repair now. The road known as the mine road passes Ballycumisk copper mine. It is a very narrow and stony road. When Ballycumisk mine was being worked some time ago it was along that road the copper was carried to the ship. The part of the road that passes the mine is steep and dangerous.[320]

Old Houses

The houses of the olden days were low one storey buildings. The walls were made of stone and clay. The roofs were thatched. The thatch was wheaten straw. Straw thrashed by the modern thrashing machines would not do for thatching at all, because it is weakened by all the beating it gets. The floors of the houses were made of clay. There were a great many houses in the country that had but two rooms. One of the rooms was used as a bedroom, the other was used as a kitchen; there was generally a bed in the kitchen also. The people of those days had not as many houses in which to store potatoes and such things as they have now, so they put potatoes and fish, which were the chief food of the people of that time, under the beds. In many places a cow was kept in the dwelling houses during the night. The fireplace was at the gable end of the house. On each side of the fireplace there was a hole in the wall called the "hob-hole" in which salt and such things were kept. There were larger holes in the wall called "oletts". The windows of the houses of the olden days were generally small. The people had not any oil lamps to give them light in the night time, but they made lights for themselves.[321]

Rossbrin
Farming, Trade and Crafts

Artificial Lights

Long ago the people of this country had to make their lights in their own homes. They dipped the hearts of rushes into some sort of animal fat and lit them, this was a very unsteady light. The next light after that was the light of the splinter. The logs of fir that were found in the peat bogs were called sculobs. These had a very fine grain, and it was possible to cut them into very thin slices or splinters. When the people went out in the nights killing birds, they carried a handful of lit splinters with them, and this was called splintering. Another light that was used in the olden times was the light of the home-made candle. This candle was made by pouring melted animal fat into a mould and placing three or four pieces of string traced together into the centre of the mould. The light that came after the light of the oil lamp. This lamp was small and cheap and had no `glass.[322]

Home Industries

There are not many home industries carried on around here at the present time, but the old people were great at working rods, and making a great many useful articles for the house. They used to make baskets which were very handy for holding potatoes, mangolds, and other things. They also made skiffs for carrying potatoes and turf. They made lobster pots of them also. The man that made them earned a great deal of money, but it was very hard work gathering the rods, and they should peel them and settle them before they made them into pots. They made handbaskets of rods also, and those baskets were used for carrying farm produce, such as butter and eggs, to town, and bringing home the provisions for the week in them.[323]

Rossbrin
Leisure

The Games I Play

There are a great many games played by the children of this locality nowadays, both at home and at school. The names of the games are as follows: Colours, Hide-and-go-seek, Gates Locked, Blind-man's-Buff, Oranges and Lemons, Frog-in-the-middle, and Four-corned-Fool. Frog-in the middle is played in the following way: A number of children stand in a circle and another child kneels in the centre of the circle, and closes his eyes, this child is called a frog. The circle of children moves around the frog and whoever is touched first by him must act as frog next. Blind-man's'-Buff also contains great amusement. It is played the following way: One person is blindfolded with a piece of cloth, a great many children run around him, and whoever is touched first by him must be blindfolded next. Four-cornered-Fool is also an amusing game. A number of children get a stone each and stand on it. Another child stands in the centre of the circle and is called a fool, then the children exchange stones with each other, and the fool watches his chance to take some other person's place.[324]

ROSSBRIN
Local Customs

Local Superstitous Practices

Long ago the people of this country had a great many superstitious practices. It was considered unlucky to redden the earth on Good Friday. If a person found a four-leaf shamrock, it was thought that the person would be lucky. If a person was going on a journey and met a black cat, it was considered lucky. If a person had a horseshoe hanging over the door, it was thought it would keep away ill-luck and bring good luck. When a person saw a number of magpies together, he began to ponder in his mind what did they betoken, and after a while the following little rhyme came to his mind.

One for sorrow.
Two for joy.
Three for a wedding.
And four for to die.
Five for silver
Six for gold.
Seven for a story that had never been told.
Eight for a shovel.
Nine for a spade.
Ten for a coffin to go down in the grave.

It was considered unlucky to go on a journey on a Monday.[325]

Easter Customs

Long ago the people of Ireland fulfilled a great many Easter customs. People went to the seashore on Good Friday to gather shellfish. When they gathered them, they washed them then they put them into a pot and boiled them rapidly, for it was feared they would toughen. It was also the custom to rise early on Easter Sunday morning to see the sun dancing. On Easter Sunday morning a pot of eggs was boiled and placed on the table, and everyone could eat as many eggs as would satisfy him. Another custom was going to devotions on Good Friday evening and making the Stations of the Cross.[326]

Local Fairs

Long ago when money was not known, fairs were not held. Another method was used for exchanging cattle for other commodities which was called swopping. When money was known, fairs were held in certain towns and villages. Ballydehob was the village where the fair was held in this locality. The fairs were held there three times in the year. After some time cattle were getting more numerous in the country and it was decided that the fairs should be held at the following dates: one on New Years Day, one on the second of February, one on the twelvth of March, one on Easter Tuesday, one on Whit Monday, one was held on the twenty ninth of June, one on the twenty fourth of July, one on the fifteenth of August, one on the eighth of September, one on the tenth of October, one was held on the eighth of November, and one was held on the eighth of December. After some time, it was observed that a great many of the fairs were held on Church holidays, so it was decided that the fairs should be held on the third Wednesday and third Thursday of each month. A great many people attended these fairs, and ballad singers, Seán Saors, and all sorts of tricksters attended them also.[327]

Lore of Certain Days

Long ago there were great superstitious beliefs connected with certain days and months. It was considered unlucky to give away or lose money on Monday. It was considered unlucky to start a new job on that day also, and it was said that whatever way Monday was spent, the rest of the week would be spent in the same manner. It was supposed unlucky to get the hair cut on Tuesday. It was considered unlucky to remove to a new house on Friday, or to draw blood by killing an animal. It was also considered unlucky to visit the sick, to get married, or to cut the hair. It was considered unlucky to get married in May. It was considered unlucky to remove to a new house in Lent or Advent. It was said to be unlucky to throw away ashes, paper, old shoes and such things on New Year's Day. It was supposed lucky to light a fire and to let the smoke float over the potato crop.[328]

Rossbrin

Local Cures

Local Cures

Long ago the people of this country did the most of their doctoring at home. For a burn the first thing done was to get stampie and cream and put it up to the burned part immediately. Also bread soda or soap. The first homecure for ringworm was a low "cutty" plant called chivers. It is a fairly long stalk with a milky substance. It has a yellow flower like the Merringold. The milky subsistance was rubbed round the ringworm. It is a sure cure for it. Watercress that grows in the streams is a good remedy for loss of appetite. Hot roasted potatoes, bran scalded with vinegar, or warm coarse salt put up to the throat at night is a good cure for sore throats. For a pain in the ear the best home cure is to get hot sweet oil and black cotton wool. Put some of the sweet oil in the wool then put it in to the ear. Paraffin oil on brown paper put up to the back between the shoulders is a good cure for colds. The first thing that was done for wildfire was to get a black cat and kill it. With the blood of the cat write the persons name around the wildfire or write the person's name with very red ink. When the whooping cough was around long ago, the people used their own remedies. First the child would get some milk that the ferret would not drink. Another cure for the whooping cough was to put the person with it under and over a donkey nine times after each other. People also go to Stouke to make rounds to Fr. John Barry's tomb on St. John's eve. They have great faith in going there and saying a decade of the rosary at each corner of the tomb if any thing was wrong with them. People also go to the Blessed well in Rossbrin strand. It is about one hundred and fifty yards east of the pier. There was an old tree over the blessed well. People always left some little thing after them on the tree.[329]

ROSSBRIN

The Natural World and Weather lore

Bird Lore

Long ago the people of this country had an idea of the weather when they saw certain birds. When sea gulls are near the land it foretells bad weather. When the starlings come to outhouses for shelter it is a sign of snow and very heavy frosts. When a robin sings on a briar on a fine day, it is a sign of rain. When the swallows are flying low it is a sign of rain. When the seagulls are not on the land or near it it is a sign of good dry weather. When the swallows are flying high it is a sign of fine weather. When the Tabhairín rúa is around in the evening, it is also a sign of fine weather. When we see the cuckoo's, corncrakes and swallows, we know that we have summer.[330]

ROSSBRIN
History and Archaeology

Local Antiquities

There are a few forts around this part of the country. There is one of them in Kielbronogue, one in Ballycumisk, Rossbrin, Cappnacolly, and Coosheen. The fort in Kielbronogue is in the north part of it. It is near the public road. There are lights seen in the field that the fort is in very often. Every year the field is tilled. Some years ago, when the field was being ploughed by the owner, his horse sank. A couple of weeks afterwards, he came with a car or two of stones and earth and covered it. Then he got a couple of flags and put them over the opened space and tilled that part of the field. There is a drain under the fort. There are lights seen there very often. In Cappnacolly the fort is in Willie Levi's land. It is said the people of old were buried there. Some people think that the forts were built by the Danes. There is a dolmen also in Kielbronogue on a hill which belongs to John ORegan. There is a very big stone on top of three other stones. It weighs one tonne. It is said that men lifted it. Some people say that Mass has been celebrated there, and others say a great chieftain was buried there. It is situated in sight of the public road. There is another dolmen in Cappnacolly between Mrs Cronen's and Jack Leadhys land on the boundary ditch. It is unknown whether Mass was celebrated on it or what use was made of it. There is a kiel in Kielbronogue and it is said that it is from this Kielbronogue got its name. There are ruins of an old Catholic church in Cooragurteen. After this, the Catholic church of this locality was in Stouke, the ruins of which are not to be seen now although it was erected many years later.[331]

On the Famine Times

This locality was thickly populated before the Famine when whole families died of hunger and of fever. Some of the corpses were never buried. Some people died in their houses and were left, and the houses were burned over them. Sometimes a pit was made, and a great many corpses were buried in it. Other corpses were buried in fields adjoining their homes. Dogs were seen eating corpses also. The people were reduced to such starvation that they ate raw vegetables, grass, nettles and other herbs. Some of the people had corn, but they kept it in order to pay the large rents of their little holdings. In the year 1846, the first year of the Famine, there were no large potatoes to be got, only small ones called Cratháins. These small potatoes were sown the following year, but they blackened and never grew. People still point out ruins and sites of houses whose occupants died of hunger and fever during the Famine years.[332]

ROSSBRIN
Songs

The Cove of Rossbrin

There is one little harbour, where kind nature smiles
Washed around by "Carbery's Hundred green Isles".
To all our four-fathers, sweet peace be with them.
Their holdings lie close by the cove of Rossbrin.

It breathes every scene most enchanting and dear.
Its school, and its copper-mines, castle, and pier.
John Collins's farm where the castle stands in.
Washed round by the waters of the Cove of Rossbrin.

It was in 1904 I travelled by rail.
To the city of Cork, to a Court of Appeal.
I saw the Lee's sparkling waters with its barques floating in.
Yet not half so charming as the Cove of Rossbrin.

It was in Autumn the fleet has repaired to our shore.
To beach in the strand until winter is o'er.
The crews have prepared as the springtime comes in.
To take their departure from the Cove of Rossbrin,

There were many dear ones who lived here as slaves.
Some have emigrated, more have filled the graves.
With rack-rented holdings, their prospects were thin.
Which forced them to rove from the Cove of Rossbrin.[333]

This was written by John Collins's Ballycumisk in the year 1904

BALLYDEHOB

Co. Chorcaighe
Bar: Cairbre Thiar
Par: Scoil Mhuire
Scoil: Béal an Dá Chab
Oide: Risteárd Ó Ligin

BALLYDEHOB, a village in the parish of Skull, western division of the barony of West Carbery, co. Cork, Munster. It stands on the road from Skibbereen to Crookhaven, and on the shore of an inlet on the west side of the bay of Roaring Water: and is grandly overhung, at a brief distance, by the imposing height of Mount Gabriel.

The Parliamentary Gazetteer of Ireland, 1843-44,
vol, 1 (Dublin: Fullarton, 1844, p.165.

`BALLYDEHOB
Local Folklore and Stories

Between a Man and a Landlord

A man lived in Ballydehob who had a great desire for shooting and hunting, and who used to have a gun and a hound always. The landlords did not like anyone to be hunting or shooting but themselves. The man was one day up in Ballyban and he met the landlord. Swanton was his name, and he was related to the Swanton of Ballydehob. This Swanton had a gun, and when he saw the man, he raised his gun and aimed at the man's house. "Who owns that hound?" says he. "I own it", says the hunter. "I will shoot it", says the landlord. "If you will shoot it", says the man, "I will shoot you." The landlord turned around and walked away.[334]

Collected by Dermot Daly, Ballydehob

Spirits in the Road

A man went for the priest long ago in the dead of night. His mother was dying. It was a sidecar he went in for the priest. On the way home the horse stopped. The man went out to lead it, but it would not go. The priest went out of the car and told the man to get in. He got a whip and beat the road in front of the horse. Then he went back into the car and the horse went on. The man asked the priest what he meant by beating the road. The priest said, "The road was swarming with them!" "With what?" said the man. "With spirits," said the priest. When they got home the woman was dead.[335]

On Great Men

There was a man who had a fishing boat in Cape Clear Island. It was more than half-a-ton in weight. The man had a son named Conchubhar Mac Eireamháin and he often used to send his son to see the boat, and the son got bored, so he brought the boat on his back up to the door of the house and left it there. There is a bridge in Ballydehob, and it is forty feet high over a river. There is a quay near this bridge and a boat had come in full of sand. The men were waiting for the tide to get higher. They came up to the bridge and one man said to the other, "I will race you over to the other end." One man ran on the wall, and the other on the ground. The fellow on the wall won. The man who ran on the ground is still living. His name is Mahony.[336]

Collected by Vincent Kelly, Ballydehob

The Horse Thief

There was once a man who was very fond of stealing horses. He took one very valuable horse, and the owner cursed him. Once when he was riding along, he saw two small men on each side of the road. When he was passing, they jumped on him and knocked his head with bottles. They flung him on the ground and rode away on the beautiful horse.[337]

The Hidden Treasure of Skehanore

A hidden treasure was buried in Skehanore, but it was found and unearthed about eighty years ago by the man who owned the farm it was in. It was buried in a kind of cave which was down by the sea. When the man with five others went into the cave, there was a foxy woman guarding the treasure. When the man's comrades saw her, they fled, but he stayed there. When the woman saw what the man wanted, she threatened him, but he took the treasure. All this wealth went bad, and that very week the man died, and his people put the treasure in the sea. It was the Danes who buried this treasure, and it must be a Danish woman was guarding the treasure. It's worth is not known. This woman guard flung a block of timber at one of the treasure seekers. There are many stories about this treasure about what happened before it was found.[338]

Collected by Vincent Kelly, Ballydehob
From Joe Kelly, Ballydehob

A Ride in a Fairy Car

Long ago a man and his son were going to a fair. The man told his son to go a different road. The man met a horse and car, and a woman and a man in the car. The man who was going to the fair asked them for a lift. They told him to come in. He went in. When he went in, he knew it was a fairy car and he knew them. They were dead, and he never knew anything until he was standing outside the Abbey graveyard. The man was waiting all the morning for his son, and the man soon died.[339]

Collected by Neil Lucey, Ballydehob
From Con Lucey, Ballydehob, Co. Cork

Strange Animals

During the time of the Land League, a man lived near Loch Ine, and he owned a small farm. He kept three cows, and they were his only means of living. One day he left the cows to graze in a field near the lake, and every two hours he used to check them. He came to see them at two o'clock one day, but there was only one cow in the field. He informed his landlord and he sent armed men to search for the lost cows. On their arrival at the place, they saw a four-footed animal coming out of the lake to take the third cow with it. The men shot the animal, and it made a loud roar, and its mate came to the rescue, but she too was shot. A collection was made for the man, and he bought two other cows.[340]

Collected by Eileen Coughlan, Ballydehob

The Bootmaker and the Hare

There was a bootmaker who lived in a remote district. He got short of wax and hemp. The nearest town to him was four miles and that was Macroom. He started his journey. After he had bought the wax and hemp, he took a near way across the country. On his way, a hare came running towards him. The hare stopped and looked in amazement, and the bootmaker stopped and looked at the hare. The bootmaker looked around to find something to throw at it. He could not get anything so instead he threw the ball of wax at it. It hit the hare in the forehead, and it clung to it. When he hit the hare, it turned about and ran back the path. Another hare came running from the opposite direction and the two bumped their heads together and they got clung. The bootmaker was very sorry for the loss of the ball of wax. On his way along the path, he saw the hares clung, and so he picked up his two fine hares.[341]

Collected by Pat Joe Murphy, Ballydehob
From Joseph Murphy, Ballydehob

The Haunted School

A few weeks ago, everyone was talking around the town that there were lights seen in the school every night. The children were frightened and in the end a crowd of boys gathered together and went there to know would it be true. They went and waited until the light shone again. Then they saw a white figure. They got afraid and ran home. The next night they carried older men with them. Each carried a stick, and they watched until the light appeared again. One of them got courage and stole up to the window of the school. There a white figure stood in front of him. He called his companions to him, and they followed the ghost. The boys were too quick for the ghost and caught the sheet and took it away from him. Then they found out that it was a neighbour that had come to play a joke.[342]

Collected by Dermot Daly, Ballydehob
From Jeremiah Daly, Ballydehob

Nothing is Ever Got by Hard Work

In a certain town not far from here there lived a butcher. He kept an errand boy whom he called Lazy Tim, because he was very fat and lazy. One day he sent him with a leg of mutton to a gentleman's house nearby. He told him to go quickly as they wanted to cook it for dinner, and knowing how slow and lazy Tim was, he gave him extra time to do the errand. The butcher watched him out of sight, and again warned him to hurry. Lazy Tim hurried until he thought he was out of sight. "The day is very warm, and I am very hot with all this hurry," says Tim to himself, "so I will rest for a while; it is only half past twelve yet, and I can rest here until the people are again going to their dinner." He therefore sat in a nice sunny spot in the side of the road, putting his meat-basket by him. He started thinking of what he was going to buy with some money he had in his pocket. He wished for very ripe pears he saw in the shop window, and several other things, until finally he dozed off to sleep, forgetting all about his meat. Sometime after, he was awakened by the howling of dogs, and he jumped up with a start and he said to himself, "Oh boy! What is this about?" He looked at the sun and thought how low it was. "It must be dinner time now," he said, "and I will have to take along my meat." He looked around for his basket but lo! the basket was empty, and the meat was gone. "Oh! Where is it gone to?" and he looked around to try to find it and he saw a dog eating it behind the ditch. He went to take the meat which the dog had mostly eaten. "Ha, ha, my boy, you won't have that," he said snapping the remainder from him. Wrapping it up in his basket he delivered the bone. The maid asked him why he hadn't the meat in time for dinner. He said he thought it was for tomorrow's dinner. He wanted to get away quickly in case she would open the parcel of meat and see what he had. He was hurrying off when the maid said I must give you something for yourself, giving him a shilling. On his way back he said to himself how well he's done it. "Oh! How lucky I am nothing is never got by hard work."[343]

Collected by John Joe McCarthy, Ballydehob
From Michael McCarthy, Ballydehob

The Murder of the Wife of Donal O'Sullivan

At the time the English were taking the castles, Donal O'Sullivan was chieftain in Castletownbere. He sent his wife to Gaugane for safety. The English commander and his men were out sporting, and he saw the lady whom he wanted to take by force, but she did not want to go. When she resisted, he stabbed her. The funeral came to Bantry Abbey by night. It happened that Donal was there and when he saw she was stabbed, he swore that neither food nor drink would he taste until he would lay the enemy low. He dressed up in a monk's habit and went to the castle where the English man was. From outside the door Donal heard him say these words. "Some demon haunts me since my pride urged me to stab that outlaw's bride. His form I see. Each sound I hear. Her dying threats are in my ears." When Donal went in, he was taken up to the top room. The English man was sure that his visitor was a spy. When he asked questions, Donal said he would like to know who stabbed the outlaw's wife. The English man answered, "I tore her from St Finbar's Shrine, amidst her tears and she was mine. She proudly scorned my fond embrace and cursed my land and all its race. I stabbed her – it was a deed of guilt. But then it was Donal's blood I spilt."

"Monster", said Donal, "behold my promise is free. 'Tis Donal himself you see." They fought hard but Donal won. As he was throwing him out the window he said, "Saxon! Behold 'tis Eara is giving you this grave", and he flung him into the wave. As the soldiers were coming Donal jumped out of the window, crossed the river which was flowing past the castle, and went off safely.[344]

Collected by Mary Sullivan (aged 16), Ballydehob
From Mr J. Bennett (aged 73), farmer, Ballydehob

Ballydehob
People, Places and Property

The Swantons

The Swantons were the landlord of Ballydehob. We do not know how long they have been in this place, but we know they are here a couple of hundred years at least. They were middling good landlords. They had only seven farms, and the rest of the place was the town. I did not here that they threw anyone out of their places. It was the tenants who put up the town of Ballydehob. It is not known how these landlords got possession of the place. The land was divided into farms.[345]

Collected by Frankie Coughlan, Ballydehob

Local Heroes

A man named Michael Brien, Skehanore, lifted from a dike a sack of corn weighing thirty-three stones which fell from a horse's back. There were onlookers at the scene. Another man named MacCarthy of Sherkin Island jumped across a chasm of sixteen feet in breadth. The jump was done in Cape Clear. A man named Tim Desmond of the Skames Island was a good swimmer and singer. His favourite songs were the Valley of Sliab na mBan and the Bonny Banks of Lock Lomond.[346]

One of the local heroes is Dan O'Mahony who was born at Dreenlomane, about two miles from Ballydehob. He is a great weight thrower and wrestler also. He is able to throw the half cwt. over fifteen feet over the bar, and he can throw it over thirty-two feet with follow. He has held the heavy-weight championship of the world without defeat.

The father of Dan O'Mahony was another hero. In a village called Goleen he did 50 feet in a hop-step and jump. Micheal Cahalane from Ballybrawn was another one of our local heroes. He jumped six-feet five inches in height, and he was able to do forty-eight feet in the hop-step and jump.[347]

Collected by Jerry O'Brien, Michael O'Regan
and Cormac O'Donovan Ballydehob

DROGHEDA ARGUS AND LEINSTER JOURNAL

[5 September 1936, p.4]

Plays and Pastimes

Danno O'Mahony, Champion All-in Wrestler of the World, at present home in his native County Cork on holidays, at Kilkenny Championship Sports at Callan on Sunday last, threw the 56lbs weight 28 feet 7 ins., thus beating Guard Tobin's record throw of 28 feet 3 ins. made recently. It has been stated that Danno hurled the missile almost 30 feet in private practice in his home town, Ballydehob. This is not to be wondered at when O'Mahony can give a 17st opponent the "Irish Whip" – which consists of twirling him a couple of time round his head, flinging him over his shoulder and slamming him flat on his back to register a "throw," which is only accomplished when the opponents' two shoulders tip the mat.

Travellers

Men come selling things very rarely now, but they come begging. One man named Tom Malone comes often. He was rich once, but now he is poor. He was at college to be a priest, but he failed. He keeps himself very well dressed and wears a foxy whisker. He was born in Listowel in Kerry and is a great handball player and footballer. He is very well educated. Hennesy is the name of another traveller. He sells pots and saucepans. There was a family of people named Cordeys, and they were foxy, and they used to steal geese and ducks. They used to make tables and fight with bottles over the money. There is a house on the road to Bantry, a mill, and they used to sleep in it. The guards used to hunt them away. They beat a boy and stole money from him because he did not know where they could swim.[348]

Collected by Vincent Kelly, Ballydehob
From C. Kelly, Ballydehob

Travelling people call to our homes still. The people have been going around for many years. The most of them are very poor, but others are not too poor. They sell small articles. People buy from them on fair days and other days like that. They buy their supplies, and they don't mind what water they drink. They are not generally welcome. Some stay for a few nights and others don't stay a night at all. Some of them have covered cars, and they sleep in them, and others sleep by the ditches. The most of them travel in families. They come too on the day of the races selling small things, and when the evening comes, they sell all the things cheap in order to get rid of them, and when they have them all sold, they go away and spend every bit of it in drink, or some other thing.[349]

Collected by Frank Coughlan, Ballydehob
From Matthew Coughlan, Ballydehob

Local Poets

There was a poet long ago named Jonney Collins. He was never known beyond Ballydehob. He lived in Ballycummisk. He died in 1920. He made songs about his own place. One was called "Ballycummisk". He used to get a headache before every song, and while in bed he used to make his songs. He died at the age of 45.

Collected by Vincent Kelly, Ballydehob
From Patrick Collins, Ballydehob

On Old Roads

There was a road going through the Ballydehob Railway Station during the time of the famine down to a building by the sea. It was used as a public road too. Houses are built now where it was. This road was made in 1750. According to old people there is a place near Ballydehob which was a swampy place during the famine. A path led through this swamp, and it was made of stones. This place was called Black Pool. There is no sign of the swamp now, and a house is built in that place which is owned by a Duggan man.[350]

Collected by Vincent Kelly, Ballydehob
From John Hickey, Ballydehob

The road leading from Skibbereen to Schull passes my house. It is made over a hundred years. Before the bridge across the river was made the river was crossed by a ford. There is an old road from the school across up through Sweetnam's land, and it comes out into the new road at Greenmount cross. This road is seldom used now.[351]

Collected by Michael O'Regan, Ballydehob
From Nora Levis, Ballydehob

The road leading from the ruined workhouse at Schull, through the gap of Mount Gabriel, and connecting at Laharn with the road from Ballydehob to Dunbeacon, was constructed in the year 1838. Before then, a path led through the lowest part of the valley between Mount Gabriel and Letter Hill, over the gap, and went straight down the northern side. About ten years before the construction of this road, a wood was planted at the northern side of Mount Gabriel level with the gap. The area of this wood was about thirty acres, this wood was cut down about forty years ago. It was planted by a Dr Hicks, who also built a residence at Dreenatra. This Dr Hicks was landlord of the townland of Dreenatra, perhaps of other places too. The residence and wood and land attached to it now belongs to Mr O'Keefe of Schull. The main road from Ballydehob to Skibbereen was constructed in the year 1828. The old road from Ballydehob to Schull led up through Stobhall Hill. It then went along the present road to Schull as far as Car a' Chúinne. From it followed the present old road through Ceapach na Cailligh e, and westwards through north Cill broin óig and Gort na Ceardchan and the Woodlands. Before the construction of the present main, road the principal shops of Ballydehob were in Stobhall Hill.[352]

Collected by Paddy Lyons, Schull
From William Burke, Schull

The road leading to my house branches from the main road from Ballydehob to Skibbereen, and ends at the quay. It was made about the year 1883. The men working on the road got nine shillings a week. The people paid extra rates for the making of the road. It is called the Wester-land road, beginning below where Lynch lived, and passing Burke's house and ending at the tide. It was used before the new road was made.[353]

Collected by Neil Lucey, Ballydehob
From Nora Levis, Ballydehob

Knockroe

I am living in the townland of Knockroe, in the parish of Kilcoe, and in the Barony of the west division of West Carbery. There are fourteen families in the townland of Knockroe, and these are fifty-seven people. Sweeny is the most common name. The houses are slated, and the land is hilly. There are two people over seventy, and one of them is able to speak Irish. The one that cannot speak Irish has the following address: Mrs Cotter, Station Road, Ballydehob, Co. Cork. The name and address of the person who can speak Irish is: John MacCarthy, Knockroe, Ballydehob. People used to emigrate from Knockroe to America. There are streams and rivers in the townland. Some of the land is boggy. Houses were more numerous in the townland long ago. There are ruins in the townland. The meaning of Knockroe is the Red Hill. Knockroe is the next place to Ballydehob. There is a bridge there, and there are twelve arches in it, and six arches are in Knockroe and six are in Ballydehob.[354]

Collected by Vincent Kelly, Ballydehob

Ballydehob

The name Ballydehob is got from the Irish word *Béal-átha-an-dá-chab* which means the mouth of the ford of the two jaws. There are one hundred families in the townland of Ballydehob. There are three hundred and sixty-seven of population in the townland of Ballydehob. The townland is very hilly. There are a few elm trees growing there.[355]

Collected by Paddy Lyon, Schull

Gurteenroe

The name of my townland is Gurteenroe. It is in the parish of Schull, and it is in the west division of West Carbery. There are four families in the townland, and there are twelve people in the townland. There are two people over seventy living in it. They can tell stories in English. Their names are Mrs Driscoll and Mrs Sullivan. The houses are slated. The Donovan families are most common. People emigrated from it in former times. Most of the land is good land. There are three streams in the land.[356]

Collected by John Donovan, Ballydehob

Skehanore

My townland is Skehanore, and it is in the parish of Kilcoe, and in the Barony of the west division of West Carbery. There are twenty-six families, and one hundred and seventy people in the townland. Hickey is the family name most common. All the houses are slated except three that are thatched. The townland got its name from a place in the Rinn called the Cill where there is a bush, and it is said that there is gold hidden under that bush. The following are the names of old people over seventy: Mr James J. Hickey and Mrs Hickey, Mr Dannie Hickey, Mrs Young, Mrs Beamish, Mrs Burke, Mr Daniel Sullivan, Mr Patrick Sullivan, Miss Mary Sullivan, Miss Katey Levis, Miss Nora Lewis, and Mrs Margaret Mahony. Houses were more numerous in it in former times. The western part of the townland is hilly, and the northern part is boggy, and the remainder is good land.[357]

Collected by Michael O'Brien, Ballydehob

Names of Fields

Páirc na trága is near the townland of Greenmount. The following are near Skibbereen: páirc dubh;[xlviii] cúilín,[xlix] the middle rock, páirc mór;[l] páirc an tobair;[li] páirc na righte;[lii] and the field of the fort.[358]

The Local Forge

The local forge is situated very close to the town of Ballydehob. It is built of stone, with two windows, and one chimney. The name of the smith is Jack Driscoll, and his ancestors had been smiths. The forge is near a cross. There is only one bellows and one fireplace in the forge. The smith shoes horses and asses. The smith uses a sledge, tongs, a poker, a shovel, anvil, and an iron.[372]

Collected by Dermot Daly, Ballydehob
From Jeremiah Daly, Ballydehob

[xlviii] Páirc dubh – black field.
[xlix] Cúilín – wedge – possibly referring to a wedge tomb.
[l] Páirc mór – big field.
[li] Páirc an tobair - well field.
[lii] Páirc na righte – field of the kings.

Figure 28. Main St. Ballydehob (c1880-1900) (top), call no. L_ROY_10261.
Looking towards Ballydehob (bottom), call no. OCO347.
Images Courtesy of the National Library of Ireland.

BALLYDEHOB

Farming, Trade and Crafts

Local Fairs

Fairs are held in the town of Ballydehob. They are held only in the town. Sometimes the buyers go out to the country, and they buy animals. Two fairs are held in Ballydehob each month, one for the pigs and bonnives,[liii] and the other for cows and sheep. The fair is held in the street. It isn't held in any special place. When an animal is sold, luck is given. Two shillings are given for a car of bonnives; a half-crown is given for a cow. When the bargain is being made, the buyer strikes the hand of the seller. The animals are marked with chalk. The halter is not given with the animal when sold. The best fairs of the year were held on the feast of the Blessed Virgin. People came to the town without any business, but for sport on these days.[359]

Collected by Pat Joe Murphy, Ballydehob

Clothes Made Locally

There is a tailor in this district, and he cuts the suits and measures them. He doesn't sew them, but he has three tailors working for him. They do not go round from house to house as formerly when required. This tailor stocks and sells cloth, but the tailors who work for him do not. Cloth is not spun and woven locally, but it was some years ago. People do not wear clothes made of such cloth because they buy them in shops. Cloth made of linen and cotton are the types of cloth used at the present time. The following are the implements which the tailor uses in his work: a sewing machine, scissors, a measure, and a thimble. He also has a lapboard and an iron. He presses the cloth down on the lapboard with the iron. People do not make shirts in their homes now because they buy them made. Socks and stockings are knitted locally but the thread is not spun in the homes. At the death of a relative, women wear black clothes and men wear crapes.[360]

Collected by Michael O'Brien, Ballydehob

[liii] Bonnive – a suckling pig

The Nailer

A nailer worked in Ballydehob about 50 years ago. His name was James Punch. He made nails for boots, boats, and for house work. His forge was about where the post office is now. Factory-made nails killed his trade, and he and his family emigrated to America. A weaver worked in Ballydehob over 50 years ago. His name was Riardon. He lived at the eastern end of the town opposite where Mr Michael Minihane lives now. The weaver's loom was in the house for some time. It is 50 years at least since he worked.[361]

Collected by Patrick Lyons, Schull
From Richard Lyons, Schull

The Weaver

A weaver by the name of Tim Duggan used to do work at a place called Cordura, but he is now dead. His son is living. This man used to carry the stuff he used to weave to Bantry to get it tucked. He had some kind of machine, and he had balls of the stuff to weave in timber balls, and he used to throw them around the top of the machine. Long ago every farmer made his own baskets, and they're very few who did not make them. There were lime kilns in the district long ago, and there are signs of them there still. There is one about half a mile south on the Greenmount road in Mike Sweetman's land. A gap is called the lime kiln gap. Where the limestone came from is not known.[362]

Collected by Vincent Kelly, Ballydehob
From C. Kelly, Ballydehob

Barrel Making

A barrel maker was in this district whose name was Peter Barry. He lived in Ratravane. A weaver lived in Ardura, whose name was Tead Duggan. A great thatcher lived in Ardura also whose name was Patrick Hayes. A spinner named Mrs Sweeney lived in Knockroe.[363]

Collected by John Sweeney, Ballydehob
From Dan Sweeney, Ballydehob

The Basket Maker

Basket making is still going on in the district, but on a small scale. It is done by the people of the islands around the district. Rope making is still carried on at the time of the haystacks. The ropes are made of hay and straw and do not last very long. They are called sugans. Gate making is still carried on by the smiths of the district. Pail making was carried on in the district. There was a nailer in Ballydehob, and his name was James Punch. He used to make nails out of rod.[364]

Collected by Pat Joe Murphy and Michael O'Regan, Ballydehob
From Joseph Murphy and C. Kelly, Ballydehob

Thatching

A man named Tim Driscoll, who was a great thatcher, lived in Letter about 80 years ago. He had a good deal of fittings for the thatching. This man went around for hire. Sometimes he carried a man around with him to help him. He commenced thatching at the right-hand side of the house. He tied a rope to each thaovan. He began the thatching at the bottom. He made the bottom of the straw even. As soon as he reached the rope, he tied a piece of cord to it that was put in a timber needle. He drove the needle in through the thatch, and the person inside drove it out at that other side. The work was carried on like that until the thatching was finished.[365]

Collected by John Donovan, Ballydehob
From Tim Foley, Ballydehob

Sheep Shearing, Carding and Spinning

Long ago nearly every farmer kept sheep. The farmer's wife shore the wool off the sheep in the summer. She washed the wool then, and dried it, and sent it to the carding mill to be carded. After it was carded, she brought it home, and spun it into thread with a spinning wheel, which she kept in her home. Then the thread was sent to a weaver named Scanlan of Hollyhill and he wove the thread into cloth. It is about fifty years since that work was carried on.[366]

Collected by Michael O'Brien, Ballydehob
From John O'Brien, Ballydehob

BALLYDEHOB
Leisure

Games Played in this Locality

I play the following games. Sometimes I go out in the winter splintering with a lantern and stick. When the birds are amongst the bushes, the light dazzles them, and they fall on the ground, and I kill them with the stick. In November I also go bowling with a circular wheel and drive it with a stick. I pick blackberries in autumn. I play handball in the winter.[367]

Collected by Dermot Daly, Ballydehob

The following are the games played in this locality. In winter snares are made for catching rabbits. Splintering birds, fishing, Ludo, Draughts, and Snakes and Ladders are also done in winter. Handball, hurling, and football are played in the summer. Rounders are played in the locality also; they can be played by four persons or more. Blackberry picking is done in the autumn. In the winter nights boys get lights and go out into fields, and if they saw a bird, they would dazzle it with the light and while it is dazzled, they kill it.[368]

Collected by Michael O'Regan, Ballydehob

The following are the games I play. The winter games are four-corner-fool, blindman's buff, making snares for catching hares and rabbits, pitching with money, bird basket making, and splintering. The summer games are bowling, pitching quoits, and fowling. Hunting hares and rabbits is carried on from October till March. Splintering is carried out from November to January.[369]

Collected by Michael Mahony, Ballydehob

Some girls make strings of flowers for necklaces, and boys make snares to catch rabbits and hares. Some boys trap wild birds. They trap wild ducks, and they make bird baskets to catch blackbirds or thrushes, and other wild birds.[370]

Collected by Paddy Donnell, Ballydehob

Toys in Former Times

Pop guns were very popular toys long ago. A piece of elder used to be got about one foot and a half long, and a hole used to be burned through it, and another piece used to be got about one foot three inches long and it used to be used as a ramming rod through the big piece. Two pieces of paper used then be got and made hard with spit and rolling. When the rod is shoved out, the outer piece will fly out. A ball used to be made from horsehair. Spit on your hand and on the hair and roll up the hair, and it will be as hard as a rock. A basket used to be made from rushes, and if you wanted to put anything in, it should be put in while making. All the rushes used to be put through each other and tied on top. Cat-a-pults were made with a gabhlóg,[liv] and rubber and leather. The rubber should be strong. It used to be tied on to the gabhlóg, and leather was attached to the ends of the rubber.[371]

Collected by Vincent Kelly, Ballydehob

[liv] Gabhlóg – a small forked stick.

BALLYDEHOB
Local Customs

Local Customs

On St Brigid's day candles are blessed in the churches. On St Patrick's day sprigs of shamrocks are worn. Pancakes are made on Shrove Tuesday night. On Good Friday those who live by the sea go to the strand for mussels. On Easter Sunday people eat large numbers of eggs. On St John's day bonfires are lit. On Hallow'een various games are played. It is sometimes called snap-apple night. Apples are hung from the ceiling by means of strings, people try to catch them with their mouths. Apples are also put floating in water. On St Stephen's day boys go from house to house singing the wren song. They wear masks over their faces as a disguise. In the evening they divide the money they get between them. On New Year's night men go around the town singing and playing musical instruments. A little feasting is done on Little Christmas. It is sometimes called the Women's Christmas.

Care of the Feet

People used not to wear boots in olden times till they were sixteen years of age, and they used only wear them to mass or to town then only. The children of the present wear shoes all the year round except in the summertime. Boots are made and repaired locally. There are three shoemakers in this district. Clogs were worn in former times, and are worn in a small scale at present in the district. Leather was never made in this district.[372]

Collected by Michael O'Regan, Ballydehob

On the Straw Boys

The straw boys, about ten in number, one a captain, used to go where the wedding feast is held. They are dressed in straw. They sing and dance, and some of them get money. If not treated well, they do damage.[373]

Collected by Pat Joe Murphy, Ballydehob
From Joseph Murphy, Ballydehob

Marriage Customs

Marriages are most frequent in Shrove in this district. Mondays, Wednesday and Fridays are regarded as unlucky days for marriages. Marriages are not frequent in the months of May, October, and December. Matches are made by the parents or friends, or sometimes the boy and girl make their own matches. Marriages were held in houses up to twenty-five years ago. Money is always given as fortune. When the wedding party comes home a feast is partaken of. The wedding party used to race with horses long ago but now the guests go in motorcars. The guests use to go inside cars, and the man and wife used to come home in a covered car.[374]

Lore of Certain Days

Mondays are regarded as unlucky days for parting with money. If a person gave money on a Monday, it is thought that he would be giving out money all that week. It was a custom long ago that any water which was to be thrown out after twelve o'clock midnight, or on a Friday night, should be left inside. On a Thursday evening it was thought that certain illnesses could be cured by bending under a certain tree and praying.[375]

Collected by Vincent Kelly, Ballydehob
From J. H. Kelly, Ballydehob

The days considered unlucky days to visit a sick person are Fridays and Mondays. Also, it is unlucky to have a sick person rise out of bed on a Friday. It is said that a farmer should not plough or dig on Good Friday. It is also thought unlucky to remove into a house during Lent or Advent. It is thought unlucky for thirteen people to sleep in one house.[376]

Collected by Dermot Daly, Ballydehob
From Jeremiah Daly, Ballydehob

BALLYDEHOB
Local Cures

Local Cures

A nettle and wild sage would cure rheumatism. It was thought that if a person who was born before his father died blew three times into a person's throat, the person would be cured from sore throat.[377]

Collected by Patrick Lyons, Schull

Besom is a kind of shrub which is used for curing pains. Wild sage is a plant which is supposed to cure bronchitis. There is a place called Ballycumusk, and in this land there is a holy well at which people used to be cured long ago. This well was supposed to cure any disease. If any person was cured, he should leave something after him.[378]

Collected by John Sweeney, Ballydehob
From Dan Sweeney, Ballydehob

To cure whooping cough, two cures used to be used. They used to get a snail and put it in a pot and boil it with sugar, and give the water to drink to the sick person. The other was the leaving of a ferret. Soot was the cure for burns, and penny leaf was the cure for bad cuts. Nettles were used for a pain in the arms or legs, but besom was mostly used. The people used to hit their legs with nettles and burn pains out of them. They used to drink besom; it is very sour. Bainne cíċe na n-eán was used for ringworm.[lv] [379]

Collected by Vincent Kelly, Ballydehob
From C. Kelly, Ballydehob

[lv] The translation of bainne cíċe na n-eán is not clear, though it likely to be the fluid from a plant, bainne meaning milk.

People in olden times used to drink the milk of a ferret for whooping cough. If a bag of stones is left on the road, and if another person takes them up, warts would leave the first person and would come on the second person. If you had a toothache, and put a frog into your mouth, when the frog would croak the toothache would leave. Besom is a cure for pains. It grows wild.[380]

Collected by Pat Joe Murphy, Ballydehob
From Joseph Murphy, Ballydehob

Long ago the people had several cures for their diseases. When they had the measles, they used to eat or drink food left behind by a ferret, or when they had a toothache, they used to put pepper into the tooth. Holy wells were often visited by those people to cure several ailments, such as the whooping cough, the measles, etc.[381]

Collected by John Joe McCarthy, Ballydehob
From Michael McCarthy, Ballydehob

It is said that if anyone who has measles drinks the milk left after a ferret it would cure them. There is an old well in Skehanore and if you visited it on Friday, Saturday, and Sunday, and said certain prayers, it would cure eyes. By washing the eyes with the water of the well any sores would be cured. It is said that if you licked an eascu-luachra,[lvi] it would cure a burn.[382]

Collected by Neil Lucey, Ballydehob
From Nora Levis, Ballydehob

[lvi] Eascu-luachra – a lizard.

BALLYDEHOB

The Natural World and Weather lore

The Great Snowstorm of 1854

Great snow fell in the year 1854. It was snowing for seven days. The snow was very high. Anyone couldn't go out for a month. Their cattle had to be kept inside in the houses. It was the heaviest snowstorm that the people of the time remembered.[383]

Collected by Neil Lucey, Ballydehob
From Nora Levis, Ballydehob

The Great Drought of 1878

There was a great drought period in the year 1878. The drought lasted from April till November. All of the rivers and lakes of this district dried, and water could not be got anywhere except in spring wells. During the droughts the farm animals were exhausted because they could not get any water.[384]

Collected by Michael Mahony, Ballydehob

The Thunderstorm of 1898

There was a great thunder storm on the 17th August 1898. This storm did many damages. The flashes broke a bridge in Ballydehob. There were floods with this storm. There was a great snow storm about 100 years ago. The snow was so high that people were starving until the snow melted.[385]

Collected by John Sweeney, Ballydehob
From Dan Sweeney, Ballydehob

The Great Storm of 1923

On the night of 26th of February 1923, a great storm arose, and two boats were driven on rocks in the western coast of Skehanore. The crew of each boat succeeded in getting safely out of the boats on the rocks. One of the boats was a trading boat between Cork and Ballydehob, and it became a total wreck. The other boat was a three-masted schooner, and it had brought a load of coal from Cardiff in Glamorganshire to Ballydehob, and it had been emptied on the day before it was driven on the rocks. Sometime afterwards it was got off the rocks, but it was badly damaged.[386]

The Storm of Christmas 1927

On Christmas night 1927 there was a great storm. Rivers rose and flooded fields and drowned cattle and sheep. The flood went into houses in the low ground and flooded them. Trees were knocked by the wind, and it caused many accidents. Boats were wrecked. Roofs were stripped of their slates. Houses were knocked. Trees were knocked across the rails of the railroad tracks causing the trains to stop til they were removed.[387]

The Storm of 1934

In the year 1934, in the month of January, a storm came which lasted one day and one night. All of the houses near the sea were stripped of their roofs on the side facing the sea, and huge big blocks were brought ashore by the sea. All the roads were impassable, and some were torn up. There were two boats, one a sand boat, and the other a motorboat, brought up against Ballydehob quay, and big cracks were put in them, and they were filled with water. Some houses had big trees around them, and they were torn down.[388]

Collected by Vincent Kelly, Ballydehob

BALLYDEHOB
Sea and Shipwrecks

The Wrecking of the Savonia

About the year 1909 a ship with 4,000 tons of timber and other things was put out of order about twenty miles out from the land, and her masts were torn off and her cabins were blown away, and something happened to her crew, and it is feared they were drowned. The ship drifted away, and it came into some small islands called the Calves, and it was broken to hundreds of pieces. The men of the mainland went out with boats and drew the timber home. This ship's name was the Savonia.[389]

Collected by Vincent Kelly, Ballydehob
From C. Kelly, Ballydehob

Skehanore wrecks

A boat was wrecked in the rocks near the Reen which is in Skehanore. The boat was going to Ballydehob with clothes. A gale blew and they were blown up on the rocks. The boat's name was called the Alma. It got wrecked in the year 1922. No one got drowned. A boat named the Inis Arcain got burned when she was going to Cork. A ship stopped and took the men in. One man was burned very badly. The man's name was Timmy MacCarthey.[390]

Collected by Neil Lucey, Ballydehob
From Con Lucey, Ballydehob,

A Shipwreck

On a dark and dreary night in the year 1857 a ship laden with Indian corn sailed round the Mizen Head. A gale blew from the south-west which tore her sails to ribbons. She drifted inland before the gale until she was tossed on the Barrel Rocks where she became a total wreck. Early the following morning the people of Gunpoint and Ballybrack saw the wreckage. Six men manned a boat and went out towards the rocks on which they saw the survivors of the wreck. At first, they saw no hope of saving the poor men because their little boat was in danger of being smashed in the wild sea which was covered by floating timber. They reached the shipwrecked men who were unconscious. They picked them up and brought them to the boat. The three rescued men were Captain, Mate, and Cabin boy, the remainder were drowned. They were rowed home to Gunpoint and taken to the homes of the rescuers. At that time there were only three houses there. The shipwrecked men got food and warm clothes and revived quickly. They were Italians and could speak only a few words of English. They seemed to relish the oatmeal porridge which was the principal food then used by the people of Ireland. When the Captain, who was kept at Denis Callaghan's house, had his bowl of porridge eaten, he kept repeated "more munjee". At first nobody could think what he meant, but after a while one of them, named Denis Callaghan, filled up another bowl of porridge and handed it to him. He took it, ate it, and was satisfied. That boy was nicknamed 'Munjee' until his death and the nickname followed his children and grandchildren. After a few days when the shipwrecked men were strong enough to be removed, the Schull Coastguards came and took them away. On leaving, the shipwrecked men showed their gratitude by kissing the women's hands and saying, "Good mother, good mother". The names of the men who went out to the wreck were John Donovan of Gunpoint, his son Jeremiah then aged 16 years, James, Mick and Denis Callaghan (brothers). Jeremiah Donovan who is mentioned in the above is still living and is now 97 years. The name of the ship was Lady Charlotte.[391]

Collected by Nora Donovan (aged 16), Ballydehob

BALLYDEHOB
History and Archaeology

Food in Former Times

Some people used to have three meals long ago, but there were people who had only two meals. The people that had three meals used to eat their meals in the morning, in the middle of the day, and in the night, but the other people had their meals in the morning and in the evening. Work used to be done long ago before the breakfast. The people used to have their breakfast at nine o'clock, but now they do not go out before their breakfast. They used to have to eat potatoes and sour milk at each meal. When the times used to be improving, they used to have bread and milk for breakfast. The table used not to be in the middle of the floor but beside the wall hanging on hinges, and when it was not in use it was lifted up and there was a board holding it up.

Food was not eaten often long ago. They used to eat salted meat. It was seldom fresh meat was used. It was the meat of the pig they used to eat. The people near the sea used to eat fresh fish, and the people in the middle of the country used to eat salted fish. The vegetables they used to have was cabbage. They used to get curds from the sour milk, and it boiling, they used to eat porridge made of yellow meal. They used to put the wheat into an oven, and it used to be dried, and when the wheat is dried it is ground, milk is mixed with it. The used not eat late in the night. They used to eat barm bracks on November night, and eggs used to be eaten on Easter Sunday. There were basins in use before cups were in use. The following is a story about a woman and two priests. Once a woman was going to have the stations. She boiled a teapot of water, and she put a half-pound of tea into it, and she strained the water out of the tea pot, and she gave the tea leaves to the priests.[392]

Collected by Dermot Daly, Ballydehob

Penal Times

In the penal times there was a chapel about one mile distant from Ballydehob. One day while the Bishop was administering the sacrament of confirmation, Cromwell and his soldiers came into the chapel and killed the Bishop and children. Beside the road leading to Ballydehob there is a graveyard called Stouke. The murdered Bishop was buried here. Sometimes during the year, people go there making pilgrimages to his grave.[393]

Collected by Cormac O'Donovan, Ballydehob

A House Burning

The dwelling house of Mrs Sullivan of Collagh was burned by black and tans. They came in, and they threw petrol all around, and in a short time the house was in flames. When the dwelling house was burned, they threw petrol on the hay shed, and they burned all the hay, but they didn't burn the shed.[394]

Collected by Paddy Donnell, Ballydehob
From Paddy Donnell, Ballydehob

Ballydehob News – 1920s

A barrack was burned in Ballydehob in 1920. It was burned by the I.R.A. A sergeant was drowned at Ballydehob quay in the year 1924. He went for a swim by himself and he got into difficulty, and he was drowned as there was no one to help him.[395]

Collected by Dermot Daly, Ballydehob
From Denis Daly, Ballydehob

A Drowning in the Ballydehob River

A boy was drowned in the Ballydehob river on the 29th June 1910. This boy was swimming across when he got drowned in it. Patrick Collins was this boy's name. He lived near Ballydehob.[396]

Collected by John Sweeney, Ballydehob,

A Drowning in Dunmanus Bay

A drowning occurred on Sunday July 25th, 1937, in Dunmanus Bay. Peter O'Driscoll of Rathrawan and two others were crossing Dunmanus Bay in a sailing boat from Ahkista to Dunbeacon. On their way about a mile from Dunbeacon the top of the mast broke. One of them climbed up to fix the mast, and the boat overturned.[397]

The Drowning of Hare Island Men

Some years ago five men from Hare Island came to Ballydehob to get twigs in the neighbourhood for making lobster pots. It was late in the evening when they started for home. When they were about halfway a hurricane blew, and their boat being full of twigs capsized, and they were all thrown into the sea. They clung to the overturned boat, and they tried to turn it over again, but they failed. Only one of them was able to swim. His name was Cahalane. He told the other men to cling on to the boat, and himself would swim ashore for help. After swimming a long time, he got to shore, and after climbing some very high cliffs he saw a light at a distance. He came to the house and he knocked, and it was opened for him, and he was taken in. He told the people of the house what happened. He was not able to go himself as he was tired and injured from having to climb the rocks, besides swimming in the cold water, it being the depth of winter. The people of the house soon got a rescue party and went to sea. After some time in the water searching for the up-turned boat they saw it, but too late as the last man had fallen into the sea and was drowned. It happened about the year 1912 in the month of November. The names of two of the men that were drowned were Harte and Piel.[398]

Collected by Cormac O'Donovan, Ballydehob

Famine Times

The famine caused great harm to this district. All the potatoes rotted. There was a building by the sea full of biscuits but the food was thrown into the sea, although the people were starving all around. The building was by my house. Some Catholics sold their religion for soup and are called soupers since then. Sometimes the potatoes rotted in pits. There are places which are said to have been places into which the dead people were thrown.[399] The great famine of 1846-1847 affected this district very much. Only for charity, several families would have died of starvation. Some families were wiped out altogether for want of food. They also got bad fever, and many were not buried for days.[400]

Collected by Dermot Daly, Ballydehob
From Jeremiah Daly, Ballydehob

Famine Times in Skehanore

The great famine of 1846-47 affected this district very much. The townland of Skehanore was very thickly populated before the famine times. There was a street of houses in one part of Skehanore and thirty-five families were living there. Most of them died of famine and fever, and they were buried in the Cill in the southern end of Skehanore which is called the Reen. In another place in the townland there was a street of twelve houses, and twelve families lived there, and most of them died of famine and fever too, and they were buried in the Cill uncoffined. Several bodies were put in one grave. Scarcely had the people seeded potatoes for 1848, they cut the eyes out of the potatoes, and sowed them broadcast like grain, and they produced a wonderful crop of potatoes. The people ate turnips and seaweed, and shellfish, and boiled nettles. There are several ruins of houses, which were then occupied, to be seen in the townland at present.[401]

The Drowned Priest

There is an old church in Gurteenroe which was built during the penal times. People used to come from all parts of the country around it to hear mass in the church. The church was never attacked. All the people used not get room in the church. Some of them used to pray around the church. One Sunday a man went up the hills to try to see was the priest coming. He saw the priest coming pursued by three men with horses in full speed. He thought that they were soldiers pursuing the priest, and he shouted at the priest that there were soldiers in pursuit of him. The priest got a fright, and he forced his horse across the river. There was a great flood in the river, and it carried away the priest off the horse's back, and he was drowned. A few days after, the body was washed up in a field about fifty yards from the drowning. The field where he was washed up on is called páirc an t-sagairt.[lvii] The place around the church is called gleann an tSéipél.[lviii] [402]

Collected by John Donovan, Ballydehob
From Jack Sullivan, Ballydehob

[lvii] Páirc an t-sagairt – Priest's field or place.
[lviii] Gleann an tSéipél – valley of the chapel.

Fairy Forts

There is a fort in a place called Ballycummisk. It is near the sea, and was first found about two years ago by people who were ploughing. It is a hole going down through the ground with four stonewalls. You could not see down now because it was filled in. They could only see the walls. They dug down about a yard, and then drove down a ten-foot crowbar but the bottom could not be found. Very small pipes were found and shells. This field is sloping to the sea. A stone about a yard long was also found. They believed it to be a handle for some old stone weapon. There is another fort called Fortview. There is a wood near it. It is about two miles from Ballydehob.[403] There are several forts in this district. There are three forts in Cooragurteen about two miles from the town.[404] There is one fort in Gurteenroe and is said that fairies used to live in it long ago. It is said also that when a priest was going to mass one morning on a horse, and when he was crossing a river near the fort, he fell in an was drowned. Some say there is a hole from the river into the fort.[405] There is a fort in Derryconnell. It has three rings around it. The door of the fort is at the end of one of the rings. Lights are seen around the fort often. Once a man went to till around the fort, and he was found dead by a man who was coming from a fair.[406] There is a fort in the land of Stephen Sullivan, Glaun. The wall around the fort is round.[406]

Collected by Vincent Kelly, Dermot Daly, Frank Coughlan, John Donovan, and Michael O'Regan, Ballydehob

Skehanore Holy well

There is a holy well in the southern part of Skehanore in a place called the cíll which is now a disused burial place. The well is on the side of a rock, and the water flows out of the rock into the well. People used to make rounds to the well long ago, but rounds are not made now. The people who used to make the rounds used to leave bottles, coins, and strips of cloth. Any person doesn't know now the origin of the sanctity of the well. There is a furze bush growing over the well.[407]

Collected by Michael Mahony, Ballydehob

Ballycummish Holy Well

There is a holy well in the townland of Ballycummish about three miles from Ballydehob. The well is called the Blessed Well. There is a whitethorn tree growing around it. A man wanted to thatch his house with a branch from that tree, and the house fell that night. The well is coming from a rock and is not deep. People call there on Wednesdays, Fridays, and Saturdays to pray. If a person had a toothache and took a drink from the well on any one of these days which I have named, he would be cured. There is no account of the origin of the well's holiness, but there is a slope about three hundred yards from the well calls *Learca na h-Alcóra* which means the slop of the altar. There is a big stone on the slope, and it may have been used as an altar long ago, and perhaps water from the well-used to be used as the water for the wine at mass. Maybe that is how the people considered it holy.[408]

Collected by Vincent Kelly, Ballydehob
From Patrick Collins, Ballydehob

BALLYDEHOB
Songs

The Wife of the Bold Tenant Farmer

One evening of late 'twas from Bandon I strayed,
Bound for Clonakilty I was making my way,
In Ballinascarthy some time I delayed,
And I wetted my whistle with porter.

I kindled my pipe, and I spat on my stick,
And away to the town like a hare I did trip,
I cared for no bailiff, nor landlord or old kick,
But I sang like a lark in the morning.

I scarcely had travelled a mile of a road,
When I heard a dispute on a farmer's abode,
By the son of a landlord, an ill-looking rogue,
And the wife of a bold tenant farmer.

He said! "What the dickens came over you all?
Not a penny of rent can we get for our call,
But after the sessions, you'll pay for it all,
You'll get the high road for your bargain."

"Your Gaffer", the bold tenant wife – she replied,
"You're as good as your daddy on the other side,
Our plan of campaign it will pull down your pride,
It is able to bear every storm."

"Your husband I've seen in the town every night,
Drinking and shouting for bold tenants' rights."
"If my husband was drinking what has it to do,
I'd rather he'd drink it than give it to you.
So, make up your mind or you'll not get a screw,
For your poor, marshy land is no bargain."

Here's to Father O'Leary, the pride of our Isle;
'Tis the priest that can title bad landlord in style,
And brave Father Fahy who carried the field,
To march with us all in good order.[409]

Collected by Kitty Cronin (aged 14½), Ballydehob

O'Donovan Rossa

Adieu my friends in Dublin, I bid you all adieu,
I cannot yet appoint the day, that I'll return to you.
I wrote those lines on board a ship where stormy billows roar.
May heaven bless those Fenian boys, till I return once more.

Let no one blame the turnkey, nor any of his men.
There's no one now but the two of us, the man who stood my friend.
I robbed no man, I shed no blood, though they sent me on to fail.
Because I was a son of Granuaile.

My curse attend those traitors false who did our cause betray,
I would tie a millstone round their necks and drown them in the sea,
Nagle, Newno and O'Brien and power to make four.
Like Davis for his conduct, in hell do loudly roar.

There was O'Leary and young Mackey, and brave O'Donovan Rossa.
It grieved me for to part with them when we left O'Carroll's Cross.
If we live, and prosper, the truth I do declare.
Like O'Mahony in America, the green flag we shall wear.

Cheer up my gallant Fenian boys, the day is not far away.
Now Fenian boys the flag we'll raise and trample tyranny.
Our gallant sons beyond the sea will gain in unity.
We'll raise the flag of freedom and fight for liberty.[410]

Collected by Rosaleen O'Donovan (aged 13½), Ballydehob
From Ned Jones (aged 87), farmer, Ballydehob

John Bull

John Bull, an English man,
He went on tramp one day,
With three pence in his pocket,
To take him on his way,
He travelled miles and miles,
And no one did he see,
Until he fell in with an Irish man,
By the name of Paddy McGee.

"Good morning sir," said Johnny,
"Good morning sir," said pat,
"Where are you going?" says Johnny,
"I'm going the road that's flat."
"Have you got any money about you?",
says Johnny unto Pat.
"Faith tis the only think I wanted,
for I haven't got a rap."

They trudged along together,
Met a Scotchman on the way,
"Lend us a bob now Scotty,
For to help us on our way."
"Lend you a bob?" says Scotty.
"Faith and sure," said he,
"Tis the only thing I wanted,
For I'm not worth a Bobbie."

"I have threepence", said the English man,
"What can I do with that?"
"Buy threepence worth of whiskey,
And it will cheer us up", said pat.
"Don't do that", said the Scotch man,
"But I'll tell you what to do.
Buy threepence worth of oatmeal,
And we'll all have brugoo."[411]

Collected by Noreen Keane, Ballydehob
From Mr J. Bennet (aged 73), farmer, Ballydehob

The Mantle of Green

As I was a-walking one morning in June,
To view the gay fields and meadows in bloom,
I espied a young female, she appeared like a queen,
With costly fine robes, and a mantle of green.

I stood in amaze and gazed with surprise,
I thought her an angel just fell from the skies,
Her eyes shone like diamonds, her cheeks like the roses,
She is one of the fairest that nature composes.

I said, "My lovely fair one, if you will agree,
We will join in wedlock and married you'll be,
I'll dress you in rich attire, you'll appear like a queen,
With costly fine robes around your mantle of green.

She quickly made answer, "I must be excused,
For I'll wed with no man, so you must be refused,
To the green woods I'll wander, and shun all men too,
For the lad I loved fell in famed Waterloo."

"Then if you'll not marry, tell me your lover's name,
For I've been a soldier and might know the same."
"Draw near to my garment and soon will be seen,
His name is embroidered on my mantel of green."

Then raising her mantle it is there I did behold,
His name and his surname, in letters of bright gold.
Young William O'Reilly appeared to my view.
He was my commander of famed Waterloo.

He fought on so victorious when the bullets did fly,
In the field of honour your true love did die,
He fought for three days until the third afternoon,
And received his death wound on the 18th of June.

When he was dying, I heard his last sigh,
"Were you here, lovely Nancy contented I'd die.
Peace is proclaimed, now the truth I declare,
Here is your love's token, the gold ring I wear."

The longer she views it, the paler she grew,
And fell into my arms – her heart full of woe;
To the green words I'll wander, for the boy that I love,
Rise up lovely Nancy, your grief I'll remove.

Nancy, lovely Nancy, I have won your heart,
In your father's garden no more we will part,
In your father's garden, so cool and so serene,
I'll fold you in my arms in your mantle of green.

This couple got married, I heard people say,
They had nobles attending on their wedding day,
Peace is proclaimed, and the war is all o'er,
You are welcome to my arms, my Nancy, once more.[412]

Collected by Minnie Sullivan (aged 13½), Ballydehob
From Guard Maloney (aged 36), Ballydehob

The Bonney Bunch of Roses O

By the dangers of the ocean,
one morning in the month of June,
When the feather warbling songsters
their charming notes did sweetly tune,
It was then I spied my fair maid,
seemingly to be in grief and woe,
Conversing with Napoleon,
concerning the Bonney bunch of roses O.

"Then," said young Napoleon,
as he grasped his mother by the hand,
"Oh! Mother pray have patience,
until I am able to command,
I will raise a powerful army,
through tremendous dangers I will go,
In spite of all the universe,
I will gain the Bonney bunch of roses O."

"Oh! Son don't speak so venturesome,
for England has a heart of oak,
England, Ireland, and Scotland,
their unity was never broke,
Think of your aged father,
in St Helena his body lies low,
And you will follow after,
So beware! Of the Bonney bunch of roses O."

"The first time you saw great Bonaparte,
You fell upon your bended knees,
You asked your father's life of him,
And he granted it most manfully,
'Twas then he raised an army,
and over the plains did go,
Saying:- "First I'll conquer Moscow,
and I'll gain the Bonney bunch of roses O."

He took 800,000 men,
likewise, a king to join his throng,
He was so well provided,
enough to sweep the world along,
But when he came near Moscow,
he was over-powered by the driven snow,
Moscow fell a blazing,
and he lost the Bonney bunch of roses O.

"Oh! Mother he was loyal,
and he always did prove true to you,
Until that fatal morning,
when he went to the plains of Waterloo,
He left thousands there,
lying on the ground,
Their blood like fountains, there did flow,
Until Grouchy proved a traitor;
and he lost the Bonney bunch of roses O.

Then mother, adieu! forever,
It's now I'll droop my youthful head,
If I had lived, I would be clever,
but it's now I'm on my dying bed,
And when my bones are mouldering,
and the weeping willow o'er us grow,
The deeds of brave Napoleon,
will conquer the Bonney bunch of roses O.[413]

Collected by Kitty Cronin, Ballydehob
From Mr J. O'Donovan (aged 36), Ballydehob

The Bad Landlords of Ireland

Ye bad landlords of Ireland, I'll have ye beware,
And on your poor tenants to take special care,
To give them abatement and show them fair play,
Or the devil a halfpenny at all will they pay.

Hurrah for the Land League each farmer unite,
The land sharks, me boys, we'll muzzle them tight,
May the banners of freedom and green laurels wave,
O'er the men of the Land League and Parnell the brave.

The bad landlords, they feed on the fat of the soil.
The sweat of the poor man, his labour and toil.
With poor rates and taxes at every call,
I am surprised how poor tenants are living at all.

Chorus

By all the improvements they make on their land,
They get no compensation as you may understand,
The tenant each morning is up with the lark,
And must work for the landlord from dawn until dark.

Chorus

The bare barren mountain and bogs I do state,
The poor Irish farmer he must cultivate,
While the landshark is waiting his chance underhand,
To grab at his labour, his house and his land.

Chorus

The devil is fishing and will soon have a pull,
With bad landlords of Ireland his net will be full.
It is in his warm corner they will sorely repent,
And Esker and Havines will pay them in rent.

Collected by Mary O'Sullivan (aged 16), Ballydehob

Paradise Alley

In a little side street, such as often you meet,
Where the boys on a Sunday rally,
It's not very wide, and its dismal beside.
Yet they called the place Paradise Alley.

Chorus
Every Sunday down to her home we go,
All the boys and the girls love her so,
Always a jolly heart, that is true you know.
She's the sunshine of Paradise Alley.
She's the daughter of widow McNally,
She has bright golden hair,
and the boys all declare,
She's the sunshine of Paradise Alley.

She has offers to wed, by the dozen 'tis said.
But she always refuses politely,
And at last she'll be seen with young Tommy Killen,
Going out for a promenade nightly.

Chorus

When O'Brien's little lad got the fever so bad,
That no one would dare go near him,
This girl so brave, says, "She thinks she could save.
Or at least she would comfort and cheer him."
So, the youngster got well, and the neighbours all tell,
She's the sunshine of Paradise Alley.

Chorus[414]

Collected by Nora Donovan (aged 16), Ballydehob
From Mr J. Cronin (aged 50), Ballydehob

The Brave, Bold Fenian Boy of Dublin

In Dublin town I was brought up,
That city of great fame,
My parents reared me honestly,
And many will tell the same.
But being a brave bold Fenian boy.
Was sent across the main.

For seven long years
to New South Wales,
To wear a convict chain.
There were seven long links
upon this chain,
And in every link a year.
Before I can return
to the country I love dear.

No longer than I was six months,
On the Australian shore,
I turned to be a Fenian again,
As I was one before.
There was Mac na Mára
and Underwood,
And Captain Mackey too,
They were the chief associates,
Of brave Jack Donoghue.

O'Donoghue went walking
one evening after noon,
But little was his notion
his death would be so soon.
The sergeant of the horse police,
Discharged the carabine,
And quickly said to Donoghue,
To fight or to resign.

Resign to you, you British coward,
That I will never do,
But now I'll fight with all my might,
Said brave Jack Donoghue
Nine rounds of this brave fight
went round,
He let a fatal ball,
Lie in the heart of Donoghue,
And caused him quick to fall.

And as he closed his mournful eyes,
To this world he bid adieu,
And people all, both great and small,
Pray still for Donoghue.[415]

Collected by Nora Donovan (aged 15½), Ballydehob
From Mr J. O'Donovan, farmer, Ballydehob

One Christmas Eve in Dublin

Come buy my nice fresh ivy,
And my holly sprigs so green.
I have the finest branches,
That ever yet were seen.
Come buy from me, good Christians,
And let me home I pray!
And I'll wish you Merry Christmas times.
And a happy New Year's Day.

Ah! Won't you take my ivy,
The loveliest ever seen.
Ah! Won't you have my holly boughs,
All you who love the green,
Do take a little bunch of each,
On my knees I'll pray,
That God may bless your Christmas,
And be with you New Year's Day.

This wind is black and bitter,
And the hailstone does not spare,
My shivering form, my bleeding feet,
And stiff entangled hair,
Then when the skies are pitiless,
Be merciful, I say,
So, Heaven will light your Christmas,
And the coming New Year's Day.

'Twas thus a dying maiden sais,
Whilst the cold hail rattled down,
And fierce winds whistled mournfully,
O'er Dublin's dreary town,
One stiff hand clutched her ivy sprigs,
And holly boughs so fair,
With the other she kept brushing,
The hail drops from her hair.

So grim and statue like she seemed,
'Twas evident that death,
Was lurking in her footsteps,
Whilst her hot impeded breath,
Too plainly told her early doom,
Though the burden of her lay,
Was still of life and Christmas joys,
And a Happy New Year's Day.

'Twas in that broad, bleak Thomas St,
I heard the wanderer sing.
I stood a moment in the mire,
Beyond the ragged ring.
My heart felt cold and lonely,
And my thoughts were far away,
Where I was many a Christmas tide,
And a Happy New Year's Day.

I dreamed of wanderings in the woods,
Amongst the holly green,
I dreamed of my own nation's cot,
And with the ivy screen.
I dreamed of lights forever dimmed,
Of hopes that can't return,
And dropped a tear on Christmas fires,
That never again can burn.

The ghost like singer skill sang on,
But no one came to buy,
The hurrying crowd passed to and fro,
But did not heed her cry,
She uttered one low, piercing moan,
Then cast her bough away.
And smiling cried "I'll rest with God,
Before the New Year's Day."

On New Year's Day I said my prayers,
Above a new made grave,
Dug recently in sacred soil,
By Liffey's murmuring wave.
The minstrel maid from earth to heaven,
Had winged her happy way,
And now enjoys with sister saints,
An endless New Year's Day.[416]

Collected by Bernadette O'Regan,Ballydehob
From Charles MacCarthy (aged 65), Ballydehob

The Exile's Dream

It's ten weary years since I left Erin's shore,
In a far distant country to roam,
How I long to return to my own native land,
To my friends and the old folks at home.
Last night as I slumbered, I had a sad dream,
'Twas a dream that brought distant friends near,
I dreamt of the old Ireland, the land of my birth,
To hear of her sons ever dear.

I saw the old homestead and faces I loved,
As I saw Ireland's valley's and dells,
I listened with joy as I did when a boy,
To the sound of the old village bell,
The logs were burning brightly,
'Twas a night that should banish all sin,
For the bells were ringing the old year out,
And the New Year in.

As the joy bells were ringing, I wended my way,
To the cot where I lived when a boy,
As I stood by the window, yes, there by the fire,
Saw my parents, with hearts filled with joy.
The tears trickled down my bronze furrowed cheeks,
As I gazed on my mother so dear,
For I knew in my heart she was singing a song,
For the boy whom she dreamt was not near.

At the door of the cottage we met face to face,
'Twas the first time in ten weary years,
Soon, the past was forgotten, we stood hand in hand,
Father and mother and wanderer in tears,
So now in my old home happy at last,
I promised no more would I roam,
And I sat in the old vacant chair by the hearth,
And sang the old song. "Home Sweet Home."[417]

The Green Isle of Erin

There's a voice in the silence, a voice ever calling,
A voice like the sound of a far distant sea,
A music, the sound of the wandered enthralling,
It floats like a dream o'er the waters to me.
I hear it with tears and a heart wildly beating,
Whilst far and alone, in a strange land I roam,
I weep as I list, and my prayers give it greeting,
The voice of the green Isle, my country and home.

Oh, green isle of Erin, that waits for me yonder,
Though faith has decreed, 'tis for ever we part.
Still exile and lonely, where e'er I wander,
The green isle of Erin remains in my heart.
Oh, green isle of Erin remains in my heart.

There's nowhere a sea like that blue rippling ocean,
That surges around and above that dear strand.
There's nowhere a star will shine down with devotion,
As bright as are those that shone down on that land.
I hear it with tears, tears beyond all controlling,
Wake and remember, an exile am I.
And I pray, though between us the wide seas are rolling,
To come home to thee, if t'were only to die.

Chorus[418]

Collected by Claire O'Donovan, Ballydehob
From Ned Jones (aged 87), Ballydehob

Ireland's Hurling Men

Who says our country's soul has fled?
Who says our country's heart is dead?
Come let them hear the marching tread,
Of twice five thousand hurling men,
They hold the hopes of bygone years,
They love the past its smiles and tears.
But quavering doubts and shrinking fears,
Are far from Ireland's hurling men.

Hurrah! Hurrah the stout Camán.
Not Seánin's steel can match its blow.
Hurrah! The arms of might and brawn,
And hearts with freedom's fame aglow.

They sing the songs their father's sang,
When to the breeze the green they flung.
They speak their own sweet Gaelic tongue,
That fires the blood of fighting men.
When all around was dark as night,
With scarce a gleam of cheering light,
When traitors fled their country's fight,
She still had hope in hurling men.

Chorus

On Irish fields when heroes died,
And foemen thronged on every side.
Our leader's joy, their hopes and pride,
Were gleaming pikes and hurling men.
And if God wills that wars red train,
Shall sweep again o'er hill and plain.
Our land shall call and not in vain,
On fighting lines of hurling men.

Chorus

But meanwhile, let each true heart tell,
The foeman's every plan to foil.
And raise, like strong plants from the soil,
Men hosts of Irish hurling men.
To guard their name and love their land,
With her through gloom and joy to stand,
And each one's gift a heart and hand,
And will to strive with Irishmen.

Chorus

When comes the day as come it must,
When Seanins rule of greed and lust,
Shall lie all broken in the dust,
We'll still have Irish hurling men.
Then here's to her the land we love,
Each grand old hill and glen and grove,
Her plains below, her skies above.
And best of all her hurling men.[419]

Collected by Rosaleen O'Donovan, Ballydehob
From Pat Donovan (aged 74), Ballydehob

Ninety-Eight

In the old marble town of Kilkenny,
With its abbey, cathedral and halls,
Where the Norman bells ring out at nightfall,
And the relics of great crumbling walls,
Show the traces of Celt and Saxon,
In bastions, and towers and keeps,
And graveyards and tombs tell the living,
Where glory of holiness sleeps.

Where the nuncio brought the pope's blessing,
And money and weapons to boot,
Whilst Owen was mad to be plucking,
The English clan up by the root.
Where regicide Oliver revelled,
With his puritan ironside horse,
And cut down both marble and monarchy,
Grimly and grave with the sword.

There in that old town of history,
England in famed Ninety-eight,
Was busy with gallows and yeomen,
Propounding the laws of the state.
They were hanging a young lad, a rebel,
On the gibbet before the old jail,
As they marked his weak spirit to falter,
And his white face to quiver and quail.

As he spoke of his mother whose dwelling,
Was but a short distance away,
A poor, lorn, heart-broken widow,
And he her sole solace and stay.
"Bring her here" cried the chief of the yeomen,
A lingering chance let us give,
To this spawn of a rebel to babble,
And by her sage counsel to live.

A quick red trooper came trotting,
From the town to the poor cabin door,
And he found the old lone woman spinning,
And sitting on the bare floor.
"Your son is in trouble old damsel,
They have him within in the town,
And he wishes to see you so bustle,
Put on your trucker and gown."

The old woman rose from her spinning,
With a frown on her deep-wrinkled brow,
"I know how it is cursed yeoman,
I am ready – I'll go with you now."
He seized her, enraged, by the shoulder,
And lifted her up on his steed,
Struck the spurs and away to the city,
Right ahead, and with clattering speed.
stopped at the foot of the gallows,
And the mother confronted her son,
And she hugged his young heart to her bosom,
And kissed his face pallid and wan.

And as the rope dangles before her,
She held to loop fast in her hand,
For though her proud soul was unflinching,
Her frail limbs were failing to stand,
And while the raw yeomen came crowding,
To witness that harrowing scene,
The brave mother flushed to the forehead,
And spoke with the air of a queen.

"My son they are going to hang you,
For loving your faith and your home,
They called me to urge you and save you,
And in God's name I've answered and come.
They murdered your father before you,
And I knelt on the red, reeking sod,
And I watched his hot blood streaming upwards,
To call down the vengeance of God.

No traitor was he to his country.
No blot did he leave on his name,
Oft I kneel at his grave in the eventide,
Oh, the priest could kneel there without shame."
"To hell with your priest and your rebels,"
The captain called out with a yell,
Whilst from the tall tower of the temple,
Rang out the sweet angelus bell.

"Blessed mother" appealed the poor widow,
"Look down on my child and on me."
"Blessed mother" sneered out the wild yeoman,
"Tell your son to confess and be free."
"Never! Never! He'll die like his father,
My boy, give your life to the Lord,
But of treason to Ireland, mavourneen,
Never speak on dishonouring word."

His white cheek flushed up at her speaking,
His head bounded up at her call,
And his hushed spirit seemed at awaking,
To scorn death, yeomen and all.
"I'll die and I'll be no informer,
My kin I will never disgrace,
And when God lets me see my poor father,
I can lovingly look in his face."

"You'll see him in hell" sneered the yeoman,
As he flung the sad widow away,
And the youth in a moment was strangling,
In the broad eye of shuddering day.
"Give the gallows a passenger outside",
A tall Hessian spluttered aloud,[lix]
As he drove a huge nail in the timber,
Mid the curse and cries of the crown.

[lix] Hessian – a person born is Hess, the reference her denotes a mercenary who fought for Britain during the revolutionary war.

Seizing the poor bereaved mother,
He passed his broad belt round his throat,
Whilst her groaning was last in the drumbeat,
And her shrieks in the shrill bugle note,
And mother and son were left choking,
And struggling and writhing in death,
Whilst angels looked down on that murder,
And the devils were wrangling beneath.

"For this" cries the exile defiant,
"For this" cried the patriot brave,
"For this" cries the lonely survivor,
O'er many a horror marked grave.
"For this" cries the priest and the peasant,
The student, the lover, the lost,
The stalwart who pride in their vigour,
The frail as they give up the ghost.

For this we curse Saxon dominion,
And join them in the world-wide cry,
That wails up to heaven for vengeance,
Through every blue gate in the sky.[420]

Collected by Mary M. Bennett (aged 14½), Ballydehob
From William Bennett (aged 38), Ballydehob

The Flower of Finae

Bright red was the sun on the waves of Loch Sheelin,
A cool gentle breeze from the mountain is stealing,
Fair 'round its islets the small ripples play,
But fairer than all is the Flower of Finae,

Her hair is like night and her eyes like grey morning,
She trips on the heather as if its touch scorning,
Her hair and her lips are as mild as May Day,
Sweet Eileen McMahon, the Flower of Finae.

But, who, down the hillside, than red deer runs faster,
Or who, on the lakeside is hastening to greet her,
Who, but Fergus O'Farrel, the fiery and gay,
The darling, the pride, and the Flower of Finae.

For Fergus O'Farrell was true to his sireland,
And the dark hand of tyranny drove him from Ireland,
He joined his brigade in the wars far away,
And he vowed he'd come back to the Flower of Finae.

One kiss, and one clasp and one wild look of gladness,
Ah! Why do they change on a sudden to sadness?
He has told his hard fortune no more he can stay,
He must leave his poor Eileen to pine at Finae.

He fought at Cremona, she hears of his story,
He fought at Cassino she's proud of his glory,
Yet, sadly she sings "Siúbhail a ruin" all the day,
Oh! Come; come my darling, home, home to Finae.

Eight long years have passed, 'till she'd nigh broken-hearted,
Her reel and her rock and her flax she has parted,
She sails with the "Wild Geese" to Flanders away,
And she leaves her sad parents alone in Finae.

On the slopes of Lá-Judon, the French men are flying,
Lord Clare and his squadrons the foe still defying,
Outnumbered and wounded retreat and array,
And bleeding writes Fergus and shouts for Finae.

In the cloister of Ypres, a banner is swaying,
And by it a pale weeping maiden is praying,
That flags the sole trophy of Ramillies Frae,
That nun is poor Eileen, the Flower of Finae.[421]

Collected by Kitty Cronin (aged 15), Ballydehob

INDEX

References

Altar School, vol. 287
Crookhaven School, vol. 287
Goleen School, vol. 287
Dunmanus School, vol. 288
Rossbrin School, vol. 288
Lowertown School, vol. 289
Ballydehob School, vol. 290
Schull School, vol. 291
Schull School, vol. 292

1 Vol. 287, pp.1-2.
2 Vol. 287, pp.149-150.
3 Vol. 287, pp.20-21
4 Vol. 287, p.130
5 Vol. 287, pp.18-19
6 Vol. 287, pp.32-33
7 Vol. 287, pp.6-7
8 Vol. 287, p.24
9 Vol. 287, pp.8-10
10 Vol. 287, pp.127-129
11 Vol. 287, p.31
12 Vol. 287, p.140
13 Vol. 287, p.141
14 Vol. 287, p.137
15 Vol. 287, p.142.
16 Vol. 287,.149
17 Vol. 287, pp.143-144
18 Vol. 287, pp.38-40.
19 Vol. 287, p.22
20 Vol. 287,.84-85
21 Vol. 287, pp.15-18
22 Vol. 287,.22-23
23 Vol. 287, p.83.
24 Vol. 287, pp.145-146
25 Vol. 287,.135-136
26 Vol. 287, pp.138-139.
27 Vol. 287,.87-88.
28 Vol. 287, p.91
29 Vol. 287, p.92
30 Vol. 287, pp.48-49
31 Vol. 287, pp.50-51
32 Vol. 287, p.52.
33 Vol. 287, pp.52-53.
34 Vol. 287, pp.53-54.
35 Vol. 287, pp.55-55.
36 Vol. 287, p.55.
37 Vol. 287, p.57.
38 Vol. 287, p.100
39 Vol. 287, p.56.
40 Vol. 287, pp.59-62.
41 Vol. 287, pp.59-60.
42 Vol. 287, pp.61-62.
43 Vol. 287, pp.57-58.
44 Vol. 287, pp.98-99
45 Vol. 287, pp.133-134
46 Vol. 287, pp.96-97
47 Vol. 287, pp.69-70
48 Vol. 287, pp.108-109
49 Vol. 287, pp.80-82
50 Vol. 287, p.63
51 Vol. 287, p.76.
52 Vol. 287, p.77.
53 Vol. 287, p.76.
54 Vol. 287, pp.71-75
55 Vol. 287, p.47
56 Vol. 287, pp.104-105.
57 Vol. 287, pp.106-107
58 Vol. 287, pp.146-148
59 Vol. 287, pp.93-95
60 Vol. 287, pp.67-68
61 Vol. 287, p.86
62 Vol. 287, pp.65-66
63 Vol. 287, pp.34-35
64 Vol. 287, pp.287:
65 Vol. 287, pp.45-46
66 Vol. 287, pp.3-5
67 Vol. 287, pp.27-30
68 Vol. 287, pp.27-30
69 Vol. 287, pp.41-42
70 Vol. 287, p.43.
71 Vol. 287, pp.44 .
72 Vol. 287, pp.110-113.
73 Vol. 287, pp.11-14
74 Vol. 287, pp.114-115.
75 Vol. 287, pp.116-118.
76 Vol. 287, pp.119-121.
77 Vol. 287, pp.122-123
78 Vol. 287, pp.124-126
79 Vol. 287, p.151.
80 Vol. 287, pp.78-79.
81 Vol. 287, pp.25-26
82 Vol. 287, pp.23-24
83 Vol. 287, pp.63-64
84 Vol. 287, pp.152-153
84 Vol. 287, pp. 158-161
84 Vol. 287, pp.170-171
85 Vol. 287, pp.131-132
86 Vol. 287, pp.458-460.
87 Vol. 398, pp.461-462.
88 Vol. 398, pp.462-465.
89 Vol. 398, pp.465-467.
90 Vol. 398, pp.467-468.
91 Vol. 398, pp.468-470.
92 Vol. 398, pp.470-473.
93 Vol. 287, p.165.

94 Vol. 287, p.165.
95 Vol. 287, p.166
96 Vol. 287, pp.167-168
97 Vol. 287, p.168-169
98 Vol. 287, p.169
99 Vol. 287, pp.170-171
100 Vol. 287, p.170
101 Vol. 287, p.208.
102 Vol. 287, pp.171-172
103 Vol. 287, pp.172-173
104 Vol. 287, pp.176-178
105 Vol. 287, p.205.
106 Vol. 287, pp.173-176
107 Vol. 287, pp.178-179
108 Vol. 287, p.207.
109 Vol. 287, pp.189-190
110 Vol. 287, pp.193-194.
111 Vol. 287, pp.194-195.
112 Vol. 287, pp.197-200.
113 Vol. 287, pp.209-210.
114 Vol. 287, pp.183-186.
115 Vol. 287, pp.186-187.
116 Vol. 287, p.178.
117 Vol. 287, p.179.
118 Vol. 287, pp.158-262.
119 Vol. 288. pp.175-178.
120 Vol. 288. pp.190-191.
121 Vol. 288. pp.232-233.
122 Vol. 288. pp.244-245.
123 Vol. 288. pp.181-182.
124 Vol. 288. pp.184-185.
125 Vol. 288. pp.189-190.
126 Vol. 288. pp.186-187.
127 Vol. 288. pp.187-188.
128 Vol. 288. pp.240-241.
129 Vol. 288. pp.249-250.
130 Vol. 288. pp.151-152.
131 Vol. 288. pp.152-153.
132 Vol. 288. pp.242-243.
133 Vol. 288. pp.149a.
134 Vol. 288. pp.147a-148a
135 Vol. 288. p.242.
136 Vol. 288. pp.145a-146a
137 Vol. 288. pp.120a-121a
138 Vol. 288. pp.166-167.
139 Vol. 288. pp.170-171.
140 Vol. 288. pp.171-172a.
141 Vol. 288. p.178.
142 Vol. 288. pp.236-237.
143 Vol. 288. pp.206-208.
144Vol. 288. pp.213-214.
145 Vol. 288. pp.211-212.
146 Vol. 288. pp.220-221.
147 Vol. 288. pp.198-199.
148 Vol. 288. pp.168-170.
149 Vol. 288. pp.179-180.
150 Vol. 288. pp.179-180.
151 Vol. 288. pp.221-222.
152 Vol. 288. pp.224-225.
153 Vol. 288. pp.227-228.
154 Vol. 288. pp.247-248.
155 Vol. 288. pp.157-158.
156 Vol. 288. p.148.
157 Vol. 288. pp.255-256.
158 Vol. 288. p.197.
159 Vol. 288. p.217.
160 Vol. 288. p.131.
161 Vol. 288. pp.161-163.
162 Vol. 288. pp.173-175.
163 Vol. 288. pp.192-196.
164 Vol. 288. p.203.
165 Vol. 288. pp.200-202.
166 Vol. 288. pp.218-219.
167 Vol. 288. pp.228-239.
168 Vol. 288. pp.124a-125a
169 Vol. 1128. pp.67-68.
170 Vol. 1128. p.68.
171 Vol. 1128. pp.68-69.
172 Vol. 1128. pp.69-70.
173 Vol. 1128. pp.70-72.
174 Vol. 1128. pp.72-74.
175 Vol. 1128. pp.53-59.
176 Vol. 1128. pp.38-43.
177 Vol. 1128. pp.46-49.
178 Vol. 1128. pp.31-34.
179 Vol. 1128. pp.14-16.
180 Vol. 1128. pp.20-21.
181 Vol. 1128. pp.24-30.
182 Vol. 1128. pp.59-63.
clxxxiii Vol. 287, pp.238-240.
clxxxiv Vol. 287, p.252.
clxxxv Vol. 287, pp.310-311.
clxxxvi Vol. 287, pp.254-256.
clxxxvii Vol. 287, pp.314-315.
clxxxviii Vol. 287, pp.316-317.
clxxxix Vol. 287, pp.330-333.
cxc Vol. 287, pp.320-321.
cxci Vol. 287, pp.322-323.
cxcii Vol. 287, pp.336-337.
cxciii Vol. 287, pp.324-329.
cxciv Vol. 287, pp.332-331.
cxcv Vol. 287, pp.378-379.
cxcvi Vol. 287, pp.372-374.
cxcvii Vol. 287, pp.276-279.
cxcviii Vol. 287, pp.367-371.

cxcix Vol. 287, pp.379-380.
cc Vol. 287, pp.381-383.
cci Vol. 287, pp.215-221.
ccii Vol. 287, pp.222-226.
cciii Vol. 287, pp.375-377.
cciv Vol. 287, pp.227-234.
ccv Vol. 287, pp.235-237.
ccvi Vol. 287, pp.247-251.
ccvii Vol. 287, pp.338-347.
ccviii Vol. 289, pp.424-427.
ccix Vol. 289, pp.427-428.
ccx Vol. 289, pp.431-432.
ccxi Vol. 289, pp.428-429.
ccxii Vol. 289, p.430.
ccxiii Vol. 289, pp.429-430.
ccxiv Vol. 289, pp.432-435.
ccxv Vol. 289, pp.274-278.
ccxvi Vol. 289, pp.334-335.
ccxvii Vol. 289, p.337.
ccxviii Vol. 289, pp.399-401.
ccxix Vol. 289, pp. 271-273.
ccxx Vol. 289, pp.401-403.
ccxxi Vol. 289, pp.377-379.
ccxxii Vol. 289, pp.384-385.
ccxxiii Vol. 289, pp.380-383.
ccxxiv Vol. 289, pp.386-391.
ccxxv Vol. 289,.395-396.
ccxxvi Vol. 289, pp.392-394.
ccxxvii Vol. 289, pp.338-342.
ccxxviii Vol. 289, pp.343-344.
ccxxix Vol. 289, pp.344-346.
ccxxx Vol. 289, pp.347.
ccxxxi Vol. 289, pp. 295-297.
ccxxxii Vol. 289, pp.304-305.
ccxxxiii Vol. 289, pp.298-299.
ccxxxiv Vol. 289, pp.299-300.
ccxxxv Vol. 289, pp.303-304;
ccxxxvi Vol. 289, p.404.
ccxxxvii Vol. 289, pp.302-303.
ccxxxviii Vol. 289, pp.405-408.
ccxxxix Vol. 289, pp.409-411.
ccxl Vol. 289, pp.411-414.
ccxli Vol. 289, pp.397-399.
ccxlii Vol. 289, pp.309-310.
ccxliii Vol. 289, pp.310-311.
ccxliv Vol. 289, pp.312-313.
ccxlv Vol. 289, pp.315-316.
ccxlvi Vol. 289, p. 317.
ccxlvii Vol. 289, pp.313-314.
ccxlviii Vol. 289, pp.285-286.
ccxlix Vol. 289, pp.293-294.
ccl Vol. 289, pp.282-284.
ccli Vol. 289, pp.287-289.
cclii Vol. 289, pp.290-291.
ccliii Vol. 289, pp.292-293.
254 Vol. 289, pp.349-352.
255 Vol. 289, pp.357-361.
256 Vol. 289, pp.415-418.
257 Vol. 289, pp.419-420.
258 Vol. 289, pp.320-322.
259 Vol. 289, pp.323-326.
260 Vol. 289, pp.366-367.
261 Vol. 289, pp.368-370.
262 Vol. 289, pp.374-375.
263 Vol.291, p.511.
264 Vol.291, pp.557-558.
265 Vol.292, pp.3-5.
266 Vol.291, pp.512-513.
267 Vol.291, pp.553-554.
268 Vol.291, p.513.
269 Vol.291, p.557.
270 Vol.291, pp.558-559.
271 Vol.291, pp.559-560.
272 Vol.291, p.564.
273 Vol.291, pp.554-556.
274 Vol.291, p.560.
275 Vol.291, p.561.
276 Vol.291, pp.569-571.
277 Vol.291, pp.520-521.
278 Vol.291, p.566.
279 Vol.291, p.563.
280 Vol.291, p.512.
281 Vol.291, p.567.
282 Vol.291, p.539.
283 Vol.291, pp.531-534.
284 Vol.291, pp.536-537.
285 Vol.291, p.568.
286 Vol.291, p.540.
287 Vol.291, pp.540-541.
288 Vol.291, p.549.
289 Vol.291, pp.538-539
290 Vol.292, pp.24-25.
291 Vol.292, pp.6-9.
292 Vol.291, pp.524-525.
293 Vol.291, p.547.
294 Vol.291, pp.542-544.
295 Vol.291, p.526.
296 Vol.291, pp.526-527.
297 Vol.291, p.552.
298 Vol.291, p.548.
299 Vol.291, p.546.
300 Vol.291, pp.545-546.

301 Vol.292, pp.39-42.
302 Vol.291, pp.528-530.
303 Vol.291, pp.518-519
304 Vol.291, p.522.
305 Vol.291, pp.523-524.
306 Vol.291, p.535.
307 Vol.291, p.565.
308 Vol.292, p.45.
309 Vol.291, pp.549-551.
310 Vol.292, pp.26-29.
311 Vol.292, pp.30-31.
312 Vol. 288, p.411.
313 Vol. 288, p.419.
314 Vol. 288, p.420.
315 Vol. 288, p.422.
316 Vol. 288, pp.389=390.
317 Vol. 288, p.392.
318 Vol. 288, p.410.
319 Vol. 288, pp.406=407.
320 Vol. 288, p.414.
321 Vol. 288, pp.423=424.
322 Vol. 288, p.402.
323 Vol. 288, p.426.
324 Vol. 288, p.421.
325 Vol. 288, p.403.
326 Vol. 288, p.404.
327 Vol. 288, p.405.
328 Vol. 288, p.425.
329 Vol. 288, pp.399-340.
330 Vol. 288, p.401.
331 Vol. 288, pp.393-394.
332 Vol. 288, p.409.
333 Vol. 288, p.408.
334 Vol 290, pp.358-359.
335 Vol 290, p.377.
336 Vol 291, pp.57-58.
337 Vol 290, pp.377-378.
338 Vol 291, p.1.
339 Vol 291, p.13.
340 Vol 290, pp.422-423.
341 Vol 291, p.22-23.
342 Vol 291, p.24.
343 Vol 291, p.32-34.
344 Vol 291, pp.175-177
345 Vol 290, pp.344-345.
346 Vol 291, p.55.
347 Vol 291, pp.56-57.
348 Vol 291, pp.149-150.
349 Vol 291, pp.150-151.
350 Vol 290, p.242.
351 Vol 290, p.247.
352 Vol 290, pp.243-245.
353 Vol 290, p.246.
354 Vol 290, pp.253-255.
355 Vol 290, pp.255-254.
356 Vol 290, pp.261-262.
357 Vol 290, pp.258-259.
358 Vol 291, pp.100-101.
359 Vol 290, pp.334-335.
360 Vol 290, pp.320-321.
361 Vol 291, p.73.
362 Vol 291, p.74.
363 Vol 291, p.77.
364 Vol 291, p.75.
365 Vol 291, pp.81-82.
366 Vol 291, p.80.
367 Vol 290, p.229.
368 Vol 290, pp.235-236.
369 Vol 290, pp.236-237.
370 Vol 291, p.141.
371 Vol 291, pp.136-137.
372 Vol 290, p.315.
373 Vol 291, p.93.
374 Vol 291, p.86.
375 Vol 291, pp.144-145.
376 Vol 291, pp.143-144.
377 Vol 291, p.133.
378 Vol 291, p.132.
379 Vol 291, p.131.
380 Vol 291, p.133.
381 Vol 291, p.134.
382 Vol 291, p.135.
383 Vol 291, p.71.
384 Vol 291, p.69.
385 Vol 291, pp.70-71.
386 Vol 291, pp.60-61.
387 Vol 291, p.70`.
388 Vol 291, p.68-69.
389 Vol 291, pp.58-59.
390 Vol 291, p.66.
391 Vol 291, pp.203-205.
392 Vol 290, pp.366-368.
393 Vol 291, p.97.
394 Vol 291, pp.59-60.
395 Vol 291, p.61.
396 Vol 291, p.62.
397 Vol 291, p.65.
398 Vol 291, p.63-64.
399 Vol 291, p.164.
400 Vol 291, pp.164-165.
401 Vol 291, pp.166-168
402 Vol 291, pp.99-100.
403 Vol 291, pp.158-159.
404 Vol 291, p.158.

405 Vol 291, p.159.
406 Vol 291, p.161.
407 Vol 290, pp.277-278.
408 Vol 290, pp.272-274.
409 Vol 291, pp.171-174
410 Vol 291, pp.178-180
411 Vol 291, pp.183-184.
412 Vol 291, pp.185-188
413 Vol 291, pp.189-191
414 Vol 291, pp.195-197
415 Vol 291, pp.208-209.
416 Vol 290, pp.384-388.
417 Vol 290, pp.393-395.
418 Vol 290, pp.397-399.
419 Vol 290, pp.400-404.
420 Vol 290, pp.405-416.
421 Vol 290, pp.417-421.

Also Available

Skibbereen: Rescued Folklore from Ireland's Southwest

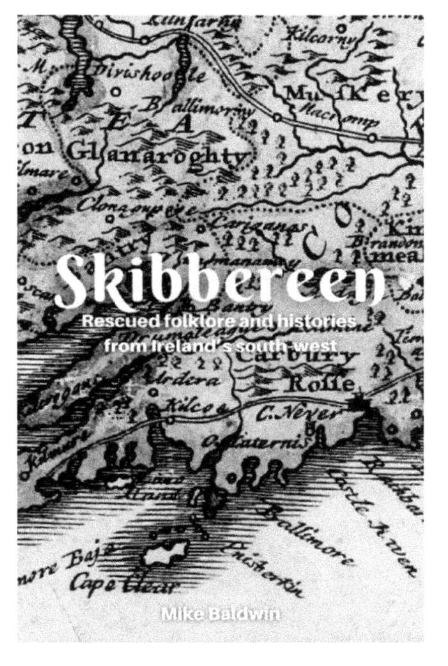

The survival of folklore is a rare thing. In a world fixated with the modern and new, many no longer see relevance in what they consider to be old. But folklore is more than a glimpse into our pasts. It is vibrant and alive, surviving and indeed thriving, layer upon layer in our environs, the places we inhabit, the people we meet, and the words we use. What is more, each generation adds its own strata.

The stories in this book are from the town of Skibbereen, situated at the heart of West Cork, Ireland. In 1937, at the behest of The National Folklore Commission, who identified the loss of this important and valuable heritage, the children from Skibbereen's schools set to work, committing tales narrated by older family members and friends to paper. Here you will find stories and histories from Abbeystrowry, Aghadown, Castlehaven, the Convent of Mercy (Skibbereen), Corravoley, Creagh, Dooneen, Drishanemore, Hare [Heir] Island, Kilcoe, Lisheen, Lissalohorig, Lough Hyne, Ringagrogy and Sherkin Islands, and the town of Skibbereen.

Ingram Content Group UK Ltd.
Milton Keynes UK
UKHW020902230723
425611UK00007B/31